Fables of La Fontaine

Fables
of La Fontaine

translated into English verse
by Walter Thornbury
with 320 illustrations
by Gustave Dore

OMEGA BOOKS

Original edition published by Cassell, Petter and Galpin

© 1982 Ebeling Publishing Ltd., London

Published by Omega Books Ltd.,
1 West Street, Ware
Hertfordshire, England

ISBN 0-907 853-45-5

Printed by Brepols, Turnhout, Belgium

Book I

The Grasshopper and the Ant

The Grasshopper, so blithe and gay,
Sang the summer time away.
Pinched and poor the spendthrift grew,
When the sour north-easter blew.
In her larder not a scrap,
Bread to taste, nor drink to lap.
To the Ant, her neighbour, she
Went to moan her penury,
Praying for a loan of wheat,
Just to make a loaf to eat,
Till the sunshine came again.
"All I say is fair and plain,
I will pay you every grain,
Principal and interest too,
Before harvest, I tell you,
On my honour – every pound,
Ere a single sheaf is bound."
The Ant's a very prudent friend,
Never much disposed to lend;
Virtues great and failings small,
This her failing least of all.
Quoth she, "How spent you the summer?"
"Night and day, to each new comer
I sang gaily, by your leave;
Singing, singing, morn and eve."
"You sang? I see it at a glance.
Well, then, now's the time to dance."

The Grasshopper and the Ant

The Raven and the Fox

Master Raven, perched upon a tree,
Held in his beak a savoury piece of cheese;
Its pleasant odour, borne upon the breeze,
Allured Sir Reynard, with his flattery.
"Ha! Master Raven, 'morrow to you, sir;
How black and glossy! now, upon my word,
I never – beautiful! I do aver.
If but your voice becomes your coat, no bird
More fit to be the Phœnix of our wood –
I hope, sir, I am understood?"
The Raven, flattered by the praise,
Opened his spacious beak, to show his ways
Of singing: down the good cheese fell.
Quick the Fox snapped it. "My dear sir, 'tis well,"
He said. "Know that a flatterer lives
On him to whom his praise he gives;
And, my dear neighbour, an' you please,
This lesson's worth a slice of cheese." –
The Raven, vexed at his consenting,
Flew off, too late in his repenting.

The Frog that wished to make herself as big as the Ox

A Frog, no bigger than a pullet's egg,
A fat Ox feeding in a meadow spied.
The envious little creature blew and swelled;
In vain to reach the big bull's bulk she tried.
"Sister, now look! observe me close!" she cried.
"Is this enough?" – "No!" "Tell me! now then see!"
"No, no!" "Well, now I'm quite as big as he?"
"You're scarcely bigger than you were at first!"
One more tremendous puff – she grew so large – she burst.

The whole world swarms with people not more wise:
The tradesman's villa with the palace vies.
Ambassadors your poorest Princelings send,
And every Count has pages without end.

The two Mules

Two Mules were journeying – one charged with oats,
The other with a tax's golden fruit.
This last betrayed that manner which denotes
Excessive vanity in man or brute.
Proudly self-conscious of his precious load,
He paced, and loud his harness-bells resounded;
When suddenly upon their lonely road,
Both Mules and masters were by thieves surrounded.
The money-bearer soon was put to death:
"Is this the end that crowns my high career?
Yon drudge," he murmured with his latest breath,
"Escapes unhurt, while I must perish here!"
"My friend," his fellow-traveller made reply,
"Wealth cannot always at the poor man scoff.
If you had been content to do as I,
You'd not at present be so badly off."

The two Mules

The Wolf and the Dog

A Wolf, who was but skin and bone,
So watchful had the sheep-dogs grown,
Once met a Mastiff fat and sleek,
Stern only to the poor and weak.
Sir Wolf would fain, no doubt, have munched
This pampered cur, and on him lunched;
But then the meal involved a fight,
And he was craven, save at night;
For such a dog could guard his throat
As well as any dog of note.
So the Wolf, humbly flattering him,
Praised the soft plumpness of each limb.
"You're wrong, you're wrong, my noble sir,
To roam in woods indeed you err,"
The dog replies, "you do indeed;
If you but wish, with me you'll feed.
Your comrades are a shabby pack,
Gaunt, bony, lean in side and back,
Pining for hunger, scurvy, hollow,
Fighting for every scrap they swallow.
Come, share my lot, and take your ease."
"What must I do to earn it, please?"

"Do? – why, do nothing! Beggar-men
Bark at and chase; fawn now and then
At friends; your master always flatter.
Do this, and by this little matter
Earn every sort of dainty dish –
Fowl-bones or pigeons' – what you wish –
Aye, better things; and with these messes,
Fondlings, and ceaseless kind caresses."
The Wolf, delighted, as he hears
Is deeply moved – almost to tears;
When all at once he sees a speck,
A gall upon the Mastiff's neck.
"What's that?" – "Oh, nothing!" "Nothing?" – "No"
"A slight rub from the chain, you know."
"The chain!" replies the Wolf, aghast;
"You are not free? – they tie you fast?"
"Sometimes. But, law! what matters it?" –
"Matters so much, the rarest bit
Seems worthless, bought at such a price."
The Wolf, so saying, in a trice,
Ran off, and with the best goodwill,
And very likely's running still.

The Heifer, the She-Goat, and the Lamb,
in partnership with the Lion

The Heifer, Lamb, and Nanny-goat were neighbours,
With a huge Lion living close at hand,
They shared the gains and losses of their labours
   (All this was long ago, you understand).
One day a stag was taken as their sport;
   The Goat, who snared him, was of course
                       enraptured,
And sent for all the partners of her toil,
   In order to divide the treasure captured.
They came. The Lion, counting on his claws,
   Quartered the prey, and thus addressed the trio –
"The parts are four. I take the first, because
   I am your monarch, and my name is Leo:
Being the strongest, I annex the second;
   As bravest, I can claim another share,
Should any touch the fourth, or say I reckoned
   Unjustly, I shall kill him. So beware."

The Wallet

Said Jupiter one day, "Let all that breathe
Come and obeisance make before my throne.
If at his shape or being any grieve,
Let them cast fears aside. I'll hear their groan.
Come, Monkey, you be first to speak. You see
Of animals this goodly company;
Compare their beauties with your own.
Are you content?" "Why not? Good gracious me!"
  The monkey said,
  No whit afraid –
"Why not content? I have four feet like others,
My portrait no one sneers at – do they, brothers?
But cousin Bruin's hurriedly sketched in,
And no one holds his likeness wirth a pin."
Then came the Bear. One thought he would have
                                          found
Something to grumble at. Grumble! no, not he.
He praised his form and shape, but, looking round,
Turned critic on the want of symmetry
Of the huge shapeless Elephant, whose ears

Were much too long; his tail too short, he fears.
  The Elephant was next.
  Though wise, yet sadly vexed
To see good Madam Whale, to his surprise,
A cumbrous mountain of such hideous size.
Quick Mrs. Ant thinks the Gnat far too small,
Herself colossal. – Jove dismisses all,
Severe on others, with themselves content.
'Mong all the fools who that day homeward went,
Our race was far the worst: our wisest souls
Lynxes to others', to their own faults moles.
Pardon at home they give, to others grace deny,
And keep on neighbours' sins a sleepless eye.
  Jove made us so,
  As we all know,
We wear our Wallets in the self-same way –
This current year, as in the bye-gone day:

In pouch behind our own defects we store,
The faults of others in the one before.

The Swallow and the little Birds

A Swallow, in his travels o'er the earth,
Into the law of storms had gained a peep;
Could prophesy them long before their birth,
   And warn in time the ploughmen of the deep.
Just as the month for sowing hemp came round,
   The Swallow called the smaller birds together.
"Yon' hand," said he, "which strews along the ground
   That fatal grain, forbodes no friendly weather.
The day will come, and very soon, perhaps,
   When yonder crop will help in your undoing –
When, in the shape of snares and cruel traps,
   Will burst the tempest which to-day is brewing.
Be wise, and eat the hemp up now or never;
   Take my advice." But no, the little birds,
Who thought themselves, no doubt, immensely
                            clever,
   Laughed loudly at the Swallow's warning words.
Soon after, when the hemp grew green and tall,
   He begged the Birds to tear it into tatters.
"Prophet of ill," they answered one and all,
   "Cease chattering about such paltry matters."

The hemp at length was ripe, and then the Swallow,
  Remarking that "ill weeds were never slow,"
Continued – "Though it's now too late to follow
  The good advice I gave you long ago,
You still may manage to preserve your lives
  By giving credit to the voice of reason.
Remain at home, I beg you, with your wives,
  And shun the perils of the coming season.
You cannot cross the desert or the seas,
  To settle down in distant habitations;
Make nests, then, in the walls, and there, at ease,
  Defy mankind and all its machinations."
They scorned his warnings, as in Troy of old
  Men scorned the lessons that Cassandra taught.
And shortly, as the Swallow had foretold,
  Great numbers of them in the traps were caught.

To instincts not our own we give no credit,
And till misfortune comes, we never dread it.

The Swallow and the little Birds

The Town Rat and the Country Rat

A Rat from town, a country Rat
 Invited in the civilest way;
For dinner there was just to be
 Ortolans and an entrement.
Upon a Turkey carpet soft
 The noble feast at last was spread;
I leave you pretty well to guess
 The merry, pleasant life they led.
Gay the repast, for plenty reigned,
 Nothing was wanting to the fare;
But hardly had it well begun
 Ere chance disturbed the friendly pair.
A sudden racket at the door
 Alarmed them, and they made retreat;
The City Rat was not the last,
 His comrade followed fast and fleet.
The noise soon over, they returned,
 As rats on such occasions do;
"Come," said the liberal citizen,
 "And let us finish our ragout."
"Not a crumb more," the rustic said;
 "To-morrow you shall dine with me;
Don't think me jealous of your state,
 Or all your royal luxury;
"But then I eat so quiet at home,
 And nothing dangerous is near;
Good-bye, my friend, I have no love
 For pleasure when it's mixed with fear."

The Town Rat and the Country Rat

The Wolf and the Lamb

The reasoning of the strongest has such weight,
None can gainsay it, or dare prate,
No more than one would question Fate.
A Lamb her thirst was very calmly slaking,
   At the pure current of a woodland rill;
A grisly Wolf, by hunger urged, came making
   A tour in search of living things to kill.
"How dare you spoil my drink?" he fiercely cried;
   There was grim fury in his very tone;
   "I'll teach you to let beasts like me alone.
"Let not your Majesty feel wrath," replied
The Lamb, "nor be unjust to me, from passion;
I cannot, Sire, disturb in any fashion
The stream which now your Royal Highness faces,
I'm lower down by at least twenty paces."

"You spoil it!" roared the Wolf; "and more, I know,
You slandered me but half a year ago."
"How could I do so, when I scarce was born?"
The Lamb replied; "I was a suckling then."
"Then 'twas your brother held me up to scorn."
"I have no brother." "Well, 'tis all the same;
At least 'twas some poor fool that bears your name.
You and your dogs, both great and small,
Your sheep and shepherds, one and all,
Slander me, if men say but true,
And I'll revenge myself on you."
Thus saying, he bore off the Lamb
Deep in the wood, far from its dam.
And there, not waiting judge nor jury,
Fell to, and ate him in his fury.

The Wolf and the Lamb

The Man and his Image

For M. the Duke de la Rochefoucauld

A Man who had no rivals in the love
He hore himself, thought that he won the bell
From all the world, and hated every glass
That truths less palatable tried to tell.
Living contented in the error,
Of lying mirrors he'd a terror.
Officious Fate, determined on a cure,
Raised up, where'er he turned his eyes,
Those silent counsellors that ladies prize.

Mirrors old and mirrors newer;
Mirrors in inns and mirrors in shops;
Mirrors in pockets of all the fops;
Mirrors in every lady's zone.
What could our poor Narcissus do?
He goes and hides him all alone
In woods that one can scarce get through.
No more the lying mirrors come,
But past his new-found savage home
A pure and limpid brook runs fair. –
He looks. His ancient foe is there!
His angry eyes stare at the stream,
He tries to fancy it a dream.
Resolves to fly the odious place, and shun
The image; yet, so fair the brook, he cannot run.

My meaning is not hard to see;
No one is from this failing free.
The man who loved himself is just the Soul,
The mirrors are the follies of all others.
(Mirrors are faithful painters on the whole;)
And you know well as I do, brothers, that the brook
Is the wise "Maxim-book."

The Dragon with many Heads, and the Dragon with many Tails

An Envoy of the Grand Signor
(I can't say more)
One day, before the Emperor's court,
Vaunted, as some historians report,
That his royal master had a force
Outnumbering all the foot and horse
The Kaiser could bring to the war.
Then spoke a choleric attendant:
"*Our* Prince has more than *one* dependant
That keeps an army at his own expense."
The Pasha (man of sense),
Replied: "By rumour I'm aware
What troops the great electors spare,
And that reminds me, I am glad,
Of an adventure I once had,
  Strange, and yet true.
  I'll tell it you.

Once through a hedge the hundred heads I saw
Of a huge Hydra show.
My blood, turned ice, refused to flow:
And yet I felt that neither fang nor claw
Could more than scare me – for no head came near.
There was no room. I cast off fear.
While musing on this sight,
Another Dragon came to light.
Only one head this time;
But tails too many to count up in rhyme.
The fit again came on,
Worse than the one just gone.
The head creeps first, then follows tail by tail;
Nothing can stop their road, nor yet assail;
One clears the way for all the minor powers:
The first's *your* Emperor's host, the second *ours*."

The Robbers and the Ass

Two Thieves were fighting for a prize,
A Donkey newly stolen; sell or not to sell –
That was the question – bloody fists, black eyes:
  While they fought gallantly and well,
    A third thief happening to pass,
    Rode gaily off upon the ass.
The ass is some poor province it may be;
  The thieves, that gracious potentate, or this,
Austria, Turkey, or say Hungary;
Instead of two, I vow I've set down three
(The world has almost had enough of this),
  And often neither will the province win:
  For third thief stepping in,
    'Mid their debate and noisy fray,
    With the disputed donkey rides away.

Simonides rescued by the Gods

Three sorts of persons can't be praised too much:
　　The Gods, the King, and her on whom we doat.
So said Malherbe, and well he said, for such
　　Are maxims wise, and worthy of all note.
Praise is beguiling, and disliked by none:
A lady's favour it has often won.
Let's see whate'en the gods have ere this done
　　To those who praised them. Once, the eulogy
Of a rough athlete was in verse essayed.
Simonides, the ice well broken, made
　　A plunge into a swamp of flattery.
The athlete's parents were poor folk unknown;
The man mere lump of muscle and of bone –
　　No merit but his thews,
　　A barren subject for the muse.
The poet praised his hero all he could,
Then threw him by, as others would.
　　Castor and Pollux bringing on the stage,
He points out their example to such men,
　　And to all strugglers in whatever age;
Enumerates the places where they fought,
And why they vanished from our mortal ken.

In fact, two-thirds of all his song was fraught
With praise of them, page after page.
A Talent had the athlete guaranteed,
But when he read he grudged the meed,
And gave a third: frank was his jest, –
"Castor and Pollux pay the rest;
Celestial pair! they'll see you righted, –
Still I will feast you with the best;
Sup with me, you will be delighted;
　　The guests are all select, you'll see,
　　My parents, and friends loved by me;
　　Be thou, too, of the company."
Simonides consents, partly, perhaps, in fear
　　To lose, besides his due, the paltry praise.
He goes – they revel and discuss the cheer;
　　A merry night prepares for jovial days.
A servant enters, tells him at the door
　　Two men would see him, and without delay.
He leaves the table, not a bit the more
　　Do jaws and fingers cease their greedy play.
These two men were the Gemini he'd praised.
They thanked him for the homage he had paid;

Then, for reward, told him the while he stayed
The doom'd house would be rased,
And fall about the ears
Of the big boxer and his peers.
The prophecy came true – yes, every tittle;
Snap goes a pillar, thin and brittle.
The roof comes toppling down, and crashes
The feast – the cups, the flagons smashes.
Cupbearers are included in the fall;
  Nor is that all:
To make the vengeance for the bard complete,
The athlete's legs are broken too.
A beam snapped underneath his feet,
  While half the guests exclaim,
"Lord help us! we are lame."

Fame, with her trumpet, heralds the affair;
Men cry, "A miracle!" and everywhere
They give twice over, without scoff or sneer,
To poet by the gods held dear.
No one of gentle birth but paid him well,
Of their ancestors' deeds to nobly tell.

Let me return unto my text: it pays
The gods and kings to freely praise;
Melpomene, moreover, sometimes traffic makes
Of the ingenious trouble that she takes.
Our art deserves respect, and thus
The great do honour to themselves who honour us.
  Olympus and Parnassus once, you see,
  Were friends, and liked each other's company.

Death and the unhappy Man

A Miserable Man incessant prayed
   To Death for aid.
"Oh Death!" he cried, "I love thee as a friend!
Come quickly, and my life's long sorrows end!"
Death, wishing to oblige him, ran,
Knocked at the door, entered, and eyed the man.
"What do I see? begone, thou hideous thing!
   The very sight
Strikes me with horror and affright!
Begone, old Death! – Away, thou grisly King!"
Mecænas (hearty fellow) somewhere said;
   "Let me by gouty, crippled, impotent and lame,
   'Tis all the same,
So I but keep on living. Death, thou slave!
Come not at all, and I shall be content."
And that was what the man I mention meant.

Death and the Woodcutter

A poor Woodcutter, covered with his load,
Bent down with boughs and with a weary age,
Groaning and stooping, made his sorrowing stage
To reach his smoky cabin; on the road,
Worn out with toil and pain, he seeks relief
By resting for a while, to brood on grief. –
What pleasure has he had since he was born?
In this round world is there one more forlorn?
Sometimes no bread, and never, never rest.
Creditors, soldiers, taxes, children, wife,
   The corvée. Such a life!
The picture of a miserable man – look east or west.
He calls on Death – for Death calls everywhere –
   Well, – Death is there.
   He comes without delay,
And asks the groaner if he needs his aid.
"Yes," said the Woodman, "help me in my trade.
Put up these faggots – then you need not stay."

Death is a cure for all, say I,
   But do not budge from where you are;
Better to suffer than to die,
   Is man's old motto, near and far.

Death and the Woodcutter

The Middle-Aged Man and the two Widows

A Man of middle age,
   Fast getting grey,
Thought it would be but sage
   To fix the marriage day.
     He had in stocks,
     And under locks,
   Money enough to clear his way.
Such folks can pick and choose; all tried to please
The moneyed man; but he, quite at his ease,
   Showed no great hurry,
   Fuss, nor scurry.
   "Courting," he said, "was no child's play."
Two widows in his heart had shares –
   One young; the other, rather past her prime,
By careful art repairs
   What has been carried off by Time.
The merry widows did their best
To flirt and coax, and laugh and jest;

Arranged, with much of bantering glee,
His hair, and curled it playfully.
The eldest, with a wily theft,
Plucked one by one the dark hairs left.
The younger, also plundering in her sport,
   Snipped out the grey hair, every bit.
Both worked so hard at either sort,
   They left him bald – that was the end of it.
"A thousand thanks, fair ladies," said the man;
"You've plucked me smooth enough;
Yet more of gain than loss, so *quantum suff.*,
For marriage now is not at all my plan.
She whom I would have taken t'other day
   To enroll in Hymen's ranks,
Had but the wish to make me go *her* way,
     And not my own;
     A head that's bald must live alone:
   For this good lesson, ladies, many thanks."

The Fox and the Stork

The Fox invited neighbour Stork to dinner,
    But Reynard was a miser, I'm afraid;
He offered only soup, and that was thinner
    Than any soup that ever yet was made.
The guest – whose lanky beak was an obstruction,
    The mixture being served upon a plate –
Made countless vain experiments in suction,
    While Reynard feasted at a rapid rate.
The victim, bent upon retaliation,
    Got up a little dinner in return.
Reynard accepted; for an invitation
    To eat and drink was not a thing to spurn.
He reached the Stork's at the appointed hour,
    Flattered the host, as well as he was able,
And got his grinders ready to devour
    Whatever dishes might be brought to table.
But, lo! the Stork, to punish the offender,
    Had got the meat cut very fine, and placed
Within a jug; the neck was long and slender,
    Suited exactly to its owner's taste.
The Stork, whose appetite was most extensive,
    Emptied the jug entirely to the dregs;
While hungry Reynard, quite abashed and pensive,
    Walked homewards with his tail between his legs.
      Deceivers reap the fruits of their deceit,
      And being cheated may reform a cheat.

The Child and the Schoolmaster

This fable serves to tell, or tries to show
    A fool's remonstrance often is in vain.
A child fell headlong in the river's flow,
    While playing on the green banks of the Seine:
A willow, by kind Providence, grew there,
The branches saved him (rather, God's good care);
Caught in the friendly boughs, he clutched and clung.
    The master of the school just then came by.
"Help! help! I'm drowning!" as he gulping hung,
    He shouts. The master, with a pompous eye,
Turns and reproves him with much gravity.
    "You little ape," he said, "now only see
What comes of all your precious foolery;
A pretty job such little rogues to guard.
Unlucky parents who must watch and thrash
Such helpless, hopeless, good-for-nothing trash.
I pity them; their woes I understand."
Having said this, he brought the child to land.

In this I blame more people than you guess –
    Babblers and censors, pedants, all the three;
Such creatures grow in numbers to excess,
    Some blessing seems to swell their progeny.
In every crisis theories they shape,
    And exercise their tongues with perfect skill;
Ha! my good friends, first save me from the scrape,
    Then make your long speech after, if you will.

The Pullet and the Pearl

A Fowl, while scratching in the straw,
Finding a pearl without a flaw,
   Gave it a lapidary of the day.
"It's very fine, I must repeat;
And yet a single grain of wheat
   Is very much more in my way."

A poor uneducated lad
A manuscript as heirloom had.
   He took it to a bookseller one day:
"I know," said he, "it's very rare;
But still, a guinea as my share
   Is very much more in my way."

The Drones and the Bees

A Workman by his work you always know.
Some cells of honey had been left unclaimed.
   The Drones were first to go
   The Bees, to try and show
That they to take the mastership were not ashamed.
Before a Wasp the cause at last they bring;
It is not easy to decide the thing.
The witnesses deposed that round the hive
They long had seen wing'd, buzzing creatures fly,
Brown, and like bees. "Yes, true; but, man alive,
The Drones are also brown; so do not try
To prove it so." The Wasp, on justice bent,
   Made new investigations
   (Laws of all nations).
To throw more light upon the case,
Searched every place,
Heard a whole ants' nest argue face to face,
Still it grew only darker; that's a fact
   (Lease or contract?)
"Oh, goodness gracious! where's the use, my son?"
   Cried a wise Bee;
   "Why, only see,
For six months now the cause is dragging on,
And we're no further than we were at first;

But what is worst,
The honey's spoiling, and the hive is burst.
'Tis time the judge made haste,
The matter's simmered long enough to waste,
Without rebutters or *fi, fa,*
Without rejoinders or *ca, sa,*
John Doe,
Or Richard Roe.
Let's go to work, the wasps and us,
We'll see who best can build and store
The sweetest juice." It's settled thus.
The Drones do badly, as they've done of yore;
The art's beyond their knowledge, quite beyond.
The Wasp adjudges that the honey goes
Unto the Bees: would those of law so fond
Could thus decide the cases justice tries.
Good common sense, instead of Coke and code,
(The Turks in this are really very wise,)
Would save how many a debtor's heavy load.
Law grinds our lives away
With sorrow and delay,
In vain we groan, and grudge
The money given to our long-gowned tutors.
Always at last the oyster's for the judge,
The shells for the poor suitors.

The Oak and the Reed

The Oak said one day to a river Reed,
"You have a right with Nature to fall out.
Even a wren for you's a weight indeed;
    The slightest breeze that wanders round about
        Makes you first bow, then bend;
While my proud forehead, like an Alp, braves all,
Whether the sunshine or the tempest fall –
A gale to you to me a zephyr is.
Come near my shelter: you'll escape from this;
    You'll suffer less, and everything will mend.
        I'll keep you warm
        From every storm;
And yet you foolish creatures needs must go,
And on the frontiers of old Boreas grow.
    Nature to you has been, I think, unjust."
"Your sympathy," replied the Reed, "is kind,
        And to my mind
Your heart is good; and yet dismiss your thought.
For us, no more than you, the winds are fraught
With danger, for I bend, but do not break.
As yet, a stout resistance you can make,
And never stoop your back, my friend;
But wait a bit, and let us see the end."
Black, furious, raging, swelling as he spoke,
The fiercest wind that ever yet had broke
From the North's caverns bellowed through the sky.
The Oak held firm, the Reed bent quietly down.
The wind blew faster, and more furiously,
    Then rooted up the tree that with its head
Had touched the high clouds in its majesty,
    And stretched far downwards to the realms of dead.

The Oak and the Reed

Book II

Against those who are hard to Please

Had I when born, from fair Calliope
Received a gift such as she can bestow
Upon her lovers, it should pass from me
To Æsop, and that very soon, I know;
I'd consecrate it to his pleasant lies.
Falsehood and verse have ever been allies;
Far from Parnassus, held in small esteem,
I can do little to adorn his theme,
Or lend a fresher lustre to his song.
I try, that's all – and plan what one more strong
   May some day do –
   And carry through.
Still, I have written, by-the-bye,
The wolf's speech and the lamb's reply.
What's more, there's many a plant and tree
Were taught to talk, and all by me.
Was that not my enchantment, eh?
"Tut! Tut!" our peevish critics say,
"Your mighty work all told, no more is
Than half-a-dozen baby stories.
Write something more authentic then,
And in a higher tone." – Well, list, my men! –

After ten years of war around their towers,
The Trojans held at bay the Grecian powers;
A thousand battles on Scamander's plain,
Minings, assaults, how many a hero slain!
Yet the proud city stoutly held her own.
Till, by Minerva's aid, a horse of wood,
Before the gates of the brave city stood.
Its flanks immense the sage Ulysses hold,
Brave Diomed, and Ajax, churlish, bold;
These, with their squadrons, will the vast machine
Bear into fated Troy, unheard, unseen –
The very gods will be their helpless prey.
Unheard-of stratagem; alas! the day,
That will the workmen their long toil repay. –
"Enough, enough!" our critics quickly cry,
"Pause and take breath; you'll want it presently.
Your wooden horse is hard to swallow,
With foot and cavalry to follow.
Why this is stranger stuff, now, an' you please,
Than Reynard cheating ravens of their cheese;
What's more, this grand style does not suit you well,
That way you'll never bear away the bell."

Well, then, we'll lower the key, if such your will is. –
Pensive, alone, the jealous Amaryllis
Sighed for Alcippus – in her care,
She thinks her sheep and dog alone will share.
Tircis, perceiving her, slips all unseen
Behind the willows' waving screen,
And hears the shepherdess the zephyrs pray,
To bear her words to lover far away. –
"I stop you at that rhyme,"
   Cries out my watchful critic,
   Of phrases analytic;
"It's not legitimate; it cannot pass this time.
And then I need not show, of course,
The line wants energy and force;
   It must be melted o'er again, I say."
You paltry meddler, prate no more,
   I write my stories at my ease.
Easier to sit and plan a score,
   Than such a one as you to please.

    Fastidious men and overwise,
    There's nothing ever satisfies.

The Council held by the Rats

A Tyrant Cat, by surname Nibblelard,
Through a Rat kingdom spread such gloom
By waging war and eating hard,
    Only a few escaped the tomb;
The rest, remaining in their hiding-places,
    Like frightened misers crouching on their pelf,
Over their scanty rations made wry faces,
    And swore the Cat was old King Nick himself.
        One day, the terror of their life
        Went on the roof to meet his wife:
        During the squabbling interview
        (I tell the simple truth to you),
The Rats a chapter called. The Dean,
        A cautious, wise, old Rat,
        Proposed a bell to fasten on the Cat.
"This should be tried, and very soon, I mean;
    So that when war was once begun,
    Safe underground their folk could run, –
    This was the only thing that could be done."
With the wise Dean no one could disagree;
Nothing more prudent there could be:
    The difficulty was to fix the bell!
One said, "I'm not a fool; you don't catch me:"
"I hardly seem to see it!" so said others.

The Council held by the Rats

The meeting separated – need I tell,
The end was words – but words. Well, well, my brothers,
There have been many chapters much the same;
Talking, but never doing – there's the blame.
Chapters of monks, not rats – just so!
Canons who fain would bell the cats, you know.

To talk, and argue, and refute,
  The court has lawyers in long muster-roll;
But when you want a man who'll execute,
  You cannot find a single soul.

The Wolf pleading against the Fox before the Ape

A Wolf who'd suffered from a thief,
  His ill-conditioned neighbour Mr. Fox
Brought up (and falsely, that is my belief)
  Before the Ape, to fill the prisoner's box.
The plaintiff and defendant in this case
    Distract the place
With questions, answers, cries, and boisterous speeches,
    So angry each is.
In an Ape's memory no one saw
An action so entangled as to law.
Hot and perspiring was the judge's face,
He saw their malice, and, with gravity,
Decided thus: – "I know you well of old, my friends,
  Both must pay damages, I see;
You, Wolf, because you've brought a groundless charge:
You, Fox, because you stole from him; on that I'll not enlarge.

The judge was right; it's no bad plan,
To punish rascals how you can.

The two Bulls and the Frog

Two Bulls were butting in rough battle,
For the fair belle of all the cattle;
A Frog, who saw them, shuddering sighed.
"What ails you?" said a croaker by his side.
"What? why, good gracious! don't you see
The end of all this fight will be
That one will soon be chased, and yield
The empire of this flowery field;
And driven from rich grass to feed,
Searching the marsh for rush and reed,
He'll trample many a back and head,
And every time he moves we're dead.
'Tis very hard a heifer should occasion
To us so cruel an invasion."
There was good sense in the old croaker's fear,
For soon the vanquished Bull came near:
Treading with heedless, brutal power,
He crushed some twenty every hour.

The poor in every age are forced by Fate
To expiate the follies of the great.

The Bat and the two Weasels

A Bat one day into a Weasel's hole
  Went boldly; well, it was a special blunder.
The Weasel, hating mice with heart and soul,
  Ran up to eat the stranger – where's the wonder?
"How do you dare," he said, "to meet me here,
When you and I are foes, and always were?
Aint you a mouse? – lie not, and cast off fear;
You are; or I'm no Weasel: have a care."
  "Now, pardon me," replied the Bat,
  "I'm really anything but that.
What! I a mouse? the wicked tattlers lie.
  Thanks to the Maker of all human things,
  I am a bird – here are my wings:
Long live the cleavers of the sky!"
These arguments seemed good, and so
The Weasel let the poor wretch go.

But two days later, though it seems absurd,
The simpleton into another hole intruded.
This second Weasel hated every bird,
And darted on the rash intruder.
"There you mistake," the Bat exclaimed;
"Look at me, aint I rashly blamed?
What makes a bird? its feathers? – yes.
  I am a mouse – long live the rats,
  And Jupiter take all the cats."
So twice, by his supreme address,
This Bat was saved – thanks to *finesse*.

Many there are who, changing uniform,
  Have laughed at every danger and intrigue;
The wise man cries, to 'scape the shifting storm,
  "Long live the King!" or, "Glory to the League!"

The Bird wounded by an Arrow

A Bird by well-aimed arrow shot,
Dying, deplored its cruel lot;
And cried, "It doubles every pain
When from oneself the cause of ruin's ta'en.
Oh, cruel men, from our own wings you drew
The plume that winged the shaft that slew;
But mock us not, you heartless race,
You too will some time take our place;
For half at least of Japhet's brothers
Forge swords and knives to slay the others."

The Dog and her Companion

A Dog, proud of her new-born family,
And needing shelter for her restless brood,
Begged a snug kennel with such urgency,
    A generous friend at last was found who would
Supply her pressing need – so it was lent.
After a week or so the good soul went
And asked it back. – "Only a fortnight more:"
    The little ones could hardly walk as yet;
'Twas kindly granted as before.
    The second term expired, again they met:
The friend demands her house, her room, her bed.
This time the graceless Dog showed teeth, and scowled;
"I and my children are prepared to go," she growled,
"If you can put us out and reign instead."
    By this time they were grown,
    And better left alone.

Lend to bad men, and you'll regret it much;
    To draw from them the money right,
    You must plead, and you must fight,
Or else your gold you'll never touch.
    Only the truth I mean to tell:
    Give them an inch, they'll take an ell.

The Eagle and the Beetle

John Rabbit, by an Eagle followed, fled,
And in his terror hid his head
In a poor Beetle's hole, that happened to be there.
You well may guess that this poor lair
Was insecure; but where to hide? alack!
He crouched – the Eagle pounced upon his back.
  The friendly Beetle intercedes,
  And, all in tears, he kindly pleads:
"Queen of the Birds! no doubt, in spite of me,
You can this trembling creature bear away;
But spare me this affront, this grief, I pray.
John Rabbit begs his little life of thee;
Grant it for pity's sake, sweet ma'am, now do!"
The bird of Jove disdained to make reply,
But struck the Beetle with her wing – one – two –

Then bore John Rabbit to the upper sky.
Indignant Beetle, of revenge in quest,
Flew straight to the proud Eagle's nest;
Broke in her absence all her eggs – the lot –
Her sweetest hopes – the eggs she held so dear.
  Angry people have no fear.
The Eagle, coming to the well-loved spot,
And seeing all the hideous fricassee,
Filled heaven with shrieks; but could not find
On whom to vent her wrath – you see,
Her fury made her blind.
She mourned in vain; that year it was her fate
Childless to be, and desolate.
The next she built a loftier nest – in vain,
The Beetle addled all the eggs again.

John Rabbit's death was well avenged indeed!
For six long months the Eagle's moanings flew,
And woke the echoing forest through.
The bird that bore off Ganymede,
Furious and loud remonstrance made,
And flew to Jupiter for aid.
Her eggs she placed upon the Thunderer's lap –
There could come no mishap;
Jove must defend them: who would dare
To touch the objects of his care?
The enemy now changed his note; he soared,
And let some earth fall where they're stored;
The god, his vestment shaking carelessly,
Let the eggs fall into infinity.
The Eagle, mad with rage at the event

(Merely an accident),
Swore she would leave the wicked court,
And make the desert her resort;
    With such vagaries. –
    (In rage all fair is.)
Poor Jupiter in silence heard;
The Beetle came, and charged the bird –
In the tribunal of the upper air
Related the affair.
The god pronounced the Eagle in the wrong,
But still the mutual hate was strong.
To make a truce, Jove then arranged
The time for Eagles' hatching should be changed
To winter, when the marmots sleep.
And Beetles from the daylight keep.

The Lion and the Gnat

"Go, paltry insect, refuse of the earth!"
Thus said the Lion to the Gnat one day.
The Gnat held the Beast King as little worth;
Immediate war declared – no joke, I say.
"Think you I care for Royal name?
I care no button for your fame;
An ox is stronger far than you,
Yet oxen often I pursue."
This said; in anger, fretful, fast,
He blew his loudest trumpet blast,
And charged upon the Royal Nero,
Himself a trumpet and a hero.
  The time for vengeance came;
  The Gnat was not to blame.
Upon the Lion's neck he settled, glad
To make the Lion raving mad;
The monarch foams: his flashing eye
Rolls wild. Before his roaring fly
All lesser creatures; close they hide
To shun his cruelty and pride:
And all this terror at
The bite of one small Gnat,
Who changes every moment his attack,
First on the mouth, next on the back;
Then in the very caverns of the nose,

Gives no repose.
The foe invisible laughed out,
To see a Lion put to rout;
  Yet clearly saw
  That tooth nor claw
Could blood from such a pigmy draw.
The helpless Lion tore his hide,
And lashed with furious tail his side;
Lastly, quite worn, and almost spent,
Gave up his furious intent.
With glory crowned, the Gnat the battle-ground
Leaves, his victorious trump to sound,
As he had blown the battle charge before,
Still one blast for the conquest more.
He flies now here, now there,
To tell it everywhere.
Alas! it so fell out he met
A spider's ambuscaded net,
And perished, eaten in mid-air.

What may we learn by this? why, two things, then:
First, that, of enemies, the smaller men
Should most be dreaded; also, secondly,
That passing through great dangers there may be
Still pitfalls waiting for us, though too small to see.

The Lion and the Gnat

The Ass laden with Sponges, and the Ass laden with Salt

A Peasant, like a Roman Emperor bearing
  His sceptre on his shoulder, proudly
Drove his two steeds with long ears, swearing
  At one of them, full often and full loudly.
The first, with sponges laden, fast and fleet
Moved well its feet:
The second (it was hardly its own fault)
Bore bags of salt.
O'er mountain, dale, and weary road,
The weary pilgrims bore their load,
Till to a ford they came one day;
  They halted there
  With wondering air;
The driver knowing very well the way,
Leaped on the Ass the sponges' load that bore,
And drove the other beast before.
That Ass in great dismay
Fell headlong in a hole;

Then plashed and scrambled till he felt
The lessening salt begin to melt;
His shoulders soon had liberty,
And from their heavy load were free.
His comrade takes example from his brother,
As sheep will follow one another;
Up to his neck the creature plunges
Himself, his rider, and the sponges;
All three drank deep, the man and Ass
Tipple together many a glass.
The load seemed turned to lead;
The Ass, now all but dead,
Quite failed to gain the bank: his breath
Was gone: the driver clung like death
Till some one came, no matter who, and aid.
Enough, if I have shown by what I've said,
That all can't act alike, you know;
And this is what I wished to show.

The Lion and the Rat

It's well to please all people when you can;
   There's none so small but one his aid may need.
   Here are two fables, if you give good heed,
Will prove the truth to any honest man.

A Rat, in quite a foolish way,
   Crept from his hole between a Lion's paws;
The king of animals showed on that day
   His royalty, and never snapped his jaws.
The kindness was not unrepaid;
Yet, who'd have thought a Lion would need aid
    From a poor Rat?
    Soon after that
The Lion in the forest brake,
In their strong toils the hunters take;
   In vain his roars, his frenzy, and his rage.
But Mr. Rat runs up; a mesh or two
Nibbles, and lets the Lion through

   Patience and length of time may sever,
   What strength and empty wrath could never.

The Lion and the Rat

The Dove and the Ant

The next example we must get
From creatures even smaller yet.
A Dove came to a brook to drink,
When, leaning on the crumbling brink,
An Ant fell in, and failed to reach,
Through those vast ocean waves, the beach.
The Dove, so full of charity is she,
Threw down a blade of grass, a promontory,
Unto the Ant, who so once more,
Grateful and glad, escaped to shore.
    Just then passed by
A scampish poacher, soft, bare-footed, came
      Creeping and sly;
A crossbow in his hand he bore:
Seeing the Dove, he thought the game
Safe in the pot, and ready for the meal:
Quick runs the Ant, and stings his heel;
The angry rascal turns his head;
The Dove, who sees the scoundrel stoop,
Flies off, and with her flies his soup.

The Astrologer who let himself fall into the Well

To an Astrologer, who by a blunder
   Fell in a well, said one, "You addle-head,
Blind half an inch before your nose, I wonder
   How you can read the planets overhead."
This small adventure, not to go beyond,
   A useful lesson to most men may be;
How few there are at times who are not fond
   Of giving reins to their credulity,
Holding that men can read,
    In times of need,
The solemn Book of Destiny,
That book, of which old Homer sung.
What was the ancient *chance*, in common sense,
But modern Providence?
Chance that has always bid defiance
To laws and schemes of human science.
If it were otherwise, a single glance
Would tell us there could be no fortune and no chance.
All things uncertain;
Who can lift the curtain?
   Who knows the will of the Supreme?
He who made all, and all with a design;
   Who but himself can know them? who can dream
He reads the thoughts of the Divine,
Did God imprint upon the star or cloud
The secrets that the night of Time enshroud,

In darkness hid? – only to rack the brains
Of those who write on what each sphere contains.
To help us shun inevitable woes,
And sadden pleasure long before its close;
Teaching us prematurely to destroy,
And turn to evil every coming joy,
This is an error, nay, it is a crime.
The firmament rolls on, the stars have destined time.
The sun gives light by day,
And drives the shadows of the night away.
Yet what can we deduce but that the will Divine
Bids them rise and bids them shine,
To lure the seasons on, to ripen every seed,
   To shed soft influence on men;
What has an ordered universe to do indeed,
   With chance, that is beyond our ken.
Horoscope-makers, cheats, and quacks,
On Europe's princes turn your backs,
And carry with you every bellows-working alchymist:
You are as bad as they, I wist. –
But I am wandering greatly, as I think,
Let's turn to him whom Fate forced deep to drink.
Besides the vanity of his deceitful art,
He is the type of those who at chimeras gape,
Forgetting danger's simpler shape,
And troubles that before us and behind us start.

The Hare and the Frogs

One day sat dreaming in his form a Hare,
(And what but dream could one do there?)
With melancholy much perplexed
(With grief this creature's often vexed).
"People with nerves are to be pitied,
And often with their dumps are twitted;
Can't even eat, or take their pleasure;
Ennui," he said, "torments their leisure.
See how I live: afraid to sleep,
My eyes all night I open keep.
'Alter your habits,' some one says;
But Fear can never change its ways:
In honest faith shrewd folks can spy,
That men have fear as well as I."
Thus the Hare reasoned; so he kept
Watch day and night, and hardly slept;
Doubtful he was, uneasy ever;

A breath, a shadow, brought a fever.
It was a melancholy creature,
The veriest coward in all nature;
A rustling leaf alarmed his soul,
He fled towards his secret hole.
Passing a pond, the Frogs leaped in,
Scuttling away through thick and thin,
To reach their dark asylums in the mud.
"Oh! oh!" said he, "then I can make them scud
As men make me; my presence scares
Some people too! Why, they're afraid of Hares!
    I have alarmed the camp, you see.
Whence comes this courage? Tremble when I come;
    I am a thunderbolt of war, my be;
My footfall dreadful as a battle drum!"
    There's no poltroon, be sure, in any place,
    But he can find a poltroon still more base.

The Hare and the Frogs

The Cock and the Fox

Upon a branch a crafty sentinel,
  A very artful old bird, sat.
"Brother," a Fox said, "greet you well"
  (He speaks so soft – there's guile in that);
"Our quarrel's over, peace proclaimed:
  I bring the news; come down, embrace;
Do not delay; I shall be blamed
  If soon not twenty stages from this place.
Now you and yours can take your ease:
    Do what you please,
    Without a fear;
We're brothers now, you know, my dear.
Light up the bonfires everywhere:
    Dismiss all care;
But let us first, to seal the bliss,
Have one fraternal, tender kiss."
  "Friend," said the Cock, "upon my word,
More glorious news I never heard.

    This peace,
    May it increase;
It's double joy to hear it, friend, from thee.
    Ha! there I see
Two greyhounds – couriers, doubtless, as you are –
  Coming fast down yonder scaur:
  They'll be here in a minute,
  Ah! yes, there's something in it –
I'll come down quick: – we'd better kiss all round."
"Adieu," the Fox said; "Sir, my business presses;
We shall meet shortly, I'll be bound:
  Another time we can exult
  Over this end of our distresses."
  Then off the rascal ran to ground,
Full of chagrin and discontent.
The Cock laughed loud, to see his fear,
And clapped his wings, his wives to cheer.
It is a pleasure doubly sweet
To trick the scoundrel and the cheat.

The Raven who wished to imitate the Eagle

The bird of Jove bore off a heavy "mutton;"
A Raven, witness of the whole affair,
Weaker in back, but scarcely less a glutton,
  Resolved to do the same, whate'er
    Might come of it.
    With greedy wit,
Around the flock he made a sweep,
Marking, among the fattest sheep,
    One of enormous size,
    Fit for a sacrifice.
Said Master Raven, winking both his eyes,
"Your nurse's name I cannot tell,
But such fat flesh will suit me well:
You're ready for my eating."
Then on the sheep, slow, sluggish, bleating,

  The Raven settled down, not knowing
The beast weighed more than a mere cream-cheese
                  could.
  It had a fleece as thickly growing
As beard of Polyphemus – tangled wood –
That clung to either claw; the animal could not with-
                  draw.
  The shepherd comes, and calling to his boy,
  Gives him the Raven for a toy.

We must take care; the moral is quite clear –
The footpad mustn't rob on the highway.
Example is a dangerous lure, I fear:
Men-eaters are not all great people; no, I say,
Where wasps passed last week gnats are crushed to-day.

The Peacock complaining to Juno

The Peacock to great Juno came:
"Goddess," he said, "they justly blame
The song you've given to your bird:
All nature thinks it most absurd,
The while the Nightingale, a paltry thing,
Is the chief glory of the spring:
Her note so sweet, and deep, and strong."
"I do thee, jealous bird, no wrong,"
  Juno, in anger, cried:
  "Restrain thy foolish pride.
Is it for you to envy other's song? –
You who around your neck art wearing
Of rainbow silks a hundred different dyes? –
You, who can still display to mortal's eyes
A plume that far outfaces
  A lapidary's jewel-cases?
Is there a bird beneath the skies
More fit to please and strike?
No animal has every gift alike:
We've given you each one his special dower;
This one has beauty, and that other power.
Falcons are swift; the Eagle's proud and bold;
By Ravens sorrow is foretold;
The Crow announces miseries to come;
All are content if singing or if dumb.
Cease, then, to murmur, lest, as punishment,
The plumage from thy foolish back be rent."

The Peacock complaining to Juno

The Cat changed into a Woman

A Man loved, heart and soul, his favourite Cat;
She was his pet, his beauty, and all that.
Her mewing was so sweet, and was so sad: –
He was far madder than the mad.
This man, then, by his tears and praying,
By wizard charms and much soothsaying,
Wrought things so well, that Destiny,
One fine day, changed the Cat into a Woman
    (A change uncommon),
And they were married, soon as they could be.
Mad friends became mad lovers then;
    And not the fairest dame e'er known
    Had ever such affection shown
To him she'd chosen from all men.
The love-blind fool, delighted with his bride,
    Found not a trace of Cat was left at all,
    No scratch or caterwaul;
He fondles her, she him: she is his pride;
    She is the fairest of her kind,
    A perfect woman, to his mind.
One night some mice came gnawing at the curtain;
It broke the lady's sleep, that's certain;

At once she leaped upon her feet –
To cats revenge is very sweet –
And on all-fours she ran to seize
Those creatures always prone to tease;
But she was changed – in shape and wit –
They did not care for her a bit
This aberration on her part
Was grief perpetual to his heart.
It never ceased to be the way
Whenever mice were out at play;
For when a certain time has gone,
The jug is seasoned; and the cloth gets wrinkles.
In vain we try to alter what is done,
The warning bell unheeded tinkles.
Things will not change again; one knows
There is no way to end the matter,
Neither by pitchforks nor by blows;
Though Habit you should beat and tatter.
You'll not be master of the place,
Saddle or bridle – how you will;
For if the door's slammed in its face,
It comes back o'er the window-sill.

The Lion and the Ass

The King of Animals a *battue* made
Upon his birthday, bent to fill his bags.
The Lion's game is not with sparrows played;
But boars of bulk, and good-sized portly stags.
    For an ally in this affair,
    He had an able minister.
The Ass, with Stentor's voice, served as his hunting-
                            horn;

The Lion hid deep 'mid the thickest wood,
And ordered him to bray loud as he could;
So that the clamour shrilly borne,
Might drive from every nook and lair
Those not initiated to the sound.
The hideous tempest came; the air
Shook with the dreadful discord; round
It flew, and scared the fiercest forest creatures;

They fled with terror-stricken features,
And fell into the ready snare,
Where the King Lion stood to meet his prey.
"Have I not served thee brave and true?"
The Ass said, taking to himself the palm.
"Yes," quoth the Lion, grave and calm,
"'Twas nobly brayed; I own to you,
Had I not known your name and race,
I had been almost frightened too!"
Had he been rash, the Ass, his rage
Would not have hidden, I'll engage.
Just was the rallying, though severe;
For who can bear a bragging Ass?

It does not fit their rank or class,
And very ill becomes their business here.

A Will interpreted by Æsop

If what they say of Esop's truth,
He was the oracle of Greece indeed;
And all the Areopagus, in sooth,
Was not so wise. And here, if you would plead
For proof, I'll give one, in a pleasant tale,
My friends and readers to regale.

A certain man had daughters three,
Each of a different turn of mind:
The one a toper, loving company;
The second, fond of all coquetry;
The third a miser, and to save inclined.
The man left them, by will and deed,
As laws municipal decreed,
Half his estate, divided equally;
And to their mother just the same:
But only in her power to claim
When all the daughters had their own
And nothing more but that alone.
The father dead, the daughters ran
To read the will – they were not slow
To con it; yet, do what they can,
They could not understand it – no.
What did he wish? – yes, that's the question
That took a good deal of digestion.

'Each one that had her part, no more,
Should to her mother pay it o'er.'
It was not quite the usual way,
With no gold left, to go and pay:
What meant their worthy father, then?
They run and ask the black-gowned men,
Who turn the case for many days –
Turn it a hundred thousand ways;
Yet after all, in sheer vexation,
Throw down their wigs in perturbation.
At last the judge advised the heirs
At once to settle the affairs.
As to the widow's part, the counsels say
A third each sister's bound to pay,
Upon demand, unless she choose to take
A life annuity, for quietness' sake,
Beginning from the day her husband died,
And so they all decide.
Then in three lots they part the whole estate:
In number one the plate;
The mighty cellars; summer-houses built
Beneath the vine;
The stores of rich Malvoisin wine;
The spits, the bowls of silver gilt,
And all the tribes of slaves who wait; –

In short, the perfect apparatus,
That gives an epicure his social status.
The second lot comprises
All that a flirting girl surprises:
Embroiderer's, and many a lady's maid,
Jewels, and costly robes; – be sure
The town house, and the furniture,
And stately eunuchs, rich arrayed.
Lot three comprises farming-stock,
Pastures and houses, fold and flock;
Labourers and horses, stores and herds.
This done, they fix, with many words,
That since the lottery won't select
What each one would the most affect,
The eldest have what she likes best,
Leaving the same choice to the rest.
   In Athens it fell out,
   This pleased the motley rout,
   Both great and small.
   The judge was praised by all;
   Æsop alone derided
   The way they had decided.
After much time and pains, they'd gone, he thought,
And set the wishes of the man at nought,
"If the dead came to life," he said,

"Athens aloud he would upbraid.
What! men who cherish subtlety,
To blunder o'er a will so stupidly!"
   Then quickly he divides,
   And thus the sage decides: –
To each he gave the part
Least grateful to her heart:
Pressing on them what they most hate.

To the coquette the cups and bowls
Cherished and loved by thirsty souls;
The toper had the farm; still worse than that,
The miser had the slaves and dresses.
This is the way, Æsop confesses,
To make the sisters alienate
Their shares of the bequeathed estate;
Nor would they longer single tarry,
But run post haste, and quickly marry;
So very soon the father's gold, set free,
Would to the mother come, with certainty,
Which was the meaning of the testament.

The people wondered, as they homeward went,
That he alone should have more brains
Than all the lawyers and their trains.

Book III

The Miller, his Son, and the Ass

The Arts are birthrights; true, and being so,
The fable to the ancient Greeks we owe;
But still the field can ne'er be reaped so clean
As not to let the later comers glean.
The world of fiction's full of deserts bare,
Yet still our authors make discoveries there.
Let me repeat a story, good, though old,
That Malherbe to Racan, 'tis rumoured, told;
Rivals of Horace, heirs in every way,
Apollo's sons, our masters, I should say:
They met one time in friendly solitude,
Unbosoming those cares that will obtrude.
Racan commences thus, – "Tell me, my friend,
You, who the clue of life, from end to end,
Know well, and step by step, and stage by stage,
Have lost no one experience of age;
How shall I settle? I must choose my station.
You know my fortune, birth, and education.
Shall I the provinces make my resort,
Carry the colours, or push on at court?
The world has bitterness, and it has charms,
War has its sweets, and marriage its alarms:
Easy to follow one's own natural bent,
But I've both court and people to content."

"Please everybody!" Malherbe says, with crafty eye,
"Now hear my story ere you make reply.

I've somewhere read, a Miller and his Son,
One just through life, the other scarce begun
(Boy of fifteen, if I remember well),
Went one fair day a favourite Ass to sell;
To take him fresh – according to wise rules –
They tied his feet and swung him – the two fools –
They carried him just like a chandelier.
Poor simple rustics (idiots, I fear),
The first who met them gave a loud guffaw,
And asked what clumsy farce it was he saw.
'The greatest ass is not the one who walks,'
So sneeringly the passing horseman talks.
The Miller frees the beast, by this convinced.
The discontented creature brayed and winced
In its own *patois;* for the change was bad:
Then the good Miller mounted the poor lad.
As he limped after, there came by that way
Three honest merchants, who reviling say,
'Dismount! why, that won't do, you lazy lad;
Give up the saddle to your grey-haired dad;
You go behind, and let your father ride.'
'Yes, masters,' said the Miller, 'you decide
Quite right; both ways I am content.'
He took his seat, and then away they went.
Three girls next passed: 'Oh, what a shame!' says one,
'A father treating like a slave his son!

The Miller, his Son, and the Ass

The churl rides like a bishop's calf.' 'Not I,'
The Miller made the girls a sharp reply:
'Too old for veal, you hussies, and ill-famed.'
Still with such jesting he became ashamed,
 Thought he'd done wrong; and changing his weak
                                        mind,
Took up his son upon the croup behind.
But three yards more, a third, sour, carping set,
Began to cavil, – 'Biggest fools we've met!
The beast is done – he'll die beneath their blows.
What! load a poor old servant!' so it grows:
'They'll go to market, and they'll sell his skin.'
'Parbleu!' the Miller said, 'not worth a pin
The fellow's brains who tries with toil and strife
To please the world, his neighbour, and his wife.
But still we'll have a try as we've begun:'
So off the Ass they jumped, himself and son.
The Ass in state goes first, and then came they.
A quidnunc met them –'What! is that the way?
The Ass at ease, the Miller quite foot-sore!
That seems an Ass that's greatly held in store.
Set him in gold – frame him – now, by the mass,
Wear out one's shoes, to save a paltry Ass!
Not so went Nicolas his Jeanne to woo;
The song says that he rode to save his shoe.
There go three asses.' 'Right,' the Miller cries;
'I am an Ass, it's true, and you are wise;
But henceforth I don't care, so let them blame
Or praise, no matter, it shall be the same;
Let them be quiet, pshaw! or let them tell,
I'll go my own way now;'" and he did well.

Then follow Mars, or Cupid, or the Court,
Walk, sit, or run, in town or country sport,
Marry or take the cowl, empty or fill the bag,
Still never doubt the babbling tongues will wag.

King Gaster and the Members

Had I but shown a proper loyalty,
I had begun my book with royalty.
The Belly is a king, it's true,
And in a certain point of view
His wants the other members share.
Well, once to work for him they weary were;
Each one discussed a better plan, –
To live an idle gentleman,
    Like Monsieur Gaster,
    Their lord and master.
"Without us he must feed on air;
We sweat and toil, and groan with care,
For whom? for him alone; we get no good,
And all our thought's to find him food:
We'll strike, and try his idle trade."
'Twas done as soon as said.
The hands refused to grasp, the legs to walk,
The eyes to open, and the tongue to talk;
Gaster might do whate'er he could. –
'Twas a mistake they soon repent
    With one consent.
The heart made no more blood, and so
The other members ceased to glow;
    All wanted strength,
And thus the working men at length

Saw that their idle monarch, in his way,
Toiled for the common weal as well as they.
And this applies to royalty,
It takes and gives with fair equality;
All draw from it their nourishment:
It feeds the artisan, and pays the magistrate,
Gives labourers food, and soldiers subsidies,
    Distributes in a thousand places
    Its sovereign graces;
In fact, supports the State.

Menenius told the story well,
When discord in the senate fell,
And discontented Commons taunted it
For having power and treasure, honour, dignity,
While all the care and pain was theirs,
Taxes and imposts, all the toils of war,
The blood, the sorrow, brand and scar.
Without the walls already do they band,
Resolved to seek another land.

    Menenius was able,
    By this most precious fable,
    To bring them safely back
    To the old, honest track.

The Wolf turned Shepherd

A Wolf who found in cautious flocks
  His tithes beginning to be few,
Thought that he'd play the part of Fox,
  A character at least quite new.
A Shepherd's hat and coat he took,
And from a branch he made a hook;
Nor did the pastoral pipe forget.
To carry out his schemes he set,
He would have liked to write upon his hat,
  "I'm Guillot, Shepherd of these sheep!"
And thus disguised, he came, pit-pat,
  And softly stole where fast asleep
Guillot himself lay by a stack,
His dog close cuddling at his back;
His pipe too slept; and half the number
Of the plump sheep was wrapped in slumber.

He's got the dress – could he but mock
The Shepherd's voice, he'd lure the flock:
  He thought he could.
That spoiled the whole affair – he'd spoken;
  His howl re-echoed through the wood.
The game was up – the spell was broken!
  They all awake, dog, Shepherd, sheep.
    Poor Wolf, in this distress
    And pretty mess,
In clumsy coat bedight,
Could neither run away nor fight.

  At last the bubble breaks;
  There's always some mistake a rascal makes.
  The Wolf like Wolf must always act;
  That is a very certain fact.

The Wolf turned Shepherd

The Frogs who asked for a King

Of Democrats the Frogs grew tired,
And unto Monarchy aspired;
Clamour so loud, that from a cloud
Great Jove in pity dropped a King,
Silent and peaceful, all allowed;
And yet he fell with such a splash, the thing
Quite terrified those poor marsh folks,
   Not fond of jokes,
Foolish and timid, all from him hid;
   And each one brushes
To hide in reeds, or sneak in rushes;
And from their swampy holes, poor little souls!
For a long time they dared not peep
At the great giant, still asleep.
  And yet the monarch of the bog
  Was but *A Log,*
Whose solemn gravity inspired with awe
The first who venturing saw:
He hobbled somewhat near,
With trembling and with fear;

Then others followed, and another yet,
Until a crowd there met;
At last the daring mob grew bolder,
And leaped upon the royal shoulder;
Good man, he did not take it ill,
But as before kept still.
Soon Jupiter is deafened with the din –
"Give us a king who'll move," they all begin.
The monarch of the gods sends down a Crane,
Who with a vengeance comes to reign.
  He gobbles and he munches,
  He sups and lunches;
Till louder still the Frogs complain.
"Why, see!" great Jupiter replied,
"How foolishly you did decide.
You'd better kept your first – the last is worst.
You must allow, if you are fair,
King Log was calm and *debonnair:*
With him, then, be ye now content,
For fear a third, and worse, be sent."

The Frogs who asked for a King

The Fox and the Goat

A Fox once travelled, and for company
His friend, a large-horned Goat, had he,
Who scarce could see an inch beyond his nose,
While Reynard every trick and quibble knows.
Thirst drove these folks, it so befell,
To seek the bottom of a well.
After they'd had their bout of drinking,
Says Reynard, "Comrade, I am thinking
How we can best get out from here;
Put up your feet and horns – no fear –
Rear up against the wall, my friend,
And I'll climb up – our troubles end.
One spring upon your horns will do;
And I once out can rescue you."
"Now, by my beard! I like the plan,"
The other said, "you're one that can;

Such folks as you see clear through things,
Some never learn the secret springs;
I never should have found it out,
Though I had groped a year about."
The Fox once free, the Goat compelled
To learn a sermon – the text's "patience."
"If Heaven," he said, "had only held
It right to give thee and thy dull relations
Half as much sense as beard –
(But then it hasn't, I'm afeard);
Still use your efforts, my dear sir – no perturbations.

   Certain affairs of state
   Will hardly let me longer wait;
In everything 'tis well to mind the end,
In future think of that, my friend."

The Eagle, the wild Sow, and the Cat

An Eagle lodged its young within a hollow tree;
A Sow lived at the foot; a Cat between the two.
Friendly they were, good neighbours, the whole three, –
Between the mothers there was no to-do.
At last the Cat malignant mischief made;
She climbed up to the Eagle: "Ma'am, our peace
Is ended, death," she says, "is threatening; I'm dismayed.
We perish if our children die; she'll never cease,
That Sow accursed. See! how she grubs and digs,
And mines and burrows, to uproot our oak;
She hopes to ruin us and ours, to feed her pigs
When the tree falls – Madam, it is no joke!
Were there but hopes of saving one,
I'd go and quietly mourn alone."
Thus sowing fear broadcast, she went
With a perfidious intent,
To where the Sow sat dozily.
"Good friend and neighbour," whispered she,
"I warn you, if you venture forth,
The Eagle pounces on your family;
Don't go and spread the thing about,
Or I shall fall a victim to her wrath."

Having here also sown wild fears,
And set her neighbours by the ears,
The Cat into her hole withdrew;
The Eagle after would not fly
To bring home; food; the poor Sow, too,
Was still more fearful and more shy.
Fools! not to see that one's first care
Is for one's self to find good fare;
Both stayed at home, still obstinate,
To save their young from cruel fate.
The royal bird, she feared the mine;
The Sow, a pounce upon her swine;
Hunger slew all the porcine brood,
And then the eaglets of the wood;
Not one was left – just think of that!
What a relief to Madame Cat!

A treacherous tongue sows misery
By its pernicious subtlety;
Of all the ills that from Pandora's box arose,
Not one brought half so many woes
As foul Deceit; daughter of Treachery.

The Drunkard and his Wife

Each one's his faults, to which he still holds fast,
And neither shame nor fear can cure the man;
'Tis *apropos* of this (my usual plan),
I give a story, for example, from the past.
A follower of Bacchus hurt his purse,
His health, his mind, and still grew each day worse;
Such people, ere they've run one-half their course,
Drain all their fortune for their mad expenses.
One day this fellow, by the wine o'erthrown,
Had in a bottle left his senses;
His shrewd wife shut him all alone
In a dark tomb, till the dull fume
Might from his brains evaporate.
He woke and found the place all gloom,
A shroud upon him cold and damp,

Upon the pall a funeral lamp.
"What's this?" said he; "my wife's a widow, then!"
On that the wife, dressed like a Fury, came,
Mask'd, and with voice disguised, into the den,
And brought the wretched sot, in hopes to tame,
Some boiling gruel fit for Lucifer.
The sot no longer doubted he was dead –
A citizen of Pluto's – could he err?
"And who are you?" unto the ghost he said.
"I'm Satan's steward," said the wife, "and serve the
food
For those within this black and dismal place."
The sot replied, with comical grimace,
Not taking any time to think,
"And don't you also bring the drink?"

The Gout and the Spider

When Mischief made the Spider and the Gout,,
"My daughters," said she, "you may clearly vaunt
That nowhere in a human haunt
Are there two plagues more staunch and stout;
Come, choose your dwellings where you would abide:
Here are the hovels – narrow, dark, and poor,
And there the palaces all gilt with pride.
You have your choice – now, what can I say more?
  Here is the lottery prescribed by law,
  Come, daughters, draw."
"The hovel's not my place," the Spider says;
Her sister hates the palace, for the Gout
Sees men called doctors creeping in and out,
They would not leave her half an hour at ease:
She crawls and rests upon a poor man's toe,
    Just so,
And says, "I shall now do whate'er I please.
No struggles longer with Hippocrates!
No call to pack and march, no one can displace me."
The Spider camps upon a ceiling high,
As if she had a life-long lease, you see,
And spins her web continually,
  Ready for any fly.
A servant soon, to clean the room,
Sweeps down the product of her loom.
With each tissue the girl's at issue:
Spiders, busy maids will swish you!

The wretched creature every day
Was driven from her home away;
At last, quite wearied, she gave out,
And went to seek her sister Gout,
Who in the country mourned her wretched fate:
A thousand times more hopeless her estate;
Even more miseries betide her
Than the misfortunes of the Spider.
Her host has made her dig and hoe,
And rake and chop, and plough and mow,
Until he's all but well.
"I can't resist him. Ah! *ma belle:*
Let us change places." Gladly heard,
The Spider took her at her word.
In the dark hovel she can spin:
No broom comes there with bustling din.
The Gout, on her part, pleased to trudge,
Goes straightway – wise as any judge –
Unto a bishop, and with whims
So fetters his tormented limbs,
That he from bed can never budge.
    Spasms!
    Cataplasms!
Heaven knows, the doctors make the curse
Steal steadily from bad to worse.
Both sisters gloried in the change,
And never after wished to range.

The Wolf and the Stork

Wolves are too prone to play the glutton.
One, at a certain feast, 'tis said,
Fell with such fury on his mutton,
He gave himself quite up for dead,
For in his throat a bone stuck fast.
A Stork, by special stroke of luck,
As he stood speechless, came at last.
He beckoned, and she ran to aid,
    No whit afraid.
A surgeon, and a very friend in need,
She drew the bone out. For the cure she'd made
She simply asked her fee.
"Fie!" said the Wolf, "you jeer at me,
My worthy gossip. Only see:
What! is it not enough that, sound and safe,
You drew your neck back from my gullet,
    My pretty pullet?
You are ungrateful. Now, then, go;
Beware, another time, my blow."

The Lion Defeated by Man

A picture was exhibited, one day,
In which an artisan had sought
To paint a lion which had fought,
And had been beaten in the fray.
The passers-by were full of self-applause.
A Lion who looked on reproached the crowd:
"Yes, here I see," he said, "the victory is man's:
The artisan had his own plans;
But if my brothers painted, they'd be proud
To show you man prostrate beneath our claws."

The Fox and the Grapes

A certain hungry Fox, of Gascon breed
(Or Norman – but the difference is small),
Discovered, looking very ripe indeed,
    Some Grapes that hung upon an orchard-wall.
Striving to clamber up and seize the prey,
    He found the fruit was not within his power;
"Well, well," he muttered, as he walked away,
    "It's my conviction that those Grapes are sour."

The Fox did wisely to accept his lot;
'Twas better than complaining, was it not?

The Fox and the Grapes

The Swan and the Cook

In a menagerie a Swan and Goose
Lived like sworn friends, in peace and amity.
This one was meant to please the master's eye,
The other fitted for his palate's use:
This for the garden, that one for the board.
The château's fosse was their long corridor,
Where they could swim, in sight of their liege lord,
Splash, drink, and paddle, or fly o'er and o'er,
Unwearied of their pastime, down the moat.
One day the Cook, taking a cup too much,
Mistook the birds, and, seizing by the throat,
Was just about to kill – his blindness such –
The helpless Swan, and thrust him in the pot.
The bird began to sing his dying song:
 The Cook, in great surprise,
 Opened his sleepy eyes.
"What do I do?" he said; "I had forgot:
No, no, Jove willing! may my neck be strung,
Before I kill a bird that sings so well."

Thus, in the dangers that around us throng,
Soft words are often useful, as it here befell.

The Wolves and the Sheep

After a thousand years of open war,
The Wolves signed treaty with their foes, the Sheep:
It seemed to be the best for both, by far;
For if the Wolves contrived their tithes to reap,
The shepherds liked a coat of tanned Wolf-skin.
No liberty for pasture had there been,
Neither for carnage; never was there rest!
None could enjoy what pleasures seemed the best;
Peace was concluded – hostages surrendered.
The Wolves their cubs, the Sheep their watch-dogs
                             rendered;
Th' exchange was made in form and order due,
Commissioners were there and not a few;
Some time elapsed, but soon the Wolf-cubs grew
To perfect Wolves, and with a taste for killing;
They chose a time the shepherds were away,
Choked all the fattest lambs that they could slay,
And bore them to the woods; no whit unwilling,
Their fellow-plotters waited for them there.
The dogs, who, full of trust, had thrown by care,
Were slain so quickly, that not one e'en knew
Who their assailants were that bit and slew.
War 'gainst the bad, a war that never ends;
Peace is a wholesome thing, good men are friends.
That I allow; yet peace is but a word, a senseless joke,
With wicked people, and such faithless folk.

The Wolves and the Sheep

The Lion grown old

A Lion, once the terror of the plain
(Borne down with age, and weakened by decay)
Against rebellious vassals fought in vain,
And found his foes the victors of the fray.
The Horse advanced, and gave his king a kick –
The Wolf a bite – the Ox a brutal butt:
Meanwhile the Lion, worn, and sad, and sick,
Could scarce resent this, the "unkindest cut."
But when an Ass came running to the place,
The monarch murmured, with his latest breath,
"Enough! I wished to die, but this disgrace
Imparts a twofold bitterness to death."

Philomel and Progne

Progne, the Swallow, set forth from her dwelling,
And, leaving the cities afar, took flight
For the grove that Philomel chose for telling
    Her ancient griefs to the listening night.
"Sister," said Progne, "I have not met you
    For nearly the space of a thousand years.
Why are we parted? I cannot forget you,
    Nor banish our Thracian trials and tears.
Come. leave this wood; it is dark and lonely."
    "What haunt could be pleasanter?" Philomel asked.
"And is it," said Progne, "for animals only,
    Or preasants at best, that your efforts are tasked?
With a note so rich 'tis a thousand pities
    To scatter its charms to the desert air.
Come, quit this grove to delight our cities,
    And waste no longer a gift so rare.
Theses woods, my sister, must oft remind you
    Of all the sorrow King Tereus wrought.
Leave, leave the terrible days behind you,
    And give to the past not a tearful thought."
"'Tis the memory, dear, of our Thracian troubles,"
    Said Philomel, sadly, "that bids me stay;
For the sight of humanity only doubles
The grief of the times that have passed away!"

Philomel and Progne

The drowned Woman

I am not one of those who coolly say,
"It's nought but just a woman who is drowned!"
I say it's much, yes, much in every way.
The sex I reverence. Taking them all round,
They are the joy of life, then let their praise resound.
And theses remarks are really *apropos*:
My fable treating of a woman lost
In a deep river. Ill luck willed it so.
Her husband sought her, at each ford she'd crossed,
To place her body in a fitting tomb.
And as he wandered by the fatal shore
Of the swift stream that bore his wife away,
The people passing he asked o'er and o'er,
If they had seen her on that luckless day.
They'd not e'en heard of his sad loss before.
"No," said the first; "but seek her lower down:
Follow the stream, and you will find her yet."
Another answer'd: "Follow her! no, no; that's wrong.
Go further up, and she'll be there, I bet,
Whether the current's weak, or the tide strong.
It's my conviction,

Such is a woman's love of contradiction,
She'll float the other way, your soul to fret.
The raillery was out of season;
And yet the heedless boor had reason,
For such is woman's humour still,
To follow out her own good will;
Yes, from her very birthday morn
Till to the churchyard she is borne,
She'd contradict to her last breath,
And wish she could e'en after death.

The Weasel in the granary

Once Madame Weasel, slender-waisted, thin,
Into a granary, by a narrow chink,
Crept, sick and hungry; quick she glided in,
To eat her fill, and she was wise, I think.
  There at her ease,
  No fear of fees,
She gnawed, and nibbled: – gracious, what a life!
The bacon melted in the strife.
  Plump and rotund she grew,
  As fat as two.
  A week was over,
  Spent in clover.
But one day, when she'd done – and that not badly –
  A noise alarmed her sadly.
She tried the hole she'd entered, wishing to retreat;
  'Twas no such easy feat.
Was she mistaken? – no, the selfsame door:
  She tried it, o'er and o'er.
"Yes, yes," she said, "it is the place, I know;
I passed here but a week ago."
A Rat who saw her puzzled, slily spoke –
'Your pouch was emptier then, before your fast broke.
Empty you came, and empty you must quit:
I tell you what I've told a dozen more.
But don't perplex the matter, I implore;
They differed from you in some ways, I do admit."

The cat and the old Rat

I've read in some old Fabulist, I know,
A second Nibblelard, of Cats
The Alexander, and of Rats
The Attila, struck many a fatal blow;
And this exterminating creature
Was quite a Cerberus by nature.
(The author writes) For miles away,
This Cat was feared; he'd vowed, they say,
  To clear the world of mice,
  And in a trice.
The disks within a jar hung gingerly,
"The death to Rats:" the traps, and gins, and springs,
The nooses, poisons, and such things,
Were nothing to this Cat, but merely toys.
Soon as he heard no longer stir or noise,
The mice being prisoned on each hole,
  Cheek and jowl;
So that it was in vain to hope for prey,
  He tried another "lay."
Shammed death, laid down fast holding by a cord;
A trickster, eager for the horde –
The mice, good folk, deem he is hung
For stealing meat or cheese, tight strung
For scratching some one, or for breaking done.
At last they think the monster's sand is run;
His funeral will be quite a gala day.
Then out they slowly creep,
First one small nose, and then another,

The Cat and the old Rat

Next a young mouse, then an old brother,
And then they scurry back in fright;
But four step once more to the light,
And lastly all come out to play,
And now begins another sort of treat:
The dead Cat falls upon his nimble feet,
Snaps the slowest, head and tail.
"Ha! ha!" he gobbling cried, "It could not fail,
My *ruse de guerre*; no holes avail
To save these creatures, and I warn them now,
They all will come to the same mouth, I trow."
His prophecy came true – the master of his art,
A second time played well his part.
His fur he whitened o'er with flour,
    That very hour,
    And hid within
    A white meal bin.

No bad contrivance, every one must own.
The Rats could not leave well alone;
One Rat was wary, shy to venture out,
    And pry about –
Man of the world, and master of *finesse*,
He'd lost his tail in battle, too,
And half a dozen tricks he knew.
"This mass of white may be all sham, I guess,"
He cried, still shunning the Cat's ambuscade:
"Beneath the stuff I fear some trap is laid;
    No matter if it's flour or no,
    It may be so;
But sack or not, still I won't venture near."
'Twas neatly said, his prudence and his fears
I much approve; Experience told him true,
    Suspicion's Safety's mother,
    And Wisdom's foster brother.

Book IV

The Lion in Love
To Mademoiselle de Sévigné

Lady, whose charms were meant to be
A model for the Graces three;
Lend graciously your gentle ear,
And but one simple fable hear;
You'll see, without profound alarm,
A Lion quelled by Cupid's arm.
Love rules with such a tyranny,
Happy those shunning slavery;
Who the harsh monarch only know
By song and poem, not by blow.
When I dare speak of love to you,
Pardon the fable, no whit true,
That gives me courage to bring it,
Perhaps with more of zeal than wit,
A simple offering, rough and rude,
Of my devoted gratitude.

   In times when animals could speak,
The Lion came intent to seek
Mankind's alliance – wherefore not?
Since beasts had then by nature got
Courage, intelligence, and skill;
A bearing, too, by no means ill.

Now hear what happened, if you will:
A Lion of a noble race
Saw in a vale a pretty face,
A shepherdess's, understand,
And instantly he claimed her hand.
The father, prudent and pacific,
Preferred a suitor less terrific:
To give his daughter seemed too bad,
Yet how refuse so wild a lad?
If he refused, perhaps there'd be
A marriage still clandestinely.
The maiden liked her dashing wooer,
Her boisterous, reckless, blustering suer,
And playing with the creature's main,
Combed it, and smoothed it o'er again;
The prudent father, half afraid
To spurn the lover of the maid,
Said, "But my daughter's delicate,
Your claws may hurt your litttle mate;
And when you fondle and caress,
Lion, you'll tear her and her dress;
Permit me, sir, to clip each paw,

It shall be done without a flaw,
And, by-the-by, in the meanwhile,
Your teeth 'twould be as well to file;
Your kisses then would be less rough,
And her's far sweeter – that's enough."
The Lion, blinded by affection,
Obeyed the artful man's direction;
Toothless and clawless, he grew prouder
(A fortress without guns or powder).
They loosed the mastiff on him soon,
And he was butchered before noon.
O Love! O Love! when bound by you,
Prudence, to thee we say, Adieu!

The Lion in Love

The Shepherd and the Sea

Beside his fold, and free from every care,
A Shepherd, Amphitrite's neighbour, lived for years;
Small was his fortune, yet while skies were fair,
He was contented, vexed by cares nor fears.
At last the treasures cast upon the shore
Tempted the man; he bartered flock and fold,
And sent forth ships to bring him back the more;
But tempests sank the vessels and the gold.
Once more he went to watch the silly sheep,
No longer master as he had been long,
When his own flocks he used to ward and keep,
And poets called him Tircis in their song;
Now he was Pierrot, and that was all.
After some time he, once more well to do,
Had flocks again to answer to his call;
One day when winds were low, and vessels drew

Safely towards the shore and home, the Shepherd stood
Upon the sunny cliff: "Fair nymphs," he cried,
"Seek some one else, I pray you be so good;
Ma foi, you don't catch me with any tide."

This story is not merely meant to please;
It's sober truth, I say, and serves to show
That pence are better if all safe, you know,
Than pounds of promises; when once at ease,
Remain content, and closely shut your ears
To Circe's wiles, resist her wanton smiles.
Ambition and the Sea, avoid them both,
They're full of miseries and racking fears;
For one who wins there's twenty thousand don't.
Rely on that; the winds and thieves are loth
To lose their prey (and trust to them) – they won't.

The Shepherd and the Sea

The Fly and the Ant

The Fly and Ant once quarrelled seriously:
"O Jupiter!" the first exclaimed, "how vanity
Blinds the weak mind! This mean and crawling thing
Actually ventures to compare
With me, the daughter of the air.
The palace I frequent, and on the board
I taste the ox before our sovereign lord;
While this poor paltry creature lives for days
On the small straw she drags through devious ways.
Come. Mignon, tell me plainly now,
Do you camp ever on a monarch's brow,
Or on a beauty's cheek? Well, I do so, –
And on her bosom, too, I'd have you know.
I sport among her curls; I place
Myself upon her blooming face.
The ladies bound for conquest go
To us for patches; their necks' snow
With spots of blackness well contrast,
Of all her toilette cares the last.
Come, now, good fellow, rack your brain,
And let us hear of sense some grain."
"Well, have you done?" replied the Ant.
"You haunt king's palaces, I grant;
But then, by every one you're cursed.
It's very likely you taste first
The gods' own special sacred feast:
Nor is it better, sir, for that.
The fane you enter, with the train –

So do the godless and profane.
On heads of kings or dogs, 'tis plain,
You settle freely when not wanted,
And you are punished often – granted.
You talk of patches on a belle,
I, too, should patch them just as well.
The name your vanity delights,
Frenchmen bestow on parasites;
Cease, then, to be so grossly vain,
Your aspirations, Miss, restrain;
Your namesakes are exiled or hung,
And you with famine will be clung.
With cold and freezing misery,
Will come your time of penury,
When our King Phœbus goes to cheer
And rule the other hemisphere:
But I shall live upon my store,
My labours for the summer o'er,
Nor over mountains and seas go,
Through storm and rain, and drifting snow;
No sorrow near me will alloy
The fulness of the present joy;
Past trouble bars out future care,
True not false glory is our share;
And this I wish to show to you –
Time flies, and I must work. Adieu!
This idle chattering will not fill
My little granary and till."

The Gardener and his Master

An amateur of flowers – bourgeois and yet clown –
Had made a garden far from any town;
Neat, trim, and snug, it was the village pride;
Green quickset hedges girt its every side;
There the rank sorrel and the lettuce grew,
And Spanish jasmine for his Margot, too,
Jonquils for holidays, and crisp dry thyme;
But all this happiness, one fatal time,
Was marred by a hare; his grief and woe
Compel the peasant to his lord to go.
"This cursed animal," he says, "by night
And day comes almost hourly for his bite;
He spurns my cunning, and defies my snares,
For stones and sticks he just as little cares;
He is a wizard, that is very sure,
And for a wizard is there, sir, a cure?"
"Wizard, be hanged!" the lord said; "you shall see,
His tricks and his wiles will not avail with me;
I'll scare the rascal, on my faith, good man."
"And when?" "To-morrow; I have got a plan."
The thing agreed, he comes with all his troop.
"Good! let us lunch – fowls tender in the coop?

That girl your daughter? come to me, my dear!
When you betroth her, there's a brave lad here.
I know, good man, the matrimonial curse
Digs plaguey deep into a father's purse."
The lord, so saying, nearer draws his chair,
Plays with the clusters of the daughter's hair,
Touches her hand, her arm, with gay respect,
Follies that make a father half suspect
Her coyness is assumed; meantime they dine,
Squander the meat, play havoc with the wine.
"I like these hams, their flavour and their look."
"Sir, they are yours." "Thanks: take them to my cook."
He dined, and amply; his retainers, too;
Dogs, horses, valets, all well toothed, nor few;
My lord commands, such liberties he takes,
And fond professions to the daughter makes.
The dinner over, and the wine passed round,
The hunters rise, and horns and bugles sound;
They rouse the game with such a wild halloo,
The good man is astonished at the crew;
The worst was that, amid this noise and clack,
The little kitchen garden went to wrack.

Adieu the beds! adieu the borders neat!
Peas, chicory, all trodden under feet.
Adieu the future soup! The frightened hare
Beneath a monster cabbage made his lair.
They seek him – find him; 'After him, my boys!"
He seeks the well-known hole with little noise;
Yet not a hole, rather a wound they made
In the poor hedge with hoof and hunting-blade.
"By the lord's orders it would never do
To leave the garden but on horseback, no."
The good man says, "Royal your sports may be,
Call them whate'er you like, but pity me;
Those dogs and people did more harm to-day
Than all the hares for fifty years, I say."

The Ass and the little Dog

To ape a talent not your own
Is foolish; no one can affect a grace.
A blundering blockhead better leave alone
The gallant's bows, and tricks, and smiling face.
To very few is granted Heaven's dower –
Few have infused into their life the power
To please, so better far to leave the charm
To them. And may I ask you, where's the harm?
One would not bear resemblance to the Ass,
Who wishing to be dearer to his master,
Amiably went to kiss him; so it came to pass
There followed instantly no small disaster.
"What!" said he, "shall this paltry thing
Assume by dint of toadying,
Win Madam's friendly fellowship,
And twist and gambol, fawn and skip,
While I have only blows? no, no!
What does he do? – why, all fools know –

He gives his paw; the thing is done,
And then they kiss him every one.
If that is all, upon my word,
To call it difficult 's absurd."
Full of this glorious thought, one luckless day,
Seeing his master smiling pass that way,
The clumsy creature comes, and clumsily
Chucks with his well-worn hoof quite gallantly
His master's chin; to please him still the more,
With voice, so sweet, sonorous brays his best.
"Oh, what caresses, and what melody!"
The master cires; "Ho! Martin, come, be quick!
And, Martin, bring the heaviest stick!"
Then Martin comes; the donkey changed his tune.

So ended the brief comedy
In bitter blows and misery.
Donkeys' ambitions pass so soon.

Battle between the Rats and Weasels

The Weasel nation, like the Cats,
Are always fighting with the Rats;
And did the Rats not squeeze their way
Through doors so narrow, I must say,
The long-backed creatures would slip in,
And swallow all their kith and kin.
One certain year it did betide,
When Rats were greatly multiplied,
Their king, illustrious Ratapon,
His army to the field led on.
The Weasels, too, were soon arrayed,
And the old flag again displayed.
If Fame reported just and true,
Victory paused between the two;
Till fallows were enriched and red
With blood the rival armies shed;
But soon in every place

Misfortune met the Rattish race.
The rout was so complete, the foe
More dreadful grew at every blow;
And what avails brave Artapax,
Meridarpax, Psicarpax?
Who, covered both with dust and gore,
Drove back the Weasels thrice and more,
Till driven slowly from the plain,
E'en their great courage proved in vain!
'Twas Fate that ruled that dreadful hour:
Then each one ran who had the power;
Soldier and captain, jostling fled,
But all the princes were struck dead;
The private, nimble in his feet,
Unto his hole made snug retreat.
The noble, with his lofty plume,
Found that he had by no means room.

To strike with terror – yes, or whether
A mark of honour – rose the feather,
That led to much calamity,
As very soon the nobles see;
Neither in cranny, hole, or crack,
Was space found for the plumed pack.
In the meantime, the populace
Found access to each lurking-place,
So that the largest heap of slain
From the Rat noblemen is ta'en.
    A nodding feather in the cap
Is oftentimes a great mishap;
A big and over-gilded coach
Will sometimes stop up an approach;
The smaller people, in most cases,
Escape by unregarded places:
Men soon are on great people's traces.

The Monkey and the Dolphin

It was a custom with the Greeks
For travellers by sea to take
Monkeys and fancy dogs, whose tricks
Would pastime in fair weather make.
A vessel with such things on deck,
Not far from Athens, went to wreck;
But for the Dolphins all had drowned.
This animal is friend to man:
The fact in Pliny may be found;
So must be true, say what you can.
A Dolphin half the people saves,
Even a Monkey, by-the-by,
He thought a sailor, from the waves
He kindly helped; the creature sly,
Seated upon the Dolphin's back,
Looked very grave and wise; good lack!
One would have really almost sworn
'Twas old Arion, all forlorn.
The two had nearly reached the land,
When just by chance, and such a pity!
Fish asks, "Are you from Athens grand?"
"Yes; oh, they know me in that city;

If you have any business there,
Employ me; for it is truly where
My kinsfolk hold the highest place.
My second cousin is Lord Mayor."
The Dolphin thanked him with good grace:
"And the Piræus knows your face?
You see it often, I dare say?"
"See him! I see him every day;
An old acquaintance; that is so."
The foolish chatterer did not know
Piræus was a harbour, not a man.
Such people, go where'er you can,
You meet within a mile of home,
Mistaking Vaugirard for Rome,
People who chattering dogmatise
Of what has never met their eyes.
The Dolphin laughed, and turning round
The Monkey saw, and straightway found
He'd saved mere shadow of humanity;
Then plunged again beneath the sea,
And search amid the billows made
For one more worthy of his aid.

The Monkey and the Dolphin

Man and the wooden Idol

A certain Pagan had a god of wood –
Deaf was the idol, yet had ears enough;
The Pagan promised to himself much good.
It cost as much as three men; for his fears
Induced repeated vows and offerings;
Fat oxen crowned with garlands and such things.
Never an idol – think of that –
Boasted of victims half as fat.
Yet all this worship brought no grace,
Treasure or legacy, or luck at play;
What's more, if any single storm came near the place,
This man was sure to have to pay;
Yet all the time the god dined well. Now, was this fair?
At last, impatient at the costly care,

He takes a crowbar, and the Idol smashes
    (Crashes).

Forth comes a stream of gold.
"I feasted you with offerings manifold,
And you were never worth an obolus to me;
Now leave," he said, "my hospitality,
Seek out another altar. I hold thee
One of those gross and stupid creatures
With wicked and untoward natures
Whose gratitude can never grow;
But after many a heavy blow,
The more I gave the less I got; I own
It's very well I changed my tone."

The Jay dressed in Peacock's plumes

A Peacock having moulted, the sly Jay
Put on the thrown-off plumage with delight;
Amongst some other Peacocks found his way,
And thought himself a fascinating sight.
At last the would-be beau got recognised,
A charlatan, in borrowed plumes equipt –
And laughed at, scouted, hustled, and despised,
Of all his second-hand attire got stript;
Returning to his friends, abashed and poor,
They most politely showed him to the door.
Two-footed Jays are anything but rare,
Who live on facts and fancies not their own;
But these are, luckily, not my affair,
So let me leave the plagiarists alone.

The Camel and the Drift-Wood

The first who saw a real live Camel
Ran for his life; the second ventured near;
The third, with ready rope, without a fear,
Made a strong halter the wild thing to trammel.
Habit has power to quickly change
Things that at first seem odd and strange;
Stale they grow, and quickly tame,
And hardly seem to be the same.
And since the question's open, once there stood
A look-out watching all the distant flood;
And seeing something far off on the ocean,
Could not conceal his notion
It was a man-of-war; a moment past
It turned a fire ship, all ataunt and brave,
Then a big boat, and next a bale, and last
Some mere drift timber jostling on the wave.
   How many things watched by the world agree
In this – that far away you see
That there is something, yet when sought,
And seen still nearer, it proves nought.

The Frog and the Rat

Merlin said well, that those who often cheat
Will sometimes cheat themselves – the phrase is old.
I'm sorry that it is, I must repeat
It's full of energy, and sound as gold.
But to my story: once a well-fed Rat,
Rotund and wealthy, plump and fat,
Not knowing either Fast or Lent,
Lounging beside a marsh pool went.
A Frog addressed him in the Frog's own tongue,
And asked him home to dinner civilly.
No need to make the invitation long.
He spoke, however, of the things he'd see:
The pleasant bath, worth curiosity;
The novelties along the marsh's shore,
   The score and score
Of spots of beauty, manners of the races,
The government of various places,
Some day he would recount with glee
Unto his youthful progeny;
One thing alone the gallant vexed,
And his adventurous soul perplexed;
He swam but little, and he needed aid.
The friendly Frog was undismayed;

His paw to hers she strongly tied,
And then they started side by side.
The hostess towed her frightened guest
Quick to the bottom of the lake –
Perfidious breach of law of nations –
All promises she faithless breaks,
And sinks her friend to make fresh rations.
Already did her appetite
Dwell on the morsel with delight,
    Lunch,
    Scrunch!
He prays the gods; she mocks his woe;
He struggles up; she pulls below.
And while this combat is fought out,
A Kite that's seeking all about
Sees the poor Rat that's like to drown;
And pounces swift as lightning down.
The Frog tied to him, by the way,
Also became the glad Kite's prey;
They gave him all that he could wish,
A supper both of meat and fish.
   So oftentimes a base deceit
Falls back upon the father cheat;
So oftentimes doth perfidy
Return with triple usury.

The Animals sending a Tribute to Alexander

A Fable current in the ancient times
Had surely meaning; but none clear to me.
Its moral's somewhere, reader, in these rhymes,
So here's the thing itself for you to see.
Fame had loud rumoured in a thousand places
Of Jove's great son, a certain Alexander,
Who had resolved, however sour men's faces,
To leave none free; moreover, this commander
Had summoned every living thing beneath the skies
To come and worship at his sovereign feet:
Quadrupeds, bipeds, elephants, and flies;
The bird republic, also, were to meet.
The goddess of the hundred mouths, I say,
Having thus spread a wide dismay,
By publishing the conqueror's decree,
The animals, and all that do obey
Their appetites alone, began to think that now
They should be kept in slavery,
And to fresh laws and other customs bow.
They met in the wild desert and decide,
After long sittings and conflicting chatter,

To pay a tribute, pocketing their pride.
The Monkey was to manage style and matter
(Chief of all diplomats in every way);
They write down what he has to say.
The tribute only vexed the creatures:
No money! how their cash to pay?
Well from a prince, who chanced to own
Some mines of gold, they got a loan.
To bear the tribute volunteered
The Mule and Ass, and they were cheered;
The Horse and Camel lent their aid.
Then gaily started all the four,
Led by the new ambassador.
The caravan went on till, in a narrow place,
They saw his majesty the Lion's face;
They did not like his look at all,
Still less when he began to call.
"Well met; and just in time," quoth he;
"Your fellow-traveller I will be;
Your toil I wish to freely share,
My tribute's light, yet hard to bear;

I'm not accustomed to a load; so, please,
Take each a quarter at your ease,
To you 'tis nothing, that I feel;
If robbers come to pick and steal,
I shall not be the last to fight:
A Lion is not backward in a fray."
They welcome him, and he's in pleasant plight;
So, spite of Jove-sprung hero, every day
Upon the public purse he battens,
And on good deer he quickly fattens.
They reach at last a meadow land,
With flowers besprinkled, fed by brooks;
The sheep feed there on either hand,
Unguarded by the shepherd's crooks:
It is the summer zephyr's home.
No sooner has the Lion come,
Than he of fever much complains;
"Continue, sirs, your embassy,"
Said he; "but burning, darting pains
Torment me now exceedingly.
I seek some herb for speedy cure;

You must not long delay, I'm sure;
Give me my money; quick! I'm hurried."
Then quickly out the gold was scurried.
The Lion, quite delighted, cried,
In tones that showed his joy and pride,
"Ye gods! my gold has hatched its brood;
And, look! the young ones are all grown
Big as the old ones; that is good:
The increase comes to me alone."
He took the whole, although he was not bid;
Or if he didn't, some one like him did.
The Monkey and his retinue
Half frightened and half angry grew,
But did not dare reply; so left him there.
'Tis said that they complained at court; but where
Was then the use? in vain their loud abuse.
What could he do? Jove's royal scion!
'Twould have been Lion against Lion.

'Tis said when Corsairs fight Corsairs,
They are not minding their affairs.

The Horse wishing to be revenged on the Stag

Horses were once as free as air,
When man on acorns lived content.
Ass, horse, and mule unfettered went
Through field and forest, anywhere,
Without a thought of toil and care.
Nor saw one then, as in this age,
Saddles and pillions every stage,
Harness for march, and work, and battle,
Or chaises drawn by hungry cattle.
Nor were there then so many marriages,
Nor feasts that need a host of carriages.
'Twas at this time there was a keen dispute
Between a Stag who quarrelled with a Horse,
Unable to run down the nimble brute:
To kindly Man he came, for aid, of course;
Man bridled him and leaped upon his back,
Nor rested till the Stag was caught and slain.

The Horse thanked heartily the Man, good lack:
"Adieu, yours truly, I'll trot off again,
Home to the wild wood and the breezy plain."
"Not quite so fast," the smiling Man replied,
"I know too well your use, you must remain;
I'll treat you well, yes, very well," he cried:
"Up to your ears the provender shall be,
And you shall feed in ease and luxury."
Alas! what's food without one's liberty?
The Horse his folly soon perceived;
But far too late the creature grieved.
His stable was all ready near the spot,
And there, with halter round his neck, he died,
Wiser had he his injuries forgot.

    Revenge is sweet to injured pride;
But it is bought too dear, if bought
With that without which all things else are nought.

The Fox and the Bust

The great too often wear the actor's mask;
The vulgar worshippers the show beguiles;
The ass looks on the surface; 'tis the task
Of the wise Fox to go far deeper; full of wiles,
He pries on every side, and turns, and peeps,
And watches – Reynard never sleeps.
And when he finds in many a place
The great man nothing but a pompous face,
Repeats, what once he subtly said
Unto a hero's plaster head –
A hollow bust, and of enormous size –
Praising it with contemptuous eyes,
"Fine head," said he, "but without brains."
The saying's worth the listener's pains;
To many a noble lord the *mot* applies.

The Wolf, the Goat, and the Kid

The She-Goat going out to feed
Upon the young grass in the mead,
Closed not the latch until she bid
Her youngest born, her darling kid,
Take care to open door to none,
Or if she did, only to one
Who gave the watchword of the place –
"Curse to the Wolf and all his race!"
The Wolf was just then passing by,
And having no bad memory,
Laid the spell by, a perfect treasure
Ready to be used at leisure.
The Kid, so tender and so small,
Had never seen a wolf at all.
The mother gone, the hypocrite

Assumes a voice demure and fit –
"The Wolf be cursed! come, pull the latch."
The Kid says, peeping through a chink,
"Show me a white foot" (silly patch),
"Or I'll not open yet the door, I think."
White paws are rare with wolves – not yet in fashion.
The Wolf surprised, and dumb with secret passion,
Went as he came, and sneaked back to his lair:
The Kid had lost her life without that care,
Had she but listened to the word
The watchful Wolf had overheard.
Two sureties are twice as good as one,
Without them she had been undone.
   And so I boldly say,
That too much caution's never thrown away.

The Wolf, the Mother, and the Child

This Wolf recalls another to my mind –
A friend who found Fate more unkind –
Caught in a neater way, you'll see;
He perished – here's the history:
A peasant dwelt in a lone farm;
The Wolf, his watch intent to keep,
Saw in and out, not fearing harm,
Slim calves and lambs, and old fat sheep,
And regiment of turkeys strutting out;
In fact, good fare was spread about.
The thief grew weary of vain wishes
   For dainty dishes;
But just then heard an Infant cry,
The mother chiding angrily –
   "Be quiet!
   No riot;
Or to the Wolf I'll give you, brat!"
The Wolf cried, "Now, I quite like that;"
And thanked the gods for being good.
The Mother, as a mother should,
Soon calmed the Child. "Don't cry, my pet!
If the Wolf comes, we'll kill him, there!"

"What's this?" the thief was in a fret;
"First this, then that, there's no truth anywhere;
   I'm not a fool, you know,
   And yet they treat me so.
Some day, when nutting, it may hap
I may surprise the little chap."
As these reflections strike the beast,
A mastiff stops the way, at one fierce bound,
To any future feast,
And rough men gird him round.
"What brought you here?" cries many a one;
He told the tale as I have done.
"Good Heavens!" loud the Mother cried;
"You eat my boy! what! darling here
To stop your hunger? Hush! my dear."
They killed the brute and stripped his hide;
His right foot and his head in state
Adorn the Picard noble's gate;
And this was written underneath
The shrivelled eyes and grinning teeth –
"Good Master Wolves, believe not all
That mothers say when children squall."

The Wolf, the Mother, and the Child

The Saying of Socrates

A House was built by Socrates,
That failed the public taste to please.
One thought the inside, not to tell a lie,
Unworthy of the wise man's dignity.
Another blamed the front; and one and all
Agreed the rooms were very much too small.
"What! such a house for our great sage,
The pride and wonder of the age!"
"Would Heaven," said he, quite weary of the Babel,
    "Was only able,
Small as it is, to fill it with true friends."
And here the story ends.
Just reason had good Socrates
To find his house too large for these.
Each man you meet as friend, your hand will claim;
Fool, if you trust the proffers that such bring.
There's nothing commoner than Friendship's name;
There's nothing rarer than the thing.

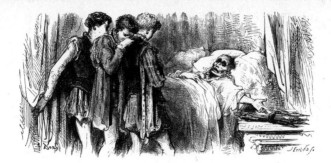

The old Man and his Children

All power is feeble, if it's disunited:
Upon this head now hear the Phrygian slave.
If I add verse to his, which has delighted,
It's not from envy; but in hopes to grave
And paint our modern manners – feeble-sighted –
Had I ambition for mere foolish aims.
Phædrus, in eager search for glory,
Enriched full many an ancient story;
Ill-fitting me were such pretentious claims.
But let us to our fable – rather history,
Of him who tried to make his sons agree.
An Old Man, when Death called, prepared to go –
"My children dear," he said, "try now to break
This knotted sheaf of arrows. I will show
The way they're tied – what progress can you make?"
The eldest, having done his very best,
Exclaimed, "I yield them to a stronger one."
The second strove across his knee and chest,
Then passed them quickly to the younger son:
They lost their time, the bundle was too strong,
The shafts together none could snap or bend.
"Weak creatures!" said their sire, "pass them along;
My single arm the riddle soon will end."
They laughed, and thought him joking; but not so,
Singly the arrows quickly fell in twain;
"Thus may you concord's power, my children, know;
Agree in love and never part again."

He spoke no more, he felt his life was done;
And then, perceiving death was very near,
"Dear sons," said he, "I go where all have gone;
Promise to live like brothers: let me hear
Your joint vow – now, grant your father this:"
Then, weeping, each one gives the parting kiss.
He joins their hands and dies; a large estate
He left, but tangled up with heavy debts.
This creditor seized land still in debate;
That neighbour brought an action for assets:
The brothers' love was short, you well may guess;
Blood joined and interest severed the brief tie;
Ambition, envy, led to base *finesse* –
The subdivision bred chicanery.
The judge by turns condemns them all,
Neighbours and creditors assail;
To loggerheads the plighted brothers fall.
The union's sundered – one agrees
To compromise; the other ventures on,
And soon the money is all gone
In wrangling about lawyers' fees.
They lose their wealth, and then, downhearted,
Regretful talk of how, in joke,
 Their father broke
Those arrows, when they once were parted.

The Oracle and the impious Man

None wish to cozen heaven but the fool;
The mystic labyrinths of the human heart
Lie open to the gods in every part:
All that man does is under their wise rule,
Even things done in darkness are revealed
To those from whom no single act's concealed.
A Pagan – a vile rogue in grain,
Whose faith in gods, it's very plain,
Was but to use them as a dictionary,
For consultation wary –
Went once to try Apollo to deceive,
With or without his leave.
"Is what I hold," he said, "alive or no?"
He held a sparrow, you must know,
Prepared to kill it or to let it fly;
To give the god at once the lie.
Apollo saw the plan within his head,
　　And answered –
"Dead or alive," he said, "produce your sparrow.
Try no more tricks, for I can always foil;
Such stratagems, you see, do but recoil.
I see afar, and far I cast my arrow."

The Miser who lost his Treasure

It's use that constitutes possession wholely;
I ask those people who've a passion
For heaping gold on gold, and saving solely,
How they excel the poorest man in any fashion?
Diogenes is quite as rich as they.
True Misers live like beggars, people say;
The man with hidden treasure Æsop drew
Is an example of the thing I mean.
In the next life he might be happy, true;
But very little joy in this he knew;
By gold the Miser was so little blessed.
Not its possessor, but by it possessed;
He buried it a fathom underground;
His heart was with it; his delight
To ruminate upon it day and night;
A victim to the altar ever bound.
He seemed so poor, yet not one hour forgot
The golden grave, the consecrated spot:
Whether he goes or comes, or eats or drinks,
Of gold, and gold alone, the Miser thinks.
At last a ditcher marks his frequent walks,
        And muttering talks,
Scents out the place, and clears the whole,
        Unseen by any spies.
On one fine day the Miser came, his soul
Glowing with joy; he found the empty nest;
Bursts into tears, and sobs, and cries,
He frets, and tears his thin grey hair;
He's lost what he had loved the best.

The Miser who lost his Treasure

A startled peasant passing there
Inquires the reason of his sighs.
"My gold! my gold! they've stolen all."
"Your treasure! what was it, and where?"
"Why, buried underneath this stone."
    (A moan!)
"Why, man, is this a time of war?
Why should you bring your gold so far?
Had you not better much have let
The wealth lie in a cabinet,
Where you could find it any hour
   In your own power?"
"What! every hour? a wise man knows
Gold comes but slowly, quickly goes;
I never touched it." "Gracious me!"
Replied the other, "why, then, be
So wretched? for if you say true,
You never touched it, plain the case;
Put back that stone upon the place,
'Twill be the very same to you."

The Eye of the Master

A stag sought refuge from the chase
Among the oxen of a stable,
Who counselled him – if he was able –
To find a better hiding-place.
"My brothers," said the fugitive,
"Betray me not; and I will show
The richest pastures that I know;
Your kindness you will ne'er regret,
With interest I'll pay the debt."
The oxen promised well to keep
The secret: couched for quiet sleep,
Safe in a tranquil privacy,
The Stag lay down, and breathed more free.
At even-time they brought fresh hay,
As was their custom day by day;
Men went and came, ah! very near,
And last of all the overseer,
Yet carelessly, for horns nor hair
Showed that the hiding stag was there.
The forest dweller's gratitude
Was great, and in a joyous mood
He waited till the labour ceased,
And oxen were from toil released,
Leaving the exit once more free,
To end his days of slavery.
A ruminating bullock cried,
"All now goes well; but woe betide
When that man with the hundred eyes
Shall come, and you, poor soul! surprise?

I fear the watchful look he'll take,
And dread his visit for your sake;
Boast not until the end, for sure
Your boasting may be premature."
She had not time to utter more,
The master opened quick the door.
"How's this, you rascal men?" said he;
"These empty racks will never do!
Go to the loft; this litter, too,
Is not the thing. I want to see
More care from those that work for me;
Whose turn these cobwebs to brush out?
These collars, traces? – look about!"
Then gazing round, he spies a head,
Where a fat ox should be instead;
The frightened stag they recognise.
In vain the tears roll from his eyes;
They fall on him with furious blows,
Each one a thrust, until, to close,
They kill and salt the wretched beast,
And cook him up for many a feast.
  Phædrus hath put it pithily,
The master's is the eye for me,
The lover's, too, is quick to see.

The Eye of the Master

The Lark and her little Ones with the Owner of a Field

"Depend upon yourself alone,"
Is a sound proverb worthy credit.
In Æsop's time it was well known,
And there (to tell the truth) I read it.
The larks to build their nests began,
When wheat was in the green blade still —
That is to say, when Nature's plan
Had ordered Love, with conquering will,
To rule the earth, the sea, and air,
Tigers in woods, sea monsters in the deep;
   Nor yet refuse a share
To larks that in the cornfields keep.
One bird, however, of these last,
Found that one half the spring was past,
Yet brought no mate, such as the season sent
To others. Then with firm intent
Plighting her troth, and fairly matched,
She built her nest and gravely hatched.
All went on well, the corn waved red
Above each little fledgling's head,
Before they'd strength enough to fly,
And mount into the April sky.
A hundred cares the mother Lark compel
To seek with patient care the daily food;
But first she warns her restless brood
To watch, and peep, and listen well,
And keep a constant sentinel;
"And if the owner comes his corn to see,
His son, too, as 'twill likely be,
Take heed, for when we're sure of it,
And reapers come, why, we must flit."

No sooner was the Lark away,
Than came the owner with his son.
"The wheat is ripe," he said, "so run,
And bring our friends at peep of day,
Each with his sickle sharp and ready."
The Lark returns: alarm already
Had seized the covey. One commences –
"He said himself, at early morn,
His friends he'd call to reap the corn."
The old Lark said –" If that is all,
My worthy children, keep your senses;
No hurry till the first rows fall.
We'll not go yet, dismiss all fear,
To-morrow keep an open ear;
Here's dinner ready, now be gay."
They ate and slept the time away.
The morn arrives to wake the sleepers,
Aurora comes, but not the reapers.
The Lark soars up: and on his round
The farmer comes to view his ground.
"This wheat," he said, "ought not to stand;
Our friends are wrong no helping hand
To give, and we are wrong to trust
Such lazy fools for half a crust,
Much less for labour. Sons," he cried,
"Go, call our kinsmen on each side,
We'll go to work." The little Lark
Grew more afraid. "Now, mother, mark,
The work within an hour's begun."
The mother answered – "Sleep, my son;
We will not leave our house to-night."
Well, no one came; the bird was right.

The third time came the master by:
"Our error's great," he said, repentantly:
"No friend is better than oneself;
Remember that, my boy, it's worth some pelf.
    Now what to do?
    Why, I and you
Must whet our sickles and begin;
That is the shortest way, I see;
I know at last the surest plan:
We'll make our harvest as we can."
No sooner had the Lark o'erheard –
"'Tis time to flit, my children; come,"
Cried out the very prudent bird.
Little and big went fluttering, rising,
Soaring in a way surprising,
And left without a beat of drum.

The Lark and her Little Ones

Book V

The Woodman and Mercury

Your taste has always been to me a guide;
I've sought in many ways to win your vote:
Fastidious cares you often would deride,
Forbad me on vain ornament to dote.
I think with you an author wastes his days,
Who tries with over-care his tale to tell;
Yet, it's not wise to banish certain traits
Of subtle grace, that you and I love well.
With Æsop's aim, I simply do my best;
And fail – well, just as little as I can.
Try to instruct by reasoning or jest;
No fault of mine if no one likes my plan.
Rude strength is not by any means my forte;
I seek to pelt, with playful ridicule,
Folly and vice; and tease the motley fool
With stinging missiles – any way, in short;
Not having brawny arms, like Hercules.
That is my only talent, that I know.
I have no strength to stem the angry seas,
Or set all honest people in a glow.
Sometimes I try to paint in fabled guise,
A foolish vanity, with envy blended;
Two of life's pivots, mocked at by the wise,
In satires long ago, and not yet ended.

Such was the miserable creature,
Mean and poor in shape, in feature,
That tried to puff herself into an ox.
Sometimes I try, by playful paradox,
To pair a vice with virtue, folly with good sense,
Lambs with gaunt wolves, the ant to match the fly;
Everywhere laughing at the fool's expense,
I mould my work into a comedy,
With countless acts, the universe its scene,
Boundless as the blue serene.
Men, gods, and brutes each play their part,
With more or less of truth and art.
Jove like the rest – come, Mercury;
Ah! look, why there he comes, I see;
The messenger who's wont to bear
Jove's frequent errands to the fair –
But more of that another day.

A Woodman's axe had gone astray,
The winner of his bread was gone;
And he sat moaning all alone.
He had no wealth to buy such things:
The axe his clothes and dinner brings.
Hopeless, and in a murky place,

The Woodman and Mercury

He sat, the tears ran down his face.
"My own, my poor old axe! Ah! me,
Great Jupiter, I pray to thee;
But give it back from down below,
And I will strike for thee a blow."
His prayer was in Olympus heard;
Mercury entered at the word.
"Your hatchet is not lost," said he;
"But will you know it, when you see?
I found an axe, just now, hard by."
A golden axe he presently
Showed to the honest man; but "Nay"
Was all the fellow cared to say.
Next one of silver he refused;
Silver or gold he never used.
Then one of simple steel and wood;
"That's mine!" he cried. "Ah! thankee – good;
I'm quite content with this, you see."

"Come," said the god, "then take the three –
That's my reward for honesty."
"In that case, then, I am content,"
The rustic said, and off he went.

Jove Mercury sent, to make reply.
To each he showed an axe of gold –
Who but a fool could it behold,
And not say, when he saw it shine –
"Hurrah! that's it – yes, that is mine?"
But Mercury gave each rogue instead
A heavy thump upon the head.
    He who with simple truth's content,
Will never of his choice repent:
To tell a lie for interest,
Was never yet of ways the best.
What does it profit thus to stoop?
Jove is not made an easy dupe.

The earthen Pot and the iron Pot

"Neighbour," said the Iron Pot,
"'et us go abroad a little."
"Thank you, I would rather not,"
Was the answer that he got.
　Earthenware, you know, is brittle;
And the weaker Pot was wiser
Than to trust his bad adviser.

"Mighty well for *you*," said he;
　"Skin like yours can hardly suffer
Very much by land or sea,
That is clear; but, as for *me*,
　Stop till I'm a little tougher.
You may roam the wide world over;
I shall stay at home in clover."

"Friend!" the Iron Pot replied,

"Don't let such a fear affect you;
I shall travel at your side:
So, whatever may betide,
　Cling to me, and I'll protect you."
Having won his friend's compliance,
Off they started in alliance.

Jigging, jogging, on they went,
　Knocking one against the other;
Till the Earthen Pot was sent
(Past the powers of cement)
　Into atoms by his brother.
'Twas his *own* imprudence, clearly,
That was paid for very dearly.

With our equals let us mate,
Or dread the weaker vessel's fate.

The little Fish and the Fisherman

A little Fish will larger grow, in time,
If God will only grant him life; and yet
To let him free out of the tangling net
Is folly; and I mean it, though I rhyme:
The catching him again is not so sure, *c'est tout*.
A little Carp, who half a summer knew,
Was taken by an angler's crafty hook.
"All count," the man said; "this begins my feast:
I'll put it in my basket." "Here, just look!"
Exclaimed, in his own way, the tiny beast.
"Now what on earth can you, sir, want with me?
I'm not quite half a mouthful, as you see.
Let me grow up, and catch me when I'm tall,
Then some rich epicure will buy me dear;

But now you'll want a hundred, that is plain,
　　　　Aye, and as much again,
To make a dish; and what dish, after all?
Why, good for nothing." "Good for nothing, eh?"
Replied the Angler. "Come, my little friend,
Into the pan you go; so end.
Your sermon pleases me, exceedingly.
　　To night we'll try
　　How you will fry."
　　The present, not the future, tense
　　Is that preferred by men of sense.

　　The one is sure that you have got:
　　The other, verily, is not.

The little Fish and the Fisherman

The Hare's ears

The Lion, wounded by some subject's horn,
Was naturally wroth, and made decree
That all by whom such ornaments were worn
From his domains forthwith should banished be.
Bulls, Rams, and Goats at once obeyed the law:
The Deer took flight, without an hour's delay.
A timid Hare felt smitten, when he saw
The shadow of his ears, with deep dismay.
He feared that somebody, with eyes too keen,
Might call them horns, they looked so very long.
"Adieu, friend Cricket," whispered he; "I mean
To quit the place directly, right or wrong.
These ears are perilous; and, though I wore
A couple short as any Ostrich wears,
I still should run." The Cricket asked. "What for?
Such ears are only natural in Hares."
"They'll pass for horns," his frightened friend replied;
"For Unicorn's appendages, I'm sure.
And folks, if I deny it, will decide
On sending me to Bedlam, as a cure."

The Fox with his Tail cut off

A sly old Fox, a foe of Geese and Rabbits,
Was taken captive in a trap one day
(Just recompense of predatory habits),
And lost his tail before he got away.
He felt ashamed at such a mutilation;
But, cunning as before, proposed a way
To gain companions in his degradation;
And spoke as follows, on a council-day: –
"Dear brother Foxes, what can be the beauty
Or use of things so cumbrous and absurd?
They only sweep the mud up. It's your duty
To cut them off – it is, upon my word!"
"Not bad advice: there *may* be wisdom in it,"
Remarked a sage, "but will you, by-the-by,
Oblige us all by turning round a minute,
Before we give a positive reply?"
You never heard such hurricanes of laughter
As hailed the cropped appearance of the rogue.
Of course, among the Foxes, ever after,
Long tails continued very much in vogue.

The old Woman and her Servants

A Beldam kept two maids, whose spinning
Outdid the Fates. No care had she
But setting tasks that, still beginning,
Went on to all infinity.
Phœbus had scarcely shaken out
His golden locks, ere wheels were winding,
And spindles whirled and danced about,
The spools of thread these captives binding:
Whiz – whiz; no resting; work and work!
Soon as Aurora showed her face,
A crowing Cock aroused the Turk,
Who, scrambling on her gown apace,
Lit up the lamp, and sought the bed
Where, with good will and appetite,
Each wretched servant's weary head
Had rested for the blessèd night.

One opened half an eye; the other stretched
A weary arm; both, under breath,
Vowed (poor worn-out and weary wretches!)
To squeeze that Chanticleer to death.
The deed was done: they trapped the bird.
And yet it wrought them little good;
For now, ere well asleep, they heard
The old crone, fearing lest they should
O'ersleep themselves, their watchful warner gone;
She never left them less alone.
    And so it is, that often men
Who think they're getting to the shore,
Are sucked back by the sea once more.

This couple are a proof again
How near Charybdis Scylla's whirlpools roar.

The old Woman and her Servants

The Satyr and the Passer-by

A savage Satyr and his brood
Once took their lodgings and their food
Within a cavern deep and drear,
Which only very few came near.

The Satyr, with his sons and wife,
Led quite an unpretending life:
Good appetite supplies the place
Of luxuries in such a case.

A Traveller, who passed that way,
Entered the cave one rainy day;
The Satyr proved a friend in need,
By asking him to stop and feed.

The other, as 'twas pouring still,
Of course, accepted with a will:

And warmed his fingers with his breath,
For he was frozen half to death:

Upon the soup then breathed a bit
(The surest way of cooling it);
Meanwhile, his host in wonder sat,
And asked, "Pray, what's the good of that?"

"Breath cools my soup," his guest replied,
"And makes my fingers warm beside."
The Satyr answered, with a sneer,
"Then, we can do without you here.

"Beneath my roof you shall not sleep;
I scorn such company to keep.
All people in contempt I hold,
Who first blow hot, and then blow cold!"

The Horse and the Wolf

A certain Wolf, in that soft, pleasant season,
When gentle zephyrs freshen every flower,
And animals leave home, for this good reason –
They want to make their hay before the shower:
A Wolf, I say, after rough winter's rigour,
Perceived a Horse newly turned out to grass.
You may imagine what his joy was. Vigour
Came to him, when he saw the creature pass.
"Good game!" he said; "I wonder for whose spit?
No sheep this time – I only wish you were.
But this wants cunning, and some little wit:
Then let's be cunning." So – with learned air,
As practised scholar of Hippocrates,
Who knew the virtues and demerits, too,
Of all the simples of the fields and leas,
And knew the way to cure (the praise is due)
All sorts of sad diseases – if Sir Horse
Would tell his malady, he'd cure the ill,
Quite gratis; for to see him course,
Wandering untethered, at his own free will,
Showed something wrong, if science did not err.
"I have an aposthume," the Horse replied,
"Under my foot." "My son," the doctor cried,
"There is no part so sensitive to blows.
I have the honour to attend your race,
And am a surgeon, too, the whole world knows."

The rascal only waited opportunity
To leap upon the invalid's sunk flanks.
The Horse, who had mistrust, impatiently
Gave him a kick, expressive of his thanks,
That made a marmalade of teeth and jaws.
"Well done!" the Wolf growled, to himself reflecting:
"Each one should stick to his own trade. My claws
Were made for butchery, not herb-collecting."

The Horse and the Wolf

The labouring Man and his Children

Work, work, with all your might and main,
For labour brings the truest gain.
A wealthy Labourer lay near to death;
And, summoning his children round the bed,
He thus addressed them, with his latest breath:
"Part not with my estate when I am dead.
My parents left me what I leave to *you*.
About the place a treasure lies concealed,
No matter where, – search every corner through,
Nor leave a spot unturned in any field.
Go, seek it from the morning till the night."
Their father dead, the loving sons fulfilled
The dying wish, that made their labour light:
From end to end the fields were duly tilled.
The harvest was enormous, though they found
No golden treasures, howsoever small.
And yet the father's last advice was sound,
For Labour *is* a treasure, after all.

The Mountain in Labour

A Mountain in labour announced the new birth
With clamour so loud that the people all thought
'Twould at least bear a city, the largest on earth.
It was merely a Mouse that the incident brought.
When I think of this fable, so false in its fact,
And so true in its moral, it brings to my mind
Those common-place authors who try to attract
Attention by means of the subjects they find.
"I will sing about Jove and the Titans," cries one;
But how often the song comes to nothing, when done!

Fortune and the little Child

Beside a well profoundly deep
A Schoolboy laid him down to sleep.
Ere care has racked with aches the head,
The hardest bank's a feather bed;
A grown-up man, in such a case,
Had leaped a furlong from the place.
Happy for him, just then came by
Fortune, and saw him heedless lie.
She woke him softly, speaking mild:
"I've saved your life, you see, my child.
Another time you close your eyes,
Be just a little bit more wise.
If you had fallen down below,
'Twould have been laid to me, I know,

Though your own fault; and now, I pray,
Before I take myself away,
In honest truth you'll own the same,
For I was hardly here to blame.
It was not *my* caprice or joke."
The goddess vanished as she spoke.
And she was right; for never yet
Have any a misfortune met,
But Fortune's blamed: she has to pay
For our misdoings every day.
For all mad, foolish, ill-planned schemes
We try to justify our dreams
By rating her with curses strong.
In one word, *Fortune's always wrong*.

Fortune and the little Child

The Doctors

One morning Doctor Much-the-Worse went out
To see a patient, who was also tended
By Doctor Much-the-Better. "Past a doubt,"
The former said, "this case is nearly ended.
There's not a chance." – The latter trusted still
In physic's aid: but while the twin concocters
Disputed hard on plaister, draught, and pill,
The patient died from this attack of doctors.
"Look there," said one, "I told you how 'twould be!"
The other said, "No doubt you're vastly clever;
But if our friend had only followed *me*,
I know he would have been as well as ever."

The Doctors

The Hen with the golden Eggs

My little story will explain
An olden maxim, which expresses
How Avarice, in search of gain,
May lose the hoard that it possesses.
The fable tells us that a Hen
Laid golden eggs, each egg a treasure;
Its owner – stupidest of men –
Was miserly beyond all measure.
He thought a mine of wealth to find
Within the Hen, and so he slew it:
He found a bird of common kind –
And lost a pretty fortune through it.
For money-worms, who now and then
Grow poor through trying to be wealthy,
I tell my fable of the Hen;
My tale is good, my moral healthy.

The Hen with the golden Eggs

The Ass that carried the Relics

An Ass, with relics loaded, thought the crowd
Knelt down to him, and straightway grew so proud;
He took to his own merit, without qualms,
Even the incense and loud chaunted psalms.
Some one, to undeceive him wisely said –
"A foolish vanity has turned your head:
They not to you, but to the idol pray;
Where glory's due, there they the honour pay."
When foolish magistrates rule o'er a town,
It's not the man we bow to, but his gown.

The Stag and the Vine

A stag behind a lofty Vine took shelter
(Such vines are met with in a southern clime);
Hunters and hounds pursued him helter-skelter,
And searched and searched, but only lost their time.
The huntsmen laid, as might have been expected,
Upon the shoulders of their dogs the blame.
The Stag, forgetting he had been protected,
Vastly ungrateful all at once became;
Upon the friendly Vine he made a dinner;
But hounds and hunters soon came back again.
Discovered quickly – now the leaves were thinner –
The Stag, of course, got set upon and slain.
"I merit this!" exclaimed the dying glutton;
"Ingratitude, like pride, must have a fall:"
Another gasp, and he was dead as mutton;
And no one present pitied him at all.
How oft is hospitality rewarded
By deeds ungrateful as the one recorded!

The Stag and the Vine

The Serpent and the File

A Serpent once and Watchmaker were neighbours
(Unpleasant neighbour for a working man);
The Snake came creeping in among his labours,
Seeking for food on the felonious plan;
But all the broth he found was but a File,
And that he gnawed in vain – the steel was tough.
The tool said, with a calm contemptuous smile,
"Poor and mistaken thing! that's *quantum suff.*
You lose your time, you shallow sneak, you do,
You'll never bite a farthing's worth off me,
Though you break all your teeth: I tell you true,
I fear alone Time's great voracity."
This is for critics – all the baser herd,
Who, restless, gnaw at everything they find.
Bah! you waste time, you do, upon my word;
Don't think your teeth can pierce the thinnest rind:
To injure noble works you try, and try, but can't,
To you they're diamond, steel, and adamant.

The Hare and the Partridge

One should not mock the wretched. Who can tell
He will be always happy? Fortune changes.
Wise Æsop, in his fables, taught this well.
My story is like his – which very strange is.
The Hare and Partridge shared the selfsame clover,
And lived in peace and great transquillity,
Till one day, racing all the meadows over,
The huntsmen came, and forced the Hare to flee,
And seek his hiding-place. The dogs, put out,
Were all astray: yes, even Brifaut erred,
Until the scent betrayed. A lusty shout
Arouses Miraut, who then loud averred,
From philosophic reasoning, 'twas the Hare,
And ardently pushed forward the pursuit.
Rustaut, who never lied, saw clearly where
Had homeward turned again the frightened brute.
Poor wretch! it came to its old form to die.
The cruel Partridge, bitter taunting, said,
"You boasted of your fleetness; now, then, try
Your nimble feet." Soon was that scorn repaid:
While she still laughed, the recompense was near.
She thought her wings would save her from man's jaws.
Poor creature! there was worse than that to fear:
The swooping Goshawk came with cruel claws.

The Eagle and the Owl

The Eagle and the Owl had treaty made –
Ceased quarrelling, and even had embraced.
One took his royal oath; and, undismayed,
The other's claw upon his heart was placed:
Neither would gulp a fledgling of the other.
"Do you know mine?" Minerva's wise bird said.
The Eagle gravely shook her stately head.
"So much the worse," the Owl replied. "A mother
Trembles for her sweet chicks – she does, indeed.
It's ten to one if I can rear them then.
You are a king, and, therefore, take no heed
Of who or what. The gods and lords of men
Put all things on one level: let who will
Say what they like. Adieu, my children dear,
If you once meet them." "Nay, good ma'am, but still,
Describe them," said the Eagle; "have no fear:
Be sure I will not touch them, on my word."
The Owl replied, "My little ones are small,
Beautiful, shapely, – prettier, far, than all.
By my description you will know the dears;
Do not forget it: let no fate by you
Find way to us, and cause me ceaseless tears."

Well, one fine evening, the old Owl away,
The Eagle saw, upon a rocky shelf,
Or in a ruin, (who cares which I say?)
Some little ugly creatures. To himself
The Eagle reasoned, "These are not our friend's,
Moping and gruff, and such a screeching, too:
Let's eat 'em." Waste time never spends
The royal bird, to give the brute his due;
And when he eats, he eats, to tell the truth.
The Owl, returning, only found the feet
Of her dear offspring: – sad, but yet it's sooth.
She mourns the children, young, and dear, and sweet,
And prays the gods to smite the wicked thief,
That brought her all the woe and misery.
Then some one said, "Restrain thy unjust grief;
Reflect one moment on the casualty.
Thou art to blame, and also Nature's law,
Which makes us always think our own the best.
You sketched them to the Eagle as you saw:
They were not like your portrait; – am I just?"

The Eagle and the Owl

The Lion going to War

The Lion planned a foray on a foe;
Held a war-council; sent his heralds out
To warn the Animals he'd strike a blow;
Soon all were ready to help slay and rout –
Each in his special way. The Elephant,
To bear upon his back the baggage and supplies,
And fight, as usual. Then the Bear, to plant
The flag upon the breach. The Fox's eyes
Brighten at thought of diplomatic guile.
The Monkey hopes to dupe with endless tricks.
"But send away the Asses," says, meanwhile,
Some courtier, in whose mind the fancy sticks;
"They're only stupid. Pack off, too, the Hares."
"No, not so," said the King; "I'll use them all:
Our troop's imperfect, if they have no shares.
The Ass shall be our startling trumpet call;
The Hare is useful for our courier, mind."
Prudent and wise the King who knows the way
For every subject fitting task to find.
Nothing is useless to the wise, they say.

The Bear and the two Friends

Two Friends, in want, resolved to sell
A Bear-skin, though the Bear was well,
And still alive. The Furrier paid
Them willingly; the bargain's made.
It was the King of Bears, they said:
They'd kill him in an hour or two,
And what more could they hope to do?
"The merchant has not such a skin,
A guarantee through thick and thin,
To fence from e'en the kneenest cold
With warm, soft, pliant fold on fold:
Better to make two cloaks than one."
The bargain's made, the business done,
The Bear, in two days, was to die
That they agreed on, presently.
They found the Bear, who, at full trot,
Came down upon them, raging hot.
The men were thunder-struck; soon done
With bargain-making, how they run!
Life against money: they are mute.
One climbs a tree, to shun the brute;
The other, cold as marble, lies
Upon his stomach – shuts his eyes;
For he has heard that Bears, instead
Of eating fear to touch the dead.

The trap deceives the foolish Bear:
He sees the body lying there,
Suspects a trick, turns, smells, and sniffs,
With many nuzzling cautious whiffs.
"He's dead," said he, "and rather high;"
Then seeks the forest that's hard by.
The merchant, from the tree descending
Quickly, to his companion's lending
The aid he needs. "A wondrous sight,
To think you've only had a fright.
But where's his skin? – and did he say
Aught in your ear, as there you lay?
For he came, as I plainly saw,
And turned you over with his paw.
"He said, 'Another time, at least,
Before you sell, first kill the beast.'"

The Bear and the two Friends

The Ass in the Lion's skin

A Donkey donned a Lion's hide,
And spread a panic, far and wide
(Although the Donkey, as a rule,
Is not a fighter, but a fool).
By chance, a little bit of ear
Stuck forth, and made the matter clear.
Then Hodge, not relishing the trick,
Paid off its author with a stick.
While those who saw the Lion's skin,
But little dreamed who lurked within,
Stood open-mouthed, and all aghast,
To see a Lion run so fast.
This tale applies, unless I err,
To many folks who make a stir;
And owe three-fourths of their success
To servants, carriages, and dress.

Book VI

The Shepherd and the Lion

Fables are sometimes more than they appear:
A crude, bare moral wearies some, I fear.
The simplest animal to truth may lead;
The story and the precept make one heed:
They pass together better than apart:
To please, and yet instruct, that is the art.
To write for writing's sake seems poor to me;
And for this reason, more especially –
Numbers of famous men, from time to time,
Have written fables in laconic rhyme,
Shunning all ornament and verbose length,
Wasting no word, unless to gain in strength.
Phœdrus was so succinct, some men found fault;
Curt Æsop was far readier still to halt.
But, above all, a Greek* did most excel,
Who in four verses told what he would tell.
If he succeeded, let the experts say;
Let's match him now with Æsop, by the way.

A Shepherd and a Hunter they will bring:
I give the point and ending as they sing,
Embroidering here and there, as on I go; –

Thus   Esop told the story, you must know.
A Shepherd, finding in his flocks some gaps,
Thought he might catch the robber in his traps,
And round a cave drew close his netted toils,
Fearing the Wolves, and their unceasing spoils.
"Grant, king of gods, before I leave the place,"
He cried, "grant me to see the brigand's face.
Let me but watch him rolling in the net,
That is the dearest pleasure I could get!"
Then from a score of calves he chose the beast,
The fattest, for the sacrificial feast.
That moment stepped a Lion from the cave;
The Shepherd, prostrate, all intent to save
His petty life, exclaimed, "How little we
Know what we ask! If I could only see
Safe in my snares, that caused me so much grief,
The helpless, panting, miserable thief,
Great Jove! a Calf I promised to thy fane:
An Ox I'd make it, were I free again."

Thus wrote our leading author of his race;
Now for the imitator, in his place.

The Lion and the Hunter

A Braggart, lover of the chase,
Losing a dog, of noble race,
Fearing 'twas in a Lion's maw,
Asked the first shepherd that he saw
If he would kindly show him where
The robber had his favourite lair;
That he might teach him, at first sight,
The difference between wrong and right.
The shepherd said, "Near yonder peak
You'll find the gentleman you seek.
A sheep a month, that is the fee
I pay for ease and liberty.
I wander where I like, you see."
And, while he spoke, the Lion ran
And put to flight the bragging man.
"O Jupiter!" he cried, "befriend,
And some safe refuge quickly send!"
The proof of courage, understand,
Is shown when danger is at hand.
Some, when the danger comes, 'tis known,
Will very quickly change their tone.

Phœbus and Boreas

Phœbus and Boreas saw a traveller,
'Fended against bad weather prudently.
Autumn had just begun, and then, you see,
Caution is useful to the wayfarer.
It rains and shines, and rainbows bright displayed
Warned those who ventured out to take a cloak:
The Romans called these months, as if in joke,
The doubtful. For this season well arrayed,
Our fellow, ready for the pelting rain,
Wore a cloak doubled, and of sturdy stuff.
"He thinks," the Wind said, "he is armed enough
To 'scape all hazards; but it's quite in vain,
For he has not foreseen that I can blow,
So that no button in the world avails:
I send cloaks flying as I do ships' sails.
It will amuse us just to let him know;
Now, you shall see." "Agreed," then Phœbus said;
"Then let us bet, without more talking, come,
Which of us first shall send him cloakless home:
You can begin, and I will hide my head."
'Twas soon arranged, and Boreas filled his throat
With vapour, till his cheeks balloons became.

A demon's holiday of lightning-flame
And storm came shistling, wrecking many a boat,
Shattering many a roof – and all for what?
About a paltry cloak. He's much ado
To save him from a precipice or two.
The Wind but wasted time – one's pleased at that –
The more it raged, but firmer still he drew
Around his breast the cloak: the cape just shook,
And here and there a shred the tempest took.
At last, the time was up, no more it blew,
Then the hot Sun dispersed the cloudy haze,
And pierced the weary horseman through and through.
Beneath his heavy mantle sprung hot dew –
No longer could he bear those fervent rays –
He threw his cloak aside (a man of sense);
Not half his power had Phœbus yet employed.
Mildness had won – the Sun was overjoyed:
Softness gains more than any violence.

Jupiter and the Farmer

Jupiter had a farm to give away;
Mercury told the world the chosen day.
The people came to offer, rough they were,
And listened grimly. One said it was bare
And stubborn land; another half agreed.
While they thus haggled, churlishly indeed,
One bolder than the rest – but wiser? – no –
Consents to take it, if Jove only grant
The climate that he wishes; he will plant,
And sow, and reap, if but the heat and cold
May come and go, like slaves, as they are told.
The seasons wait his nod: the wet and dry
Obey his bidding from a servile sky.
Jove grants his wish – our foolish fellow sways
His sceptre bravely – rains and blows for days;
Makes his own climate just as he may please:

His neighbours, no more than Antipodes,
Share his good weather. Still as well they fare;
Their barns are teeming full; but his are bare.
The next year quite a change; another way
He sets the seasons, watching day by day:
Still, there's some flaw – his crops are thin and poor,
While loaded waggons crowd his neighbour's door.

What can he do? – he falls before Jove's throne,
Confesses all his folly: he alone
Has been to blame. Jove, with much gentleness,
Like a mild master, pities his distress.
It is agreed that Providence is kind,
And knows far better than a human mind
What's good for us, and calmly bids us do it:
We seldom see our way till we are through it.

The Cockerel, the Cat, and the little Rat

A Rat, so very young that it had seen
Nothing at all, was at his setting out
Almost snapped up; and what his fears had been
He told his mother. Thus it came about –
"I crossed the mountains bordering our land,
Bold as a Rat that has his way to make;
When two great animals, you understand,
Before my eyes, their way towards me take.
The one was gentle, tender, and so mild;
The other restless, wild, and turbulent;
A screeching voice, some flesh upon its head,
A sort of arm, raised as for punishment.
His tail a plume, a fiery plume displayed
(It was a capon that the creature drew
Like a wild beast new come from Africa);
And with his arms he beat his sides, it's true,
With such a frightful noise, that in dismay,
E'en I, who pride myself on courage, ran
And fled for fear, cursing the evil creature;
As, but for him, I should have found a plan
To make acquaintance with that gentle nature –
So soft and sweet, and with a skin like ours;

Long tail, and spotted, with a face so meek;
And yet a glittering eye, of such strange powers:
A sympathiser, sure as I can speak,
With us the Rats, for he has just such ears.
I was about to make a little speech,
When, all at once, as if to rouse my fears,
The other creature gave a dreadful screech,
And I took flight." "My child," exclaimed the Rat,
"That gentle hypocrite you liked so well,
Was our malignant enemy – the Cat.
The other, on whose form so foul you fell,
Is simply harmless, and will be our meal,
Perhaps, some day; while, as for that meek beast,
On us he dearly loves to leap and steal,
And crunch and munch us for this cruel feast.
Take care, my child, in any case,
Judge no one by their look or face."

The Fox, the Monkey, and the other Animals

The Animals (The Lion dead)
Resolved to choose a King instead;
The crown was taken from its case –
A dragon guarded well the place.
They tried the crown, but, when they'd done,
It would not fit a single one.
Some heads too large, and some too small;
Many had horns, – defects in all.
The Monkey, laughing, tried it, too,
And got his mocking visage through,
With many wild, fantastic faces;
And twisting gambols and grimaces.
A hoop, at last, around his waist
He wore it, and they cried, "Well placed!
He was elected. Each one paid
Their homage to the King they'd made.

The Fox alone laments the choice,
But chokes it down with flattering voice.
Paying his little compliments,
To hide his secret sentiments.
"Sire," to the King, he said, "I've pleasure
To tell you I have found a treasure;
A secret, but to me alone –
All treasures fall unto the throne."
The young King, eager at finance,
Ran fast himself, to catch the chance.
It was a trap, and he was caught.
The Fox said, when his aid he sought,
"You think to govern us and rule;
You cannot save yourself, you fool!"
They turned him out, and, with some wit,
Agreed that few a crown will fit.

The Mule that boasted of his Family

An Episcopal Mule, of its family proud,
Would *not* keep his ancestry under a cloud,
But chattered, and bragged of his mother the mare:
Of her having done this, and her having been there;
And vowed that so famous a creature ignored,
Was a shame and disgrace to historian's record.
He frankly disdained on a doctor to wait,
And patiently stand at a poor patient's gate.
At last, growing old, in the mill he's confined,
Then his father, the donkey, came into his mind.
A misfortune is useful, if only to bring
A fool to his senses – a very good thing –
It's sent for a purpose, and always will be
Useful to some one or something, you see.

The old Man and the Ass

An Old Man, riding on a Donkey, saw
A meadow thick with flowers, and full of grass.
He instantly unbridled the poor Ass,
And let him roam for twenty minutes' law.
It scratch'd, and scratch'd, and munch'd, and chew'd, and bray'd
Nipping the best, and kicking, for sheer fun:
The meal refreshing was betimes begun.
Just then the enemy came, all arrayed:
"Fly," said the Old Man. "Wherefore?" said the beast;
"Am I to carry double burden – double load?
Am I to tramp once more upon the road?"
"No," said the Old Man; "I'll stop here, at least."
"To whom I may belong is no great matter.
Go, save yourself from an unlucky blow;
My master is my enemy, I know:
I tell you in the best French I can patter."

The Stag viewing himself in the Stream

Beside a fountain in the wood
A royal Stag admiring stood:
   His antlers pleased him well.
But one thing vexed him to the heart:
His slender legs ill matched the part
   On which he loved to dwell.

"Nature has shaped them ill," said he,
Watching their shadows peevishly:
   "Here is a disproportion!
My horns rise branching, tall, and proud;
My legs disgrace them, 'tis allowed,
   And are but an abortion."

Just then a deer-hound frightened him,
And lent a wing to every limb.
   O'er bush and brake – he's off!

At those adornments on his brow
The foolish creature praised just now
   He soon begins to scoff.

Upon his legs his life depends:
They are his best and only friends.
   He unsays every word,
And curses Heaven, that has sent
A dangerous gift. We all repent
   Speeches that are absurd.

We prize too much the beautiful,
And useful things spurn (as a rule);
   Yet fast will beauty fleet.
The Stag admired the antlers high,
That brought him into jeopardy,
   And blamed his kindly feet.

The Stag viewing himself in the Stream

The Hare and the Tortoise

It's not enough that you run fleet;
Start early, – that's the way to beat.
The Tortoise said unto the Hare,
"I'll bet you, free, and frank, and fair,
You do not reach a certain place
So soon as I, though quick your pace."
"So soon?" the nimble creature cries;
"Take physic for your brains; – be wise" –
"Fool or no fool, I make the bet."
The bet is made, the stakes are set;
But who the sporting judges were
Is neither your nor my affair.
Our Hare had but a bound to make,
From him the swiftest hounds to shake.
They run themselves almost to death,
Yet he is scarcely out of breath;
Plenty of time for him to browse,
To sleep, and then again to rouse;
Or boldly turn the while he's going,
And mark which way the wind is blowing.

Careless, he lets the Tortoise pace,
Grave as a senator. To race
With such a thing is but disgrace.
She, in the meanwhile, strives and strains,
And takes most meritorious pains;
Slow, yet unceasing. Still the Hare
Holds it a very mean affair
To start too soon; but when, at last,
The winning-post is almost past
By his dull rival, then, 'tis true,
He quicker than the arrow flew.
Alas! his efforts failed to win,
The Tortoise came the first one in.
"Well," she said then, "now, was I right?

What use was all your swiftness: light
I held your speed, and won the prize;
Where would you be, can you surmise,
If with my house upon your shoulders,
You tried to startle all beholders?"

The Ass and his Masters

A Gardener's Donkey once complained to Fate
Of having to rise earlier than the sun.
"The cocks," he said, "are certainly not late;
But I have got to rise ere they've begun.
And all for what? – to carry herbs to sell:
A pretty cause to break one's morning sleep!"
Fate, touched by this appeal, determined well
To give the beast to other hands to keep:
The Gardener to a Tanner yields him next.
The weight of hides, and their distressing fume,
Soon shock our friend; he is far worse perplexed:
His mind again begins to lower and gloom.
"I much regret," he said, "my first good man,
For when he turned his head I always got
A bite of cabbage; – that was just my plan:
It cost me not a single sous, or jot;
But here no, no rewards but kick and cuff." –
His fortune shifts; a Charcoal-dealer's stall
Receives him. Still complaints, and *quantum suff*.
"What! not content yet," Fate cries, "after all?
This Ass is worse than half a hundred kings.
Does he, forsooth, think he 's the only one
That's not content? Have I no other things
To fill my mind but this poor simpleton?"

And Fate was right. No man is satisfied:
Our fortune never fits our wayward minds;
The present seems the worst we've ever tried;
We weary Heaven with outcries of all kinds.
And yet, if Jupiter gave each his will,
We should torment his ear with wishes still.

The Sun and the Frogs

A Monarch's wedding gave his people up,
The whole day long, to dances and the cup;
But Æsop found their doings in bad taste,
And thought their joy decidedly misplaced.

"The Sun," said he, "once thought about a wife,
And fancied he could shine in married life;
But instantly there came petitions loud
From all the Frogs on earth – a noisy crowd.
'Suppose,' they said, 'the Queen should be prolific,
Our situation will become terrific.
A single sun is quite enough to bear;
The little ones will drive us to despair.
Parched as we are, in sultry summer weather,
The extra heat will roast us altogether.
Let us entreat your mercy on our race;
The river Styx is not a pleasant place!'"

Considering that Frogs are very small,
I think the argument not bad at all.

The Countryman and the Serpent

Æsop describes, as he's well able,
A Peasant, wise and charitable,
Who, walking on a winter day
Around his farm, found by the way
A snake extended on the snow,
Frozen and numb – half dead, you know.
He lifts the beast, with friendly care,
And takes him home to warmer air –
Not thinking what reward would be
Of such an unwise charity.
Beside the hearth he stretches him,
Warms and revives each frozen limb.
The creature scarcely feels the glow,
Before its rage begins to flow:
First gently raised its head, and rolled

Its swelling body, fold on fold;
Then tried to leap, and spring, and bite
Its benefactor; – was that right?
"Ungrateful!" cried the man; "then I
Will give you now your due – you die!"
With righteous anger came the blow
From the good axe. It struck, and, lo!
Two strokes – three snakes – its body, tail,
And head; and each, without avail,
Trying to re-unite in vain,
They only wriggle in long pain.
It's good to lavish charity;
But then on whom? Well, that's just it.
As for ungrateful men, they die
In misery, and as 'tis fit.

The Countryman and the Serpent

The sick Lion and the Fox

The King of Beasts was sick to death,
And, almost with his latest breath,
Made known to all his vassals he
Needed their deepest sympathy.
As in his cave he lay, he stated,
For friendly visitors he waited.
With every guarantee insured,
The deputies went, quite secured;
Upon the Lion's passport writ,
In fair round hand, each word of it —
A promise good, in eyes of law,
Whether against tooth or claw.
The Prince's will to execute
Goes every class of beast and brute.
The Foxes only kept at home;
One gave the reason he'd not come:
"The footprints of the courtiers, see,
Are all one way, that's plain to me:
But none point homeward. It is just
If I feel somewhat of distrust.
Our sick King's courtiers may dispense
With passports, for they're full of sense.
Granted, no doubt; and yet I crave
They'll show me how to leave the cave. —
I clearly see they enter. Well!
But how they leave it who can tell?"

The sick Lion and the Fox

The Bird-Catcher, the Hawk, and the Skylark

Injustice, and false people's wilful crimes,
Serve others as excuses, oftentimes,
For fresh injustice. Nature's law 's planned so;
If you wish to be spared, then give no blow.
A Countryman, with glittering looking-glass,
Was catching birds. The brilliant phantom lured
A Lark; when, suddenly, it came to pass
A Sparrow Hawk, of its sweet prey assured,
Dropped from the cloud, and struck swift to the ground
The gentlest bird that sings; though near the tomb,
She had escaped the trap; yet now she found
Beneath that cruel beak at last her doom.
Whilst stripping her, eager and all intent,
The Hawk itself beneath the net was caught.
"Fowler," he cried, "no harm I ever meant:
I never did thee ill, nor ever sought
To do." The man replied, "This helpless thing
Had done no more to thee; – no murmuring!"

The Horse and the Ass

In this world every one must help his brother.
If your poor neighbour dies, his weary load
On you, perhaps, may fall, and on no other.
An Ass and Horse were travelling on the road:
The last had but the harness on his back.
The first, borne down unto the very ground,
Besought the Horse to help him, or, alack!
He'd never reach the town. In duty bound,
Apologies he made for this request:
"To you," he said, "the load will be mere sport."
The Horse refused, and snorted at the jest.
Just as he sneered, the Donkey died. In short,
He soon perceived he had not acted right,
And had his friend ill treated; for that night
They made him drag the cart through thick and thin,
And in the cart his injured comrade's skin.

The Dog and the Shadow

We all deceive ourselves, and so we fall;
We all run after shadows, in our way:
So many madmen, one can't count them all;
Send them to Æsop's Dog, – I beg and pry.
The Dog, who saw the shadow of the meat
He carried, dark upon the liquid tide,
Dropping his prey, snapped at the counterfeit:
The river rose, and washed him from the side.
True, with much danger, he regained the shore,
But neither meat nor shadow saw he more.

The Carter stuck in the Mud

A Phaeton, who drove a load of hay,
Found himself in the mud stuck hard and fast:
Poor man! from all assistance far away.
(In Lower Brittany he had been cast,
Near Quimper-Corentin, and all may know
'Tis there that Destiny sends folks she hates.
God keep us from such journey here below!)
But to return. The Carter, in the mire,
Rages and swears, and foams and execrates –
His eyes wild rolling, and his face on fire;
Curses the holes, the horses, every stone,
The cart, and then himself. The god he prays,
Whose mighty labours through the world are known:
"O Hercules! send present aid," he says;
"If thy broad back once bore this mighty sphere,
Thy arm can drag me out." His prayer he ends.
Then came a voice from out a cloud quite near:
"To those who strive themselves he succour lends.
Work, and find out where the obstruction lies;
Remove this bird-lime mud you curse so hot;
Clear axle-tree and wheel – be quick and wise;
Take up the pick, and break that flint – why not?"

Fill up that yawning rut. Now, is it done?
"Yes," said the man; and then the voice replied,
"Now I can help you; take your whip, my son."
"I've got it. Hallo! here; what's this?" he cried;
"My cart goes nicely – praise to Hercules."
And then the voice – "You see how readily
Your horses got clear out of jeopardy."
To those who help themselves the gods send help and ease.

The Carter stuck in the Mud

The Charlatan

Of Charlatans the world has never lack:
This science of professors has no want.
Only the other day one made his vaunt
He could cheat Acheron; in white and black
Another boasted o'er the town that, lo!
He was another Cicero.

One of these fellows claimed a mastery
Of eloquence; swore he could make an ass,
"A peasant, rustic, booby, d'ye see? –
Yes, gentlemen, a dolt of basest class –
Eloquent. Bring me an ass," he cried,
"The veriest ass, and I will teach him so,
He shall the cassock wear with proper pride."
The Prince resolved the truth of this to know.
"I have," he to the rhetorician one day said,
"A fine ass from Arcadia in my stable;
Make him an orator, if you are able."

"Sire, you do what you will." The man they made
Accept a sum, for twenty years to teach
The ass the proper use of speech;
And if he failed, he in the market-place,
With halter round his neck, was to be hung;
Upon his back his rhetoric books all strung,
And asses' ears above his frightened face.
One of the courtiers said that he would go
And see him at the gibbet; he'd such grace
And presence, he'd become the hangman's show;
There, above all, his art would come in well:
A long-extended speech – with pathos, too –
Would fit the great occasion, so it fell
In the one form of those grand Ciceros
Vulgarly known as thieves. "Yes, that is true,"

The other said; "but ere I try,
The king, the ass, and you will die."

Discord

Discord, who had the gods entangled
About an apple – how they wrangled! –
Was driven from the skies at last,
And to that animal came fast
That they call Man; her brother, too,
"Whether or no," who long'd to view
Our ball of earth. Her father came –
Old "Thine and Mine" – the very same.
She did much honour to our sphere
By longing so much to be here;
She cared not for the other race
Who watch us from aerial space –
We were gross folk, not tamed the least,
Who married without law or priest –
Discord no business had at all:
The proper places where to call

Scandal has orders to find out;
She, a right busy, active scout,
Falls quick to quarrel and debates,
And always Peace anticipates:
Blows up a spark into a blaze,
Not to burn out for many days.
Scandal, at length, complain'd she found
No refuge certain above ground,
And often lost her precious time:
She must have shelter in this clime –
A point from whence she could send forth
Discord, west, east, or south, or north.
There were no nunneries then, you see:
That made it difficult, may be.
The inn of Wedlock was assign'd
At last, and suited Scandal's mind.

The young Widow

A husband isn't lost without a sigh;
We give a groan, then are consoled again;
Swift on Time's wings we see our sorrow fly;
Fleet Time brings sunshine's pleasure after rain.
    The widow of a year, the widow of a day,
    Are very different, I say:
One finds it almost hard to trust one's eyes,
Or the same face to recognise.
One flies the world, the other plans her wiles;
In true or untrue sighs the one pours forth her heart,
Yet the same note they sing, or tears or smiles –
"Quite inconsolable," they say; but, for my part,
I don't heed that. This fable shows the truth:
Yet why say fiction? – it is sooth.
The husband of a beauty, young and gay,
Unto another world was call'd away.
"My soul, wait for me!" was the Widow's moan.

The husband waited not, but went alone.
The Widow had a father – prudent man!
He let her tears flow; 'twas the wisest plan.
Then to console, "My child," he said, "this way
Of weeping will soon wash your charms away.
There still live men: think no more of the dead;
I do not say at once I would be wed;
But after a short time you'll see, I know,
A husband young and handsome that I'll show,
By no means like the sorry one you mourn."
"A cloister is my husband – ah! forlorn."
The father let these foolish groans go by;
A month pass'd – every moment tear or sigh.
Another month, and ribbons load her table;
She changed her dress, and cast away her sable.
The flock of Cupids to the dovecot back
Came flying, now unscared by scarecrow black.
Smiles, sports, and dances follow in their train,
She bathes in youth's bright fountain once again.

No more the father fears the dear deceased;
But, as his silence not one whit decreased,
The angry widow cries impatiently,
"Where's the young husband that you promised me?"

The young Widow

Book VII

To Madame de Montespan

The apologue is from the immortal gods;
   Or, if the gift of man it is,
   Its author merits apotheosis.
Whoever magic genius lauds
   Will do what in him lies
To raise this art's inventor to the skies.
   It hath the potence of a charm,
   On dulness lays a conquering arm,
   Subjects the mind to its control,
   And works its will upon the soul.
   O lady, armed with equal power,
   If e'er, within celestial bower,
   With messmate gods reclined,
   My muse ambrosially hath dined,
   Lend me the favour of a smile
     On this her playful toil.
If you support, the tooth of time will shun,
And let my work the envious years outrun.
   If authors would themselves survive,
   To gain your suffrage they should strive.
On you my verses wait to get their worth;
To you my beauties all will owe their birth, —
   For beauties you will recognize
   Invisible to other eyes.

Ah! who can boast a taste so true,
　　　Of beauty or of grace,
　　　In either thought or face?
For words and looks are equal charms in you.
Upon a theme so sweet, the truth to tell,
　　　My muse would gladly dwell:
But this employ to others I must yield; –
A greater master claims the field.
For me, fair lady, 'twere enough
Your name should be my wall and roof.
Protect henceforth the favoured book
Through which for second life I look.
　　In your auspicious light,
　　These lines, in envy's spite,
　　Will gain the glorious meed,
　　That all the world shall read.
'Tis not that I deserve such fame; –
I only ask in Fable's name,
(You know what credit that should claim;)
And, if successfully I sue,
A fane will be to Fable due, –
A thing I would not build – except for you.*

*Translated by Elizir Wright.

The Animals sick of the Plague

A malady that Heaven sent
On earth, for our sin's punishment –
The Plague (if I must call it right),
Fit to fill Hades in a night –
Upon the animals made war;
Not all die, but all stricken are.
They scarcely care to seek for food,
For they are dying, and their brood.
The Wolves and Foxes crouching keep,
Nor care to watch for timorous Sheep.
Even the very Turtle-doves
Forget their little harmless loves.
The Lion, calling counsel, spoke –
"Dear friends, upon our luckless crown
Heaven misfortune has sent down,
For some great sin. Let, then, the worst
Of all our race be taken first,
And sacrificed to Heaven's ire;
So healing Mercury, through the fire,
May come and free us from this curse,
That's daily growing worse and worse.
History tells us, in such cases
For patriotism there a place is.
No self-deception; – plain and flat
Search each his conscience, mind you that.
I've eaten several sheep, I own.
What harm had they done me? – why, none.

Sometimes – to be quite fair and true –
I've eaten up the shepherd too.
I will devote myself; but, first,
Let's hear if any has done worst.
Each must accuse himself, as I
Have done; for justice would let die
The guiltiest one." The Fox replied –
"You are too good to thus decide.
Your Majesty's kind scruples show
Too much of delicacy. No!
What! eating sheep – the paltry – base,
Is that a sin? You did the race,
In munching them, an honour – yes,
I'm free, your highness, to confess.
And as for shepherds, they earn all
The evils that upon them fall:
Being of those who claim a sway
(Fantastic claim!) o'er us, they say."
Thus spoke the Fox the flatterer's text.
The Tiger and the Bear came next,
With claims that no one thought perplexed.
In fact, more quarrelsome they were,
The fewer grew the cavillers there.
Even the humblest proved a saint:
None made a slanderous complaint.
The Ass came in his turn, and said,
"For one thing I myself upbraid.

Once, in a rank green abbey field,
Sharp hunger made me basely yield.
The opportunity was there;
The grass was rich; the day was fair.
Some demon tempted me: I fell,
And cleared my bare tongue's length, pell-mell."
Scare had he spoken ere they rose
In arms, nor waited for the close.
A Wolf, half lawyer, made a speech,
And proved this creature wrong'd them each
And all, and they must sacrifice
This scurvy wretch, who to his eyes
Was steep'd in every wickedness.
Doom'd to the rope, without redress,
"Hang him at once! What! go and eat
An Abbot's grass, however sweet!
Abominable crime!" they cry;
"Death only clears the infamy."
If you are powerful, wrong or right,
The court will change your black to white.

The Animals sick of the Plague

The Man badly married

Oh, that the good and beautiful were wedded!
From early morrow I will seek the pair;
But since they are divorced, the addle-headed
Alone would track them long through sea or air.
Few beauteous bodies shelter beauteous souls;
So don't be angry if I cease pursuit.
Marriages many I have seen. The goals
To which men strive my fancies seldom suit.

The full four-fourths of men rush reckless on,
And brave the deadliest risks; – four-fourths repent.
I'll produce one who, being woe-begone,
Found no resource but sending where he'd sent
Before his hopeless wife, jealous and miserly,
Peevish and fretful; – nothing was done right.
They went to bed too soon – rose tardily;
The white was black, the black was staring white;
The servants groaned, the master swore outright.
"Monsieur is always busy; – he, of course,
Will think of nothing – squanders everything."
So much of this, in fact, Monsieur, *par force,*
Weary of all this squabble, and the sting,
Sends her back to the country and her friends, –

Phillis, who drives the turkeys, and the men
Who watch the pigs, and very soon she mends.
Grown calmer, he writes for her kindly then: –
"Well, how did time pass? was it pleasant there?
How did you like the country innocence?"
"It's bearable," she said; "the only care
That vexed me was to see the vile pretence
Of industry. Why, those base, lazy patches
Let the herds starve; – not one of them has sense
To do their proper work, except by snatches."
" Come, madam," cried the husband in a rage,
"If you're so peevish that folk out all day
Weary of you, and long to see the stage
That bears you from them anywhere away,
What must the servants feel who, every hour,
Are chased about by your outrageous tongue!
And what the husband, who is in your power
By night and day? Adieu! May I be hung
If I again recall you from the farm;
Or if I do, may I atone the sin
By having Pluto's gloomy realms within
Two wives like you, a shrew for either arm."

The Rat who retired from the World

There is a legend of the Levantine,
That once a certain Rat, weary of strife,
Retired into a Dutch cheese, calm, serene,
Far from the bustle and the cares of life.
In solitude extreme, dim stretching far and wide,
The hermit dwelt in all tranquillity,
And worked so well with feet and teeth inside,
Shelter and food were his in certainty.
What need of more? Soon he grew fat with pride;
God showers his blessings upon those who pay
Their vows to him in faith. There came, one day,
A pious deputy, from Ratdom sent,
To beg some trifling alms, because their town –
Ratopolis – was leaguered with intent
Most deadly; they, without a crown,
Had been obliged to fly, – so indigent
Was the assailed republic. Little ask
The scared ambassadors – the succour sure,
In a few days: the loan was no hard task.
"My friend," the hermit cried, "I can endure
No more the things of this world. What have I,
A poor recluse, to give you, but a prayer?
I yield you patiently unto His care."
And then he shut the door, quite tranquilly.
Who do I mean, then, by this selfish Rat?
A monk? – no, sir; a dervish is more fat.
A monk, where'er in this world he may be,
Is always full, you know, of charity.

The Heron

One day, on his stilt legs, walked, here and there,
A Heron, with long neck and searching beak;
Along a river side he came to seek.
The water was transparent, the day fair,
Gossip, the Carp, was gambolling in the stream:
The Pike, her neighbour, was in spirits, too.
The Heron had no trouble, it would seem,
But to approach the bank, and snap the two;
But he resolved for better appetite
To calmly wait: – he had his stated hours:
He lived by rule. At last, there came in sight
Some Tench, that exercised their finny powers.
They pleased him not, and so he waited still,
Scornful, like rat of whom good Horace wrote.
"What! eat a tench? – I, who can take my fill,
Munch such poor trash?" – he'll sing another note.
The tench refused, a gudgeon next came by:

"A pretty dish for such as me, forsooth!
The gods forgive me if I eat such fry:
I'll never open beak for that:" – and yet, in truth,
He opened for far less. The fish no more
Returned. Then Hunger came; – thus ends my tale.
He who'd rejected dishes half a score,
Was forced, at last, to snap a paltry snail.
Do not be too exacting. The cleverer people are
The sooner pleased, by far.
We all may lose by trying for too much; –
   I have known such.
Hold nothing in contempt, and the less so,
If you are needing help, for know
In that trap many fall, not only birds,
Like Herons, to whom now I gave some words.
Listen, my fellow-men, – another fable;
Some lessons can be found amid your lords.

The Maiden

A certain Maiden, somewhat proud,
A husband sought from out the crowd
Of suitors. Handsome he's to be, and bold,
Agreeable, young, and neither cold
Nor jealous. Wealth she wished, and birth,
Talent; in fact, all things on earth.
Who could expect to have them all?
Fortune was kind and helped to call
Lovers of rank and eminence.
She thought them mean and wanting sense –
"What! I accept such people? Pish!
You're doting, if that is your wish.
Look at the paltry creatures. See,
Mark how they grin, and ogle me."
One's vulgar; he who dares propose
Has, goodness gracious! such a nose;
This is too short, and that too tall,
Something distinctly wrong in all.
Affected girls are hard to please,
Though lovers sue them on their knees.
After the best were spurned, there came
The humbler people of less name.
She mocked them, too, unmercifully –
"To greet such men is good of me;

Perhaps they think my chance is poor,
Even to venture near my door;
But, Heaven be thanked, I pass my life,
Although alone, quite free from strife."
The Belle was with herself content;
But age came soon, the lovers went.
A year or two passed restlessly;
Then comes chagrin, and by-and-by
She feels that every hurrying day
Chases first smiles, then love away.
Soon wrinkles make her almost faint,
And try a thousand sorts of paint;
But all in vain, when past one's prime,
To shun that mighty robber, Time:
A ruined house you can replace,
But not the ruins of a face.
Her pride abates – her mirror cries,
"A husband get if you are wise;"
Her heart, too, echoes what is said –
E'en prudes are willing to be wed.
A curious choice, at last, she made,
And not a grand one, I'm afraid;
Her choice was what most men called foolish:
A clumsy boor, ill-shaped and mulish.

The Maiden

The Wishes

In the Mogul's dominions far away,
Certain small spirits there are often found,
Who sweep the house and dig the garden ground,
And guard your equipage by night and day:
If you but touch their work, you spoil the whole.
One of these spirits near the Ganges, then,
Toiled at the garden of a citizen;
And with a silent skill worked heart and soul.
He loved his master and his mistress, too,
The garden most. The Zephyrs (Heaven knows),
Friends of the genii, as the story goes,
Perhaps assisted him, whate'er he'd do.
He toiled unceasingly to show his zeal,
Loaded his host with gifts, a brimming store,
Boundless of pleasure; indeed, wished no more
To leave those friends for whom he thus could feel.
Fickle such spirits are, yet true was he;
His brother genii, joining in a plot,
The chief of their republic quickly got,
From some caprice or jealous policy,

To order him to go to Norway straight.
To guard a hut covered with changeless snows,
From India straight to Lapland. Ere he goes
The Spirit with his master holds debate:
"They make me leave you, yet I know not why;
For some forgotten fault, and I obey;
But be the time a month, or but a day,
I'll grant you now Three Wishes ere I fly –
Three, and no more. It is not hard, I know,
For man to wish – how easy, we all see."
They wished Abundance, and then presently
Abundance came; fast from her full hands flow
The golden streams, barns brim with piles of wheat;
The cellars with rich casks are almost burst:
How to arrange the stores – that is the worst;
What ceaseless care! what toil of hands and feet!
Thieves plot against them, nobles will still borrow,
The Prince heaps taxes: hapless is their fate;
Their sorrow, too much fortune, luck too great.
They say, "Take from us wealth, let's wake to-morrow

Poor as before. Happy the indigent;
Poverty's better than such wealth," their cry:
"Treasures, begone, take wings at once, and fly;
Of that so foolish wish we both repent.
Come, Moderation, mother of Repose,
Friend of good sense, O Moderation, come!"
She comes once more unto her former home;
The door behind her joyfully they close.
Two wishes gone, and not so luckily,
Their lot was that of those who dream away
Life in vain sighings, stealing, day by day,
Time better spent in honest industry.
The Spirit smiled at them; ere taking flight,
While yet his wings were spread, the one wish more
They asked; and this time Wisdom – that's a store
That never can embarrass, day or night.

The Court of the Lion

His Majesty Leo, in order to find
The extent of his varied and ample dominions,
Had summoned his vassals of every kind,
Of all colours and shapes, and of divers opinions.
A circular, signed by His Majesty's hand.
Was the means of conveying the King's invitation –
He promised festivities regally grand
(With an evident eye to self-glorification).
His palace was open, of course, to the throng;
What a place! – a mere slaughter-house, putting it
plainly,
Where visitors met with an odour so strong,
That they strove to protect their olfactories vainly.
The Bear in disgust put a paw to his nose;
He had scarcely the time to repent his grimaces;
For Leo at once in a fury arose,
And consigned the poor brute to the Styx, to make
faces.
The Monkey, true courtier, approved of the deed –
Said the palace was fit for a king's habitation,
And thought neither amber nor musk could exceed
The rich odour that gave him such gratification.
His fulsome behaviour had little success;
He was treated the same as the previous aspirant
(His Leonine Majesty, let us confess,
Was Caligula-like, and a bit of a tyrant).
The Fox trotted up, very servile and sly;
Said the monarch, "No shuffling, but answer me frankly;
Beware how you venture to give your reply:
Do you notice that anything smells rather rankly?"
But Reynard was more than a match for his king,
And replied that his cold being rather a bad one,
He could not at present distinguish a thing
By its odour, or even assert that it *had* one.
There's a hint for plain-speakers and flatterers here –
You should ne'er be too servile nor over-sincere;
And to answer sometimes in a round-about way,
Is a dozen times better than plain yea or nay.

The Vultures and the Pigeons

Mars one day set the sky on fire:
A quarrel roused the wild birds' ire –
Not those sweet subjects of the spring,
Who in the branches play and sing;
Not those whom Venus to her car
Harnesses; but the Vulture race,
With crooked beak and villain face.
'Twas for a dog deceased – that's all.
The blood in torrents 'gins to fall;
I only tell the sober truth,
They fought it out with nail and tooth.
I should want breath for the detail,
If I told how with tooth and nail
They battled. Many chiefs fell dead,
Many a dauntless hero bled;

Prometheus on his mountain sighed,
And hoped Jove nearly satisfied.
'Twas pleasure to observe their pains –
'Twas sad to see the corpse-strewn plains.
Valour, address, and stratagem,
By turns were tried by all of them;
By folks so brave no means were lost
To fill each spare place on the coast
Of Styx. Each varied element
Ghosts to the distant realm had sent.
This fury roused, at last, deep pity,
Within the pigeons' quiet city;
They – of the neck of changing hue,
The heart so tender and so true –
Resolved, as well became their nation,

The Vultures and the Pigeons

To end the war by mediation.
Ambassadors they chose and sent,
Who worked with such a good intent,
The Vultures cried, "A truce," at last,
And war's red horrors from them cast.
Alas! the Pigeons paid for it;
Their heart was better than their wit:
The cursed race upon them fell,
And made a carnage terrible;
Dispeopled every farm and town,
And struck the unwise people down.

In this, then, always be decided:
Keep wicked people still divided;
The safety of the world depends
On that – sow war among their friends;
Contract no peace with such, I say,
But this is merely by the way.

The Coach and the Fly

Up a long dusty hill, deep sunk in sand,
Six sturdy horses drew a Coach. The band
Of passengers were pushing hard behind:
Women, old men, and monks, all of one mind.
Weary and spent they were, and faint with heat;
Straight on their heads the sunbeams fiercely beat.
In the hot air, just then, came buzzing by,
Thinking to rouse the team, a paltry Fly.
Stings one, and then another; views the scene:
Believing that this ponderous machine
Is by his efforts moved, the pole bestrides;
And now upon the coachman's nose he rides.
Soon as the wheels begin again to grind
The upward road, and folks to push behind,
He claims the glory; bustles here and there,
Fussy and fast, with all the toil and care
With which a general hurries up his men,

To charge the broken enemy again,
And victory secure. The Fly, perplexed
With all the work, confessed that she was vexed
No one was helping, in that time of need.
The monk his foolish breviary would read:
He chose a pretty time! a woman sang:
Let her and all her foolish songs go hang!
Dame Fly went buzzing restless in their ears,
And with such mockery their journey cheers.
After much toil, the Coach moves on at last:
"Now let us breathe; the worst of it is past,"
The Fly exclaimed; "it is quite smooth, you know;
Come, my good nags, now pay me what you owe."
So, certain people give themselves great airs,
And meddlers mix themselves with one's affairs;
Try to be useful, worry more and more,
Until, at last, you show the fools the door,

The Milk-maid and the Milk-pail

Perette, her Milk-pail balanced on her head,
Tripped gaily and without hindrance down the road,
So slim and trim, and gay she nimbly sped.
For more agility, with such a load,
She'd donned her shortest kirtle and light shoes.
And as she went she counted up her gains –
Her future gains – with her twice one, twice twos.
How long division racked her little brains!
"First buy a hundred eggs, then triple broods;
With care like mine the money soon will grow;
No fox so clever in our neighbour's woods
But must leave me enough, as well I know,
To buy a pig, 'twill fatten very soon;
I buy him large, and for a good round sum
I sell him, mark you that some afternoon;
A cow and calf into our stable come;
Who'll prevent that? that's what I mean to say.
I see the calf skipping among the herd."
Then Perette skipped for joy. Alack-a-day!
Down came the milk, I give you my sworn word:
Adieu cow, calf, pig, chicken, all the rest.

She left with tearful eye her fortune lost,
And ran to tell her husband, dreading lest
He'd beat her, when in anger tempest tossed.
The neighbours, doubling up with laughter,
Called her the Milk-pail ever after.

Who has not raised his tower in Spain,
And in a cloud-land longed to reign?
Picrocolles, Pyrrhus have so done,
Sages or fools, just like this one.
All dream by turns; the dream is sweet;
The world lies prostrate at our feet:
Our souls yield blindly to the vision,
Our's beauty, honour, fields Elysian.
'Tis I alone the bravest smite,
The dethroned Sophy owns my might;
They choose me king, in crowds I'm led;
Gold crowns come raining on my head.
A fly soon wakes me up once more,

And I am Big John, as before.

The Milk-Maid and the Milk-Pail

The Curate and the Corpse

A dead man, on his mournful way,
To his last lodging went one day.
A Curè, bustling gaily, came
In due form, to inter the same.
Deceased was in a coach, with care
Packed snugly from the sun and air;
Clad in a robe, alas! ye proud,
Summer or winter, called a shroud;
To change it no one is allowed.
The pastor sat the dead beside,
Reciting, without grief or pride,
Lessons, responses, and those done,
The funeral psalms; yes, every one.
Good Mr. Dead-man, let them chant,
The salary is all they want.
The Curè Chouart shut the eyes
Of his dead man, lest he surprise
The priest who snatched from him a prize.

His looks they seemed to say, "My friend,
From you I'll have, before I end,
This much in silver, that in wax,"
And many another little tax;
That soon would bring our good divine
A small cask of the choicest wine;
His pretty niece a new silk gown,
And Paquette something from the town.
Just as his pleasant thoughts took flight,
There came a crash ... Curè; good night!
The leaden coffin strikes his head.
Parishioner, lapped up in lead,
Politely you went first, you see,
Now comes the priest for company.

Such is our life, as in this tale:
See Curè Chouart counting on his fee,
Like the poor girl with the milk-pail.

The Man who runs after Fortune, and the Man who waits for her

Is there a man beneath the sun,
Who does not after Fortune run?
I would I were in some snug place,
And high enogh to watch the race
Of the long, scuffling, struggling train
That hunt Dame Fortune all in vain.
The phantom flies from land to land,
They follow with an outstretched hand.
Now they have almost caught her. No;
She's vanished like the April bow.
Poor creatures! Pity them, I do:
Fools deserve pity – the whole crew,
By no means rage – "You see, we hope;
That cabbage-planter made a Pope.
Are we not quite as good?" they cry.
"Twenty times better," my reply.
"But what avails your mighty mind,
When Fortune is so densely blind?
Besides, what use the Papacy?
It is not worth the price, may be."
Rest, rest; a treasure that's so great
'Twas once for gods reserved by Fate;
How rarely fickle Fortune sends
Such gifts unto her trusting friends.
Seek not the goddess, stay at home;

Then like her sex she's sure to come.
Two friends there lived in the same place,
Who were by no means in bad case.
One sighed for Fortune night and day:
"Let's quit our sojourn here, I pray,"
He to the other said, "You know,
Prophets in their own country go
Unhonoured; let us seek elsewhere."
"Seek!" said the other; "I'll stay here.
I wish no better land or sky:
Content yourself, and I will try
To sleep the time out patiently."
The friend – ambitious, greedy soul! –
Set out to reach the wished-for goal;
And on the morrow sought a place
Where Fortune ought to show her face,
And frequently – the Court, I mean;
So there he halts, to view the scene;
Still seeking early, seeking late,
The hours propitious to Fate;
But yet, though seeking everywhere,
He only found regret and care.
"It's of no use," at last he cried;
"Queen Fortune elsewhere must abide;
And yet I see her, o'er and o'er,

Enter by this and that man's door:
And how, then, is it I can never
Meet her, though I seek her ever?"
These sort of people, I'm afraid,
Ambition find a losing trade.
Adieu, my lords; my lords, adieu;
Follow the shadow ruling you.
Fortune at Surat temples boasts;
Let's seek those distant Indian coasts,
Ye souls of bronze who e'er essayed
This voyage; nay, diamond arms arrayed
The man who first crossed the abyss.
Many a time our friend, I wis,
Thought of his village and his farm,
Fearing incessantly some harm
From pirates, tempests, rocks and sands,
All friends of death. In many lands
Man seeks his foeman, round and round,
Who soon enough at home is found.
In Tartary they tell the man
That Fortune's busy at Japan:
Then off he hurries, ne'er downcast.
Seas weary of the man at last,
And all the profit that he gains

Is this one lesson for his pains:
Japan, no more than Tartary,
Brought good to him or wealthy fee.
At last he settles it was shame
To leave his home, and takes the blame.
Then he returns: the well-loved place
Makes tears of joy run down his face.
"Happy," he cries, "the man at ease,
Who lives at home himself to please;
Ruling his passions, by report
Knowing alone of sea or Court,
Or Fortune, of thy empire, Jade,
Which has by turns to all displayed
Titles and wealth, that lead us on
From rising to the setting sun;
And yet thy promises astray
Still lead us to our dying day.
Henceforth I will not budge again,
And shall do better, I see plain."
While he thus schemed, resolved, and planned,

And against Fortune clenched his hand,
He found her in the open air
At his friend's door, and sleeping there.

The two Fowls

Two Barn-door Fowls in peace spent all their life,
Until, at last, love, love lit up the strife:
War's flames burst out. O Love! that ruined Troy,
'Twas thou who, by fierce quarrel, banished joy,
And stained with blood and crime the Xanthus' tide!
Long, long the combat raged 'tween wrath and pride,
Until the rumour spread the whole town through,
And all the crested people ran to view.
Many a well-plumed Helen was the prize
Of him who conquered; but the vanquished flies –
Skulks to the darkest and most hidden place,
And mourns his love with a dejected face.
His rival, proud of recent victory,
Exulting crows, and claims the sovereignty.
The conquered rival, big with rage, dilates,
Sharpens his beak, and Fortune invocates,
Clapping his wings, while, maddened by defeat,
The other skulks and plans a safe retreat.
The victor on the roof is perched, to crow;
A vulture sees the bragger far below.
Adieu! love, pride, and glory, all are vain
Beneath the vulture's beak; – so ends that reign.

The rival soon returns to make his court
To the fair dame, and victory to report,
As he had half-a-dozen other wives, to say the least,
You'll guess the chattering at his wedding feast.

Fortune always rejoices in such blows:
Insolent conquerors, beware of those.
Still mistrust Fate, and dread security,
Even the evening after victory.

The two Fowls

The Ingratitude and Injustice of Men towards Fortune

A Merchant, trading o'er the seas,
  Became enriched by every trip.
No gulf nor rock destroyed his ease;
  He lost no goods, from any ship.

To others came misfortunes sad,
  ·For Fate and Neptune had their will.
Fortune for him safe harbours had;
  His servants served with zeal and skill.

He sold tobacco, sugar, spices,
  Silks, porcelains, or what you please;
Made boundless wealth (this phrase suffices),
  And "lived to clutch the golden keys."

'Twas luxury that gave him millions:
  In gold men almost talked to him.
Dogs, horses, carriages, postillions,
  To give this man seemed Fortune's whim.

A Friend asked how came all this splendour:
  "I know the 'nick of time,'" he said,
"When to be borrower and lender:
  My care and talent all this made."

His profit seemed so very sweet,
  He risked once more his handsome gains;
But, this time, baffled was his fleet:
  Imprudent, he paid all the pains.

One rotten ship sank 'neath a storm,
  And one to watchful pirates fell;
A third, indeed, made port in form,
  But nothing wanted had to sell.

Fortune gives but one chance, we know:
  All was reversed, – his servants thieves.
Fate came upon him with one blow,
  And made the mark that seldom leaves.

The Friend perceived his painful case.
  "Fortune, alas!" the merchant cries.
·"Be happy," says his Friend, "and face
  The world, and be a little wise."

To counsel you is to give health:
  I know that all mankind impute
To Industry their peace and wealth,
  To Fortune all that does not suit."

Thus, if each time we errors make,
  That bring us up with sudden halt,
Nothing's more common than to take
  Our own for Fate or Fortune's fault.

Our good we always make by force,
  The evil fetters us so strong;
For we are always right, of course,
  And Destiny is always wrong.

The Fortune-teller

Opinion is the child of Chance,
And this Opinion forms our taste.
Against all people I advance
  These words. I find the world all haste –
Infatuation; justice gone;
  A torrent towards a goal unseen.
We only know things will be done
  In their own way, as they have been.

In Paris lived a Sorceress,
  Who told the people of their fate.
All sought her: – men; girls loverless;
  A husband whom his wife thought late
In dying; many a jealous woman.
  Ill-natured mothers, by the score,
Came – for they all were simply human –
  To hear what Fortune had in store.

Her tricks of trade were hardihood,
  Some terms of art, a neat address.
Sometimes a prophecy proved good,
  And then they thought her nothing less
Than Delphi's Pythoness of yore:
  Though ignorance itself was she;
And made her wretched garret floor
  Highway for gullibility.

Grown rich, she took a house, and bought
  A place of profit for her lord.
The witch's garret soon was sought
  By a young girl, who never soared
To witchery, save by eyes and voice.
  But yet they all came, as of old –
The lucky, who in wealth rejoice,
  And poor – to have their fortunes told.

The regulation had been made
  For this poor place, by her who late
Had been its tenant; and the shade
  Sybillic hovered o'er its state.
In vain the maiden said, "You mock.
  Read Fate! – I scarcely know my letters!"
But though such words, of course, might shock,
  They never could convince "her betters."

"Predict – divine; – here's gold in pay,
  More than the learned get together."
What wonder if the maid gave way,
  Despite herself, such gold to gather?
For fortune-telling seemed the place
  All tumble-down, and weird, and broken:
A broomstick, for the witches' chase,
  And many another mystic token;

The witches' sabbath; all suggested
    The change of body, and of face;
And so in Fate fools till invested.
    But what of her who made the place?
She seeks the golden prize to gain,
    In gorgeous state, like any parrot;
But people jeer and pass. In vain;
    They all go rushing to the garret.
'Tis custom governs everything.
    I've often seen, in courts of law,
Some stupid barrister, who'll bring
    Briefs such as clever men ne'er saw.
All a mistake: his eyes may glisten;
    They'll take him for some other man:
One unto whom the world will listen.
    Explain me this, now, if you can.

The Cat, the Weasel, and the little Rabbit

A little Rabbit's charming nook
A Weasel seized upon one morn;
His household gods with him he took,
    Jane Rabbit's mansion to adorn.

At break of day departed Jane,
    To munch amongst the thyme and roses,
Returning, at her window-pane –
    "Why, there the wicked Weasel's nose is!"

"Oh, gracious goodness! what is here?
    Turned out of my paternal hall!
From this you quickly disappear,
    Or I'll give all the rats a call."

The Weasel simply said the Earth
    Always belonged to the first comer;
All other claims were little worth:
    A sufferance tenant a misnomer.

A little kingdom he had found:
    "Now, tell me, what more right have you
To these domains, this patch of ground,
    Than Tom or Dick, than Nan or Sue?"

"Usage and custom of the law,"
    The Rabbit said, "give me the place:
On sire's and grandsire's claims I stand –
    I, who here represent their race."

"A law most wise! can't be more wise!"
    Said cunning Weasel. "What of that?
Our claims to settle, I devise
    A reference to our friend the Cat."

It was a Cat of solemn mien –
    A very hermit of a Cat: –
A saint, upon whose face was seen
    Precept and practice, law, and – fat.

The Rabbit here agreed, and then
    They sought the pious Pussy's home.
"Approach – I'm deaf," he said; and when
    They came, they told him why they'd come.

"Approach, fear not, for calm is law;
    For law no one here ever lacks;"
And, stretching on each side a claw
    He broke both litigants' weak backs.

This story calls unto my mind
    The sad result which often springs
From squabbles of a larger kind,
    Which small grand-dukes refer to kings.

The Head and the Tail of the Serpent

The Snake has two parts, it is said,
Hostile to man – his tail and head;
And both, as all of us must know,
Are well known to the Fates below.
Once on a time a feud arose
For the precedence – almost blows.
"I always walked before the Tail,"
So said the Head, without avail.
The Tail replied, "I travel o'er
Furlongs and leagues – ay, score on score –
Just as I please. Then, is it right
I should be always in this plight?
Jove! I am sister, and not slave:
Equality is all I crave.

Both of the selfsame blood, I claim
Our treatment, then, should be the same.
As well as her I poison bear,
Powerful and prompt, for men to fear.
And this is all I wish to ask;
Command it – 'tis a simple task:
Let me but in my turn go first;
For her 'twill be no whit the worst.
I sure can guide, as well as she;
No subject for complaint shall be."
Heaven was cruel in consenting:
Such favours lead but to repenting.
Jove should be deaf to such wild prayers:
He was not then; so first she fares;
She, who in brightest day saw not,
No more than shut up in a pot,
Struck against rocks, and many a tree –
'Gainst passers-by, continually;
Until she led them both, you see,
Straight into Styx. Unhappy all
Those wretched states who, like her, fall.

An Animal in the Moon

Some sages argue that all men are dupes,
And that their senses lead the fools in troops;
Other philosophers reverse this quite,
And prove that man is nearly always right.
Philosophy says true, senses mislead,
If we judge only by them without heed;
But if we mark the distance and reflect
On atmosphere and what it will effect,
The senses cheat none of us; Nature's wise:
I'll give an instance. With my naked eyes
I see the sun; how large is it, think you?
Three feet at farthest? It appears so, true!
But could I see it from a nearer sky,
'Twould seem of our vast universe the eye:
The distance shows its magnitude, you see;
My hand discovers angles easily.
Fools think the earth is flat; it's round, I know;
Some think it motionless, it moves so slow.
Thus, in a word, my eyes have wisdom got,
The illusions of the senses cheat me not.
My soul, beneath appearances, sees deep;
My eye's too quick, a watch on it I keep;
My ear, not slow to carry sounds, betrays;
When water seems to bend a stick ten ways,

My reason helps me out, and if my sight
Lies always, yet it never cheats me quite:
If I would trust my senses, very soon
They'd tell me of the woman in the moon.
What is there really? – No, mistrust your eyes,
For what you see are inequalities.
The surface of the moon has many regions,
Here spread the plains, there mountains rise in legions.
In light and shade strange figures you can trace –
Not long ago, in England men perlexed,
Saw, in a telescope, what *savants* vexed,
An elephant, an ox, a human face.
A monster in this planet's mirror fair;
Wild cries of horror filled the midnight air.
Some change was pending – some mysterious change,
Predicting wars, or a misfortune strange.
The monarch came, he favoured learned men;
The wondrous monster showed itself again:
It was a mouse between the glasses shut –
The source of war – the nibbler of a nut.
The people laughed – oh, nation blessed with ease,
When will the French have time for toils like these?
Mars brings us glory's harvests; still the foe
Shrinks down before us dreading every blow;

'Tis we who seek them, sure that victory,
Slave to our Louis, follows ceaselessly
His flag; his laurels render us renowned:
Yet memory has not left this mortal round.
We wish for peace – for peace alone we sigh;
Charles tastes the joys of rest: he would in war
Display his valour, and his flag bear far,
To reach the tranquil joy that now he shares.
Would he could end our quarrels and our cares!
What incense would be his, what endless fame!
Did not Augustus win a glorious name,
Equal to Cæsar's in its majesty,
And worthy of like reverence, may be?
Oh, happy people, when will Peace come down,
To dower our nation with her olive-crown?

An Animal in the Moon

Book VIII

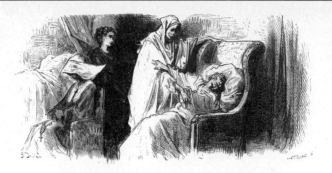

Death and the dying Man

Death never yet surprised the sage,
Who's always ready for the stage;
Knowing each hour that comes may be
His passage to eternity.
Death's rule embraces every day:
Each moment is beneath his sway.
We all pay tribute to that lord;
We all bow down beneath his sword.
The instant the king's child has birth –
And looks forth on this desert earth –
That instant Death may it surprise,
And close its scarcely-opened eyes.
Beauty, youth, virtue, every day,
Death steals so ruthlessly away.
One day the world will be his prey:
This knowledge is most largely shared;
For no event we're less prepared.
A dying man, a century old,
Complained to Death, that he was told
Too suddenly, before his will
Was made; he'd duties to fulfil;
"Now, is it just," this was his cry,
"To call me, unprepared, to die?
No; wait a moment, pray, sir, do;
My wife would wish to join me, too.
For still one nephew I'd provide:

And I have causes to decide.
I must enlarge my house, you know.
Don't be so pressing, pray, sir, go."
"Old man," said Death, "for once be wise;
My visit can be no surprise.
What! I impatient? In the throng
Of Paris who has lived so long?
Find me in all France even ten;
I should have warned you, you say then?
And so your will you would have made,
Your grandson settled; basement laid.
What! not a warning, when your feet
Can scarcely move, and fast retreat
Your memory makes, when half your mind
And wit is left a league behind?
When nearly all fails? – no more hearing –
No taste – all fading, as I'm fearing.
The star of day shines now in vain
For you: why sigh to view again
The pleasures out of reach? Just see
Your comrades drop continually,
Dead, dying: is no warning there?
I put it to you, is this fair?
Come, come, old man; what! wrangling still?
No matter, you must leave your will;
The great republic cares not, sir,

For one or no executor."
And Death was right: old men, at least,
Should die as people leave a feast,
Thanking the host – their luggage trim:
Death will not stay to please their whim.
You murmur, dotard! look and sigh,
To see the young, that daily die;
Walk to the grave or run, a name
To win of everlasting fame:
Death glorious may be, yet how sure,
And sometimes cruel to endure.
In vain I preach; with foolish zeal,
Those most akin to death but feel
The more regret in quitting life,
And creep reluctant from the strife.

The Cobbler and the Banker

A Cobbler, who would sing from dawn to dark
(A very merry soul to hear and see,
As satisfied as all the Seven Wise Men could be),
Had for a neighbour, not a paltry clerk,
But a great Banker, who could roll in gold:
A Crœsus, singing little, sleeping less;
Who, if by chance he had the happiness,
Just towards morning, to drop off, I'm told,
Was by the Cobbler's merry singing woke.
Loud he complain'd that Heaven did not keep
For sale, in market-places, soothing sleep.
He sent, then, for the Cobbler ('twas no joke): –
"What, Gregory, do you earn in the half-year?"
"Half-year, sir!" said the Cobbler, very gaily;
"I do not reckon so. I struggle daily
For the day's bread, and only hunger fear."
"Well, what a day? – what is your profit, man?"
"Now more, now less; – the worst thing is those fêtes.
Why, without them – and hang their constant dates! –
The living would be tidy – drat the plan!
Monsieur the Curé always a fresh saint
Stuffs in his sermon every other week."
The Banker laughed to hear the fellow speak,
And utter with such *naïveté* his complaint.
"I wish," he said, "to mount you on a throne;
Here are a hundred crowns, knave – keep them all,
They'll serve you well, whatever ill befall."
The Cobbler thought he saw before him thrown
All money in the earth that had been found.

Home went he to conceal it in a vault,
Safe from discovery and thieves' assault.
There, too, he buried joy, – deep under ground;
No singing now: he'd lost his voice from fear.
His guests were cares, suspicions, vain alarms;
All day he watch'd, – at night still dreading harms:
If but a cat stirr'd, robbers he could hear.
At last the poor fool to his neighbour ran;
He had not woke him lately, I'm afraid:
"Return my songs and tranquil sleep," he said,
"And take your hundred crowns, my generous man."

The Cobbler and the Banker

The Lion, the Wolf, and the Fox

A Lion, sickly, weak, and full of years,
Desired a remedy against old age
(*Impossible's* a word no monarch hears
  Without directly flying in a rage).
He sent for doctors – men of draughts and pills;
  From far and near, obedient to the call,
Came makers-up of recipes and pills:
  The Fox alone declined to come at all.
At court the Wolf malignantly referred
  To Reynard's absence, whereupon the King –
Whose anger was aroused at what he heard –
  Decided on a rather cruel thing.
He sent a force to smoke sly Reynard out,
  And bring him, willy nilly. When he came,
The Fox could scarcely entertain a doubt
  As to whose tongue had put him thus to shame.
"I greatly fear, your Majesty," said he,
  "You think me rude; you wrong me, if you do:

For I was on a pilgrimage, you see,
  And went to offer up my vows for *you*.
I scarcely need inform you I have met
  Expert physicians whilst I was away,
And hope to cure you of your sickness yet,
  Which comes from coldness of the blood, they say
You must, sire, skin a Wolf, and wrap the skin
  About you close, to get the body warmed;
And when the heat has kindled up within
  The fires of life again, the cure's performed.
Our friend, I'm sure, will take immense delight
  In lending you his coat; so, take it, sire."
The Lion supped upon the Wolf that night,
  And made the skin a part of his attire.
Courtiers, discretion is your safest plan:
  Malice is sure to find its source again;
And, while you do yourself what good you can,
  Reflect that slandering others is in vain.

The Lion, the Wolf, and the Fox

The Power of Fables

How can a great ambassador descend
To simple tales a patient ear to lend?
How could I trifling verses to you bring,
Or dare with transient playfulness to sing?
For if, sometimes, I vainly tried to soar,
Would you not only deem me rash once more?
You have more weighty matters to debate
Than of a Weasel and a Rabbit's fate.
Read me, or read me not; but, oh, debar
All Europe banding against us in war,
Lest from a thousand places there arise
Fresh enemies our legions to surprise.
England already wearies of her rest,
And vies our king's alliance as a jest.
Is it not time that Louis sought repose?
What Hercules but wearies of his blows
At the huge Hydra? – will it show its might,
And press again the lately ended fight,
By thrusting forth another head to meet,
At his strong sinewy arm, a fresh defeat?
If your mind, pliant, eloquent, and strong,
Could soften hearts, and but avert this wrong,
I'd sacrifice a hundred sheep to you –
A pretty thing for a poor bard to do.
Have then, at least, the kindness graciously
This pinch of incense to receive from me.
Accept my ardent vows, and what I write:

The subject suits you that I here indite.
I'll not repeat the praises Envy owns
Are due to you, who need not fear her groans.

In Athens' city, fickle, vain, of old,
An Orator, who dangers manifold
Saw crowding on his country, one day went
Up in the tribune, with the wise intent,
With his skill'd tongue, and his despotic art,
Towards a republic to force every heart.
He spoke with fervour 'bout the common weal;
They would not listen: they were hard as steel.
The Orator, to rouse them, had recourse
To metaphors of greater fire and force,
To sting the basest. He awoke the dead.
He, Zeus-like, flamed and thunder'd o'er each head:
The wind bore all away, – yes, every word.
The many-headed monster had not heard:
They ran to see the rabble children play,
Or two boys fighting made them turn away.
What did the speaker do? – he tried once more:
"Ceres," he said, "once made, we hear, a tour.
An Eel and Swallow follow'd her;
A river gave them some demur.
The Eel it swam: the Swallow flew,
Now what I tell you 's really true."
And as he utter'd this, the crowd

"And Ceres, what did she?" cried loud.
"Just what she did;" – then pious rage
Stirr'd him to execrate the age.
"What children's tales absorb your mind,
Careless of all the woes behind!
Thou only careless Grecian state,
What Philip does you should debate."
At this reproach the mob grew still,
And listen'd with a better will:
Such silence a mere fable won!
We're like the Greeks, all said and done.
And I myself, who preach so well,
If any one to me would tell
"Le Peau d'Ane," I should, with delight,
Listen for half the livelong night.
The world is old, as I have heard,
And I believe it, on my word;
Yet still, though old, I'm reconciled
To entertain it like a child.

The Man and the Flea

People pray to and weary the gods, now and then,
About trifles unworthy to interest men;
Thinking Providence cruel unless it contrives
To design to their likings the whole of their lives.
Why believe that Olympus should study us more
Than it studied the Greeks and the Trojans of yore?

A gaby was bit on the shoulder, one night,
By a Flea, which took refuge instanter in flight.
"O Hercules, Hercules, prithee come down,
And exterminate Fleas!" cried the suppliant clown.
"O Jupiter, strike with your lightning the beasts,
And avenge me on them and their horrible feasts!"

To punish a Flea, 'twould be rather a wonder
If gods went to work with theirclubs and their thunder.

The Woman and the Secret

A Secret is a dreadful weighty thing:
Few women carry secrets very far;
And this remark doth to my memory bring
Some men, too, born beneath the female star.
To try his wife, a husband one night cried,
"Ye gods, I perish! spare me, spare, I pray:
For, lo! I have just laid an egg." "An egg?" she sighed.
"Here it is – newly laid; but do not say
A single word, or they will call me 'hen.'
Be silent, darling." Then, in full belief,
She swore by all the gods to keep all men
Quite in the dark, so she assured her chief.
But with the shadows pass those words of hers.
Foolish and indiscreet, at earliest dawn,
She seeks her neighbour, and she thus avers:
"My gossip, such a thing took place last night!
You must say nothing, or I shall be beat.
My husband laid an egg, yes, large and white,
And big as any four; but don't repeat,
In Heaven's name, nor mention anywhere
This strange occurrence." "Now, I see you mock,"
The other said. "What! mention the affair!
You know me not. Go, I am like a rock!"

The hen's wife hastened homeward presently;
The other spreads the tale in twenty places.
The one big egg she quickly turns to three;
Nor was this all: to many startled faces
Another chatterer makes the number four.
Whispering is no more needful – all is known,
Before the day was over there had flown
A rumour that the man had forty score
Of chickens of his own all cackling round his door.

The Dog which carried round his Neck his Master's Dinner

Few eyes are against beauty proof;
Few hands from gold can keep aloof;
Few people guard a treasure well,
Or of strict faithfulness can tell.
A certain Dog, true, brave, and stout,
Carried his master's dinner out.
This self-denial pressed him hard,
When he had dainty food to guard:
Yet long he kept it safe and sound.
Well, we are tempted oft, 'tis found,
By good things near us! Strange, we learn
From dogs, and yet we hopeless turn
From men when temperance is in view!
One day this Dog, so staunch and true,
A mastiff met, who wished to seize
The dinner. Not so, if you please.
The Dog put down the food, to fight
A mighty combat. Left and right
Came other dogs, – mere thieves and foes,
Who cared not for the hardest blows.
Our Dog, who dreaded every stranger,
And saw the food was much in danger,
Wanted his share. "Come, gentlemen,
This rabbit does for me; now, then,
You take the rest!" so he leaped on it,
And then the others fell upon it.

He snapped the best, and then they flew
And shared the plunder, – the whole crew.
So, sometimes, when they yield a town,
And soldiers burghers trample down,
Sheriffs and provosts are the worst
To rob and pillage, being first:
Pleasant to see them pistoles seize,
Filling their purses at their ease!
And if, by chance, to one more cool
Some scruples come, they call him fool:
Then he repents him of the blunder,
And is the first to lead the plunder.

The Dog and his Master's Dinner

The Joker and the Fishes

He's vastly popular, your "Funny Man;"
For *my* part I avoid him when I can.
I generally find him rather hollow; –
The joker's is no easy art to follow.
I think sarcastic people were created
For fools to grin at, when exhilarated.
Let me present one at a dinner-table,
To point a moral and adorn a fable.
A wag, dining out at a banker's, one day,
    Had some very small fishes put near him.
He saw there were finer ones farther away,
    So, pretending the fishes could hear him,
He mutter'd some words to the poor little creatures,
    And feign'd to receive their replies.
It was done with such grave and unchangeable
                                        features,
    That people all opened their eyes.

Then he said that some very particular friend
    Was *en route* for the Indies, or thereabouts;
And he feared he might come to a watery end,
    So he wanted some hints of his whereabouts.
"The fishes had answered," he added, politely,
    "That *they* were too young to reply;
But they fancied their fathers could answer him
                                        rightly,
    Should one of them chance to be by."
To say that the company relished the jest,
    Or the jester, is more than I'm able;
But it answered his end, for they gave him the best
    Of the fishes that lay on the table.
'Twas a monster that might have related him stories
    As much as a century old;
Long tales of the sea, of its perils and glories,
    As wondrous as ever were told.

The Rat and the Oyster

A rustic Rat, of mighty little sense,
Weary of home, would needs go travel thence;
And quitted the paternal hearth, one day,
To study life in places far away.
At each wide prospect, hitherto unscanned,
He murmured, "Oh, how beautiful! how grand!
Yon mount is Caucasus, begirt with pines;
That range, methinks, must be the Apennines."
For every molehill, to his wondering eyes,
Became a mountain of terrific size.
He reached a province of the land, at last,
Where Tethys, deity of seas, had cast
Some Oysters on the sand, which looked at least
Like first-rate frigates to our simple beast.
"My father is a timid soul," he said,
"Who fears to travel: what an empty dread!
As to myself, what marvels I have seen;
What scores of wonders, earthly and marine!'
Thus boasted he, in magisterial tone,
And boasted loud, though speaking all alone.
Most rats, I beg to say, are more discreet,
And use their lips but when they wish to eat.

Meanwhile, one Oyster – a luxurious one –
With shells apart, was basking in the sun.
Tasting the balmy breeze, it lay agape, –
A fine fat morsel of seductive shape.
The Rat, with moistenings of the under lip
(Mistaking still the Oyster for a ship),
Ran up, and, smelling something nice to eat,
Prepared, straightway, his grinders for a treat.
"The crew," quoth he, "have left a feast on board, –
A cold collation, fit for any lord;
If it deceive me not, I've got a prize,
Or else I do not know the use of eyes."
So saying, Master Rat, resolving well,
Peered round the pearly margin of the shell.
It held him fast: the Oyster from his nap
Had woke, and sharply shut his treacherous trap.
This all arose from fatal ignorance:
The fable's useful to the folks of France, –
Nor France alone: it shows with what surprise
The simplest object strikes a booby's eyes.
And notice, oftentimes, for want of wit,
The fool, who thinks he's biting, is first bit.

The Bear and the Amateur of Gardening

A Certain Mountain Bruin once, they say,
Was wont within a lonely wood to stray, –
A new Bellerophon secluded there,
His mind had gone, and left his brain-pan bare.
Reason on lonely people sheds no ray;
It's good to speak – better to silent stay:
Both in excess are bad. No animal
Was ever seen, or was within a call.
Bear though he was, he wearied of this life,
And longed for the world's joy and the world's strife:
Then "Melancholy marked him for her own."
Not far from him an old man lived alone:
Dull as the Bear, he loved his garden well;
Was priest of Flora and Pomona; still,
Though the employment's pleasant, a kind friend
Is needful, its full charms to it to lend:
Gardens talk little, save in my small book.
Weary at last of their mere smiling look,
And those his dumb companions, one fine day,
Our man set forth upon his lonely way,
To seek a friend. The Bear, with the same thought,
Had left his mountain, satisfied with nought.

The Bear and the Amateur of Gardening

By chance most strange the two adventurers meet
At the same turning. He's afraid to greet
The Bear; but fly he can't. What can he do?
Well, like a Gascon, he gets neatly through:
Conceals his fright. The bear is not well bred;
"Here is my cottage; pray come in, my lord;
Still growls, "come see me!" but the other said,
Do me the honour at my frugal board
To lunch *al fresco*. I have milk and fruit,
That will, perhaps, your worship's pleasure suit
For once, though not your ordinary fare;
I offer all I have." With friendly air
They're chums already before reaching home;
Still better friends when there they've fairly come.
In my opinion it's a golden rule:
Better be lonely than be with a fool.
The Bear, who did not speak two words a day,

Left the drudge there to work and toil away.
Bruin went hunting, and brought in the game,
Or flapped the blow-flies, when the blow-fles came;
And kept from off his sleeping partner's face
Of wingèd parasites the teasing race.
One day a buzzer o'er the sleeping man
Poised, and then settled on his nose, – their plan.
The Bear was crazy: all his chase was vain;
"I'll catch you, thief!" he cried: it came again.
'Twas said, 'twas done; the flapper seized a stone,
And launched it bravely – bravely it was thrown.
He crushed the fly, but smashed the poor man's skull –
A sturdy thrower, but a reasoner dull.

Nothing's so dangerous as a foolish friend;
Worse than a real wise foe, you may depend.

The two Friends

Two steadfast Friends lived once in Monomtàpa;
They loved as if really they'd had the same pàpa:
What one earned the other earned. Ah! for that land;
It's worth ten such countries as ours, understand.
One night, when a deep sleep had fallen on all,
And the sun had gone off in the dark, beyond call,
One of these worthy men, woke by a nightmare,
Ran to his friend, in a shiver, and quite bare.
The other at once takes his purse and his sword,
Accosts his companion, and says, "'Pon my word
You seldom are up when all other men snore;
You make better use of the night than to pore
Over books; but come, tell me, you're ruined at play,
Or you have quarrelled with some one; now, speak
out, I say.
Here's my sword and my purse; or, if eager to rest
On a fond wife's compassionate, fondling breast,
Take this slave: she is fair." "No, no," said the other,
"'Twas neither of these things that startled me,
brother.
Thanks, thanks for your zeal; 'twas a dream that I had:
I saw you appear to me, looking so sad;
I feared you were ill, and ran to you to see:
'Twas that dream, so detestable, brought me to thee."
Which friend loved the most? – come, reader, speak
out!
The question is hard, and leaves matter for doubt.
A true friend is choicest of treasures indeed;
In the depths of your heart he will see what you need:
He'll spare you the pain to disclose woes yourself,
Indifferent to either his trouble or pelf:
A dream, when he loves, or a trifle – mere air –
Will strike him with terror, lest danger be there.

The Pig, the Goat, and the Sheep

A Goat, a Sheep, and a fat Pig were sent
To market, to their mutual discontent;
Not for the pleasures of the noisy fair,
But just to sell – the farmer's only care.
Not to see jugglers' tricks drove on the carter,
Bent only on his traffic and his barter.
Sir Porker screeched, as if he felt the knife,
Or heard ten butchers plotting 'gainst his life.
It was a noise to deafen any one:
His mild companions prayed him to have done.
The carter shouts, "Good heavens! why this riot?
You'll drive us silly; fool! can't you be quiet?
These honest folks should teach you manners, man;
So hold your tongue, you coward, if you can.
Observe this sheep, he has not said a word,
And he is wise." "Now, fool! you talk absurd.
If he the dangers knew as well as I,
Till he was hoarse and blind he'd bleat and cry.
And this my other friend, so calm and still,
Would scream his life out, as I, carter, will.
They think you're only going, on the morrow,
From this his milk, from that his wool to borrow:
They may be right or wrong, I do not know;
But *I* am certain of the deadly blow:
I'm good but for the spit. Farwell to you,
My house, and wife, and children! now, adieu."
Sir Porker reasoned with sufficient skill;
But all was useless: he was fit to kill.
Fear nor complaint could change his destiny:
He who looks forward least will wisest be.

Tircis and Amaranth

I Quitted Æsop, long ago,
For pleasant old Boccaccio;
But now a fair Divinity
Would once more from Parnassus see
Fables in my poor manner; so
To answer with a boorish "No,"
Without a valid, stout excuse,
To goddesses would be no use;
Divinities need more than this,
And belles especially, I wis.
Her wishes are all queens, you see;
She rules us all, does Sillery;
Who wishes once again to know
Of Master Wolf, and Master Crow.
Who can refuse her majesty?
None can deny her. How can I?
Well, to her mind my stories are
Obscure, and too mysterious far;
For, sometimes, even *beaux esprits*
Are puzzled and astray, you see.
Let us, then, write in plainer tune,
That she may so decipher soon.
I'll sing of simple shepherds, then,
Before I rhyme of wolves again.

Tircis to youthful Amaranth, one day,
Said, "Ah! but if you knew the griefs that slay!
Pleasing enchantments! Heaven-kindled woe!
The greatest joy of earth you then would know.
Oh, let me picture them! you need not fear.
Could I deceive you? Stay, then, sweet, and hear.
What! I betray? – I, whose poor heart is cleft
By fondest hopes that cruel Love has left?"
Then Amaranth exclaimed, "What is this pain?
How call you it? – now, tell me once again!"
"'Tis Love!" "A pretty word, its symptoms tell:
How shall I know it – I, who am so well?"
"A malady, to which all pleasant things –
Yes, even all the pleasures of great kings –
Seem poor and faded. Lovers thus are known:
In gloomy forests they will walk alone;
Muse by the river, watch the stream beside,
Yet their own faces rise not from the tide;
One image only in the flood shows day by day;
This lovely shadow comes but to betray:
To other things they're blind. A shepherd speaks;
His voice, his name, raise blushes on your cheeks:
You like to think of him, yet know not why;
You wonder at the wish, and yet you sigh;
You fear to see him, and yet, absent, cry."

Amaranth leaped for joy: "Is this, then, love?
Is that the pain you rank all things above?
It is not new to me: I think I know it."
Tircis thought he was safe, but dared not show it.
The maid said, "Yes, and that, I freely grant,
Is what I feel for dear, dear Clidamant."
Then Tircis almost burst with rage and spite;
But yet it seved the cheating fellow right.
Thinking to gain the prize, he lost the game,
And only cleared the road for him who came.

Tircis and Amaranth

The Funeral of the Lioness

The Lion lost his wife, one day;
And everybody made his way
To bring the prince that consolation
Which makes us feel our desolation.
The King announced the funeral
On such a day, to one and all.
They regulate the obsequy,
And marshal the vast company:
As you may guess, each one was there;
The prince's groanings filled the air;
And the den shook, above, below –
Lions have got great lungs, you know.
As the King does, all the others do;
So the best courtiers blubbered too.
Let me define a court: a place
Sad – gay; where every changeful face,
Careless of joy, is ready still
To change again at the King's will;
And if some cannot change, they try
To watch the change in the King's eye:
Chameleons, apes, in every feature;
Plastic and pliant in their nature.
One soul by turns fills many bodies:
These knaves are soulless, which more odd is.

But to return. The Stag alone
Uttered no single sigh or groan.
It could not well be otherwise;
This death avenged old injuries.
The Queen had cruel mischief done;
Strangled his wife, and slain his son:
Therefore he shed no single tear.
A flatterer noticed, hovering near;
Moreover, the spy saw him smile.
The anger of a King, meanwhile
(I may observe, with Solomon,
The wisest man beneath the sun),
Is terrible; but to our friend
No book could much instruction lend.
"Base creature of the woods!" with scorn
The Lion cried, "you do not mourn!
What should prevent our sacred claws
Teaching you friendship's holy laws?
Come, Wolves, avenge that Queen of mine:
Offer this victim on her shrine!"
The Stag replied, "The time for grief

Is passed; tears now are useless, Chief.
Your wife, whose features well I know,
Appeared to me an hour ago,
Half hid in flowers. 'My friend,' she said,
'For me your tears are vainly shed.

Weep not: in the Elysian fields
I've every pleasure that life yields,
Conversing with my holy friends;
But for a time the King descends
To a despair that charms me so.'"
Scarce had he spoken thus, when, lo!
"A miracle!" the courtiers cry.
The Stag's rewarded, instantly;
And safely, without punishment,
Back to his native woods is sent.

With dreams amuse a listening king,
With falsehoods sweet and flattering;
Whatever rage within may burn,
He'll gorge the bait, and friendly turn.

The Rat and the Elephant

In France there's many a man of small degree
Fond of asserting his own mightiness:
A "nobody" turns "somebody." We see
  In this the nation's natural flightiness.
In Spain men are not vain; their high-flown schools
Have made them proud, yet have not made them fools.

A tiny Rat saw a huge Elephant
  Travelling slowly with his equipage;
'Mongst beasts a sultan, knowing not a want.
  His suite comprised within a monstrous cage
His household gods, his favourite dog and cat,
His parroquet, his monkey, and all that.

The Rat, astonished to see people stare
  At so much bulk and state, which took up all
The space where he of right should have his share,
  Upon the citizens began to call:
"Fools! know you not that smallest rats are equal
To biggest elephants?" (Alas! the sequel.)

"Is it his monstrous bulk you're staring at?
  It can but frighten little girls and boys;
Why, I can do the same. You see, a Rat
  Is scarce less than an Elephant." A noise!
The Cat sprang from her cage; and, with one pant,
The Rat found he was not an Elephant.

The Rat and the Elephant

The Horoscope

A Man will sometimes meet his destiny
The moment that he turns ill-luck to flee.
A father had an only son, and dear
He held him; so, as love is kin to fear,
He with astrologers held a debate
About the stars that ruled the infant's fate.
One of these people said the father's care
Should of all lions specially beware.
Till he was twenty, he should keep him in,
And, after that, his safety would begin.
The cautious father, resolute to save
His offspring from the ever-yawning grave,
Knowing the danger turned on one neglect,
Guarded him carefully, in this respect; –
Forbad him exit; barred up every door;
But other pleasures lavished more and more.
With his companions, all the live-long day,
He was allowed to walk, and run, and play.
When he had reached the age that loves the chase,
A closer ward they kept upon the place.

They talked with scorn of all the huntsman's joys,
Spoke of the dangers – mocked the trumpet's noise.
But all in vain were sermons, though well meant;
Nothing can change the force of temperament.
The youth was restless, fiery, hot, and brave;
The stormy impulses came, wave on wave.
He sighed for pleasure; – more the obstacle,
The more desire; in vain they try to quell:
He knew the cause of all his misery.
The spacious house, so rich with luxury,
Was full of pictures, and of tapestry, –
The subjects hunting scenes, and forest glades:
Here animals, there men, strong lights, dark shades, –
The weaver made the lion chief of all:
"Out, monster!" cried the youth, and eyed the wall
With foaming rage: "'tis you that keep me here,
In gloom and fetters. Is it you I fear?"
He spoke, and struck, with all a madman's might,
The beast so innocent. There, out of sight,
Under the hanging, a sharp nail was stuck:

It pricked him deeply, by the worst of luck.
The arts of Æsculapius were in vain:
He joined the shadows that own Pluto's reign.
His death was due to his fond sire's regard,
That in the locked-up palace kept him barred.
It was precaution, too, that whilom slew
The poet Æschylus, if they say true.
It had been prophesied a house should fall
Upon his head, so he shunned tower and wall,
The city left, and camped out on the plain.
Far from all roofs and danger, he was slain:
An eagle, with a tortoise in his grip, flew by;
The poet's bald head, from the upper sky,
Looked like a smooth boulder; the bird let drop
The prey he wished to crush upon the top.
So perished Æschylus. From hence, we see,
The art, if true, led to the misery
That they would shun, all who in it had trust;
But I maintain it's false, and quite unjust.
I'll ne'er believe that Nature ties our hands,

Or would submit herself to such vile bands,
As in the skies to write our future fate;
Times, persons, places, have far greater weight
Than the conjunctions of a charlatan,
Under the self-same planet, tell the man.
Are kings and shepherds born, though one may sway
With golden sceptre, and the other play
With ashen crook? "The will of Jupiter," –
A star has not a soul, my worthy sir;
Why should its influence affect these two
So diversely? How can it pierce through
That sea of air, – those cloudy gulfs profound,
Mars and the Sun, and pass each fiery bound?
An atom would disturb it on its path.
Horoscope-mongers, let me rouse your wrath:
The state of Europe, – who predicted that?
Did you foresee it? – now, then, answer pat.
Think of each planet's distance, and its speed;
These sage's passions, it is well agreed,
Prevent their judging of our actions right.

On them our fate depends: a planet's course
Goes like our minds, with a still-varying force.
And yet these fools, with compass and with line,
Of men's whole lives would map out a design!
But do not let the tales that I repeat
Weigh in the balance more than it is meet.
The fate of boy and Æschylus came true,
Blind and deceitful though the art be, too.
Once in a thousand times the bull's eye's hit;
That is the good luck of your juggling wit.

The Ass and the Dog

We ought to help each other, wise men say:
An Ass forgot this motto, one fine day.
I know not how our beast ignored the rule,
For he's an amiable, good-natured fool.
A trusty Dog so gravely paced along,
The master took his nap at even-song:
The Ass began to roam about and feed,
And found, at last, a rank and savoury mead.
There were no thistles, – that he must endure:
One must not be too much an epicure.
The feast was still not bad: while aught remains;
'Twould pass for once, the air's fresh on these plains.
The Dog, half dead with hunger, said, at last,
"My dear companion, all this time I fast.
Stoop down a bit, and let the panniers fall;
I'll take my dinner out." No word at all

The Ass vouchsafed, fearing to lose a bite;
At length he deigned to answer the poor wight:
"Friend, when your master rouses from his nap,
He's sure at once to call you on his lap,
And give you a good meal." A Wolf, just then,
Ran forth, half famished, from his forest den.
The Ass called loudly to the Dog to aid;
The Dog stood still. "My friend," he quickly said,
"Fly till your master wakes – he'll not be long; –
Run fast. If caught, avert the coming wrong
With a hard kick, and break the wretch's jaw:
They've shod you lately, and you're right in law.
Mind, stretch him flat." The Dog spoke wise and well.
But the Wolf choked the Ass, and down he fell.
Conclusion: – We should always help each other;
And every man help carry his lame brother.

The Bashaw and the Merchant

An old Greek Merchant, one day, sought
Protection from a Bashaw, bought
At pasha's, not at merchant's, price
(Such guardians are not very nice).
It cost so much, that he complained
His purse and coffer were both drained.
Three other Turks, of lower station,
Offered, from sheer commiseration,
Their joint help, by word and deed,
For less than half the first to cede:
The Greek he listens, then agrees.
The Bashaw, cheated of his fees,
Is told that if of time the nick
He'd seize, these rascals he must trick –
Send them to Mahomet, to bear
A message for his private ear;
And quickly, too, or they united,
Knowing his friends, would see him righted;
Would send him some vile poison-broth,
To show the keenness of their wrath;
And that would send him to protect
The Stygian merchants, they expect.
The Turk – an Alexander – strode
Unto the Merchant's snug abode:
Down at the table sat – his air
Generous, bold, and free from care,
For he feared nothing, – how could he?

"My friend," he said, "you're quitting me;
And people tell me to watch keenly. –
You are too worthy: so serenely
No poisoner ever looks, I know;
So no more on that tack we'll go.
But for these patrons you have found,
Hear me, – to tell a tale I'm bound.
To wrong you I have no intent,
With reasoning, or with argument.

"Once a poor shepherd used to keep
A dog, to guard his silly sheep;
Till some one asked him, plain and pat,
How he could keep a beast like that,
With such a ravenous appetite:
It really wasn't fair or right.
'Twas their and every one's desire
He'd give the dog up to the squire.
Three terriers were best for him,
To guard his flocks, in life and limb:
The cur ate three times more than they. –
But the fool meddlers did not say
He also fought with treble teeth,
When wolves came howling out for death.
The shepherd listened – three dogs bought:
They cost him less, but never fought.
The flock discovered their ill lot

Almost as soon as you, I wot.
Your wretched choice will quickly do:
Now mark what I have said to you;
If you'll do well, return to me."
The Greek obeyed him speedily.

'Tis good the provinces should heed:
'Tis better, in good faith I plead,
Unto one powerful king to bend,
Than on poor princelings to depend.

The Bashaw and the Merchant

The Advantage of being Clever

Between two citizens there once
Arose a quarrel furious;
The one was poor, but full of knowledge
Ripe, and rare, and curious;
The other had not been to college,
And was, though rich, a perfect dunce.
He, far too fondly oft proclaiming
The items of his hoarded pelf,
Declared that learned men but came in
A rank far underneath himself.
The man was quite a fool, and I
Can never understand the why
Or wherefore wealth alone should place
A man above the learned race.
The rich one to the wise one said,
Full often, "Is your table spread
As well as mine? And if not, tell
What boots it that you read so well?
Night after night you sadly clamber
To the dull third-floor's backmost chamber;
And in December's cold you wear
What in hot June would be too bare;
Whilst as for servants, you have none,
Unless you call your shadow one.
Alack! explain to me the fate
Of this or any other State,
If all were there like you, and I

Spent nothing on my luxury?
We rich ones use our wealth, God knows!
And forth from us to artisan,
To tradesman and to courtesan,
In glorious golden floods it flows.
And even you, who write your works
Chiefly to use the knives and forks
Of rich financiers, get your meed
Of what you call our *hoarded* greed."
These foolish words, need scarce be said,
Simply contemptuous answer had.
The wise man had too much to say
In answer, and so went away.
But, worse than sarcasm, the sword
Of rough invader met the hoard
Of him who had the wealth: the town
In which he dwelt was toppled down.
They left the city, and the one
Who ignorant was was soon undone,
And met all men's contempt; whilst he
Who knew the sciences was free
Of all men call society.

The quarrel so at last was ended;
But this is what I always say:
In spite of the fool's yea or nay,
The wise must be commended.

Jupiter and the Thunderbolts

Jove, viewing from on high our faults,
Said, one day, in Cerulean vaults,
"Let us 'plenish the earth
With a race of new guests;
For those of Noah's birth
Quite weary me out with their endless requests.
Fly to hell, Mercury!
And bring unto me
The Fury most fierce and most grim of the three!
For that race that I've cherished
Will all soon have perished!"
Thus passionate Jupiter spoke,
But quickly from anger awoke.
And so, let me warn you, O Kings!
Of whom Jupiter makes the mere strings,
To rule and to guide as you will;
For a brief moment pause,
To examine the cause,
Ere you torture your subjects, or kill.
The god with light feet,
And whose tongue's honey sweet,
Went, as ordered, to visit the Fates.
Tisiphone looked at,
Megæra then mocked at;
And, after inspection,
Fixed his choice, of all persons, on ugly Alecton.

Rendered proud by this choice,
With a horrible voice,
The goddess declared,
In the caverns of Death,
That she'd stop all men's breath,
And not one live thing on the earth should be spared.
Unto Mercy's straight path
Jove came back from his wrath,
Annulled the Eumenide's oath;
Nothing loath.
Yet his thunders he threw
At the vile mortal crew;
And one might have thought
That destruction were wrought;
But the fact was just this –
The bolts managed to miss,
For the Thund'rer's pride
With our fear's satisfied.
He was father of men,
And so he knew when,
As papas mortal know too,
What distance to throw to.

But, with mercy thus treated,
Man, with wickedness heated,
Grew so vicious, at last,
That Jove swore he would cast
And crush our weak race,
Their Creator's disgrace.
But yet he still smiled;
For a father his child
Strikes with merciful hand.
So at last it was planned
That god Vulcan should have
The duty of sending us men to the grave.
With bolts of two sorts
Vulcan fills his black courts;
And of these two there's one
That Heaven throws straight,
When it fills up its hate,
And the thread of a man's life is done.
The other falls only
On mountain tops lonely;
And this kind alone
By great Jupiter's thrown.

The Falcon and the Capon

A treacherous voice will sometimes call;
Hear it, but trust it not at all.
Not meaningless the thing I tell,
But like the dog of Jean Nivelle.
A citizen of Mons, by trade,
A Capon, one day, was dismayed,
Being summoned, very suddenly,
Before his master's Lares; he
Disliked that tribunal, the spit
(It was a fowl of ready wit).
Yet all the folks, their scheme to hide,
"Coop, coop, coop, coop," so softly cried.
"Your servant; your gross bait is vain;
You won't catch me, I say again."
All this a Falcon saw, perplexed:
What had the silly creature vexed?
Instinct, experience, or no,
Fowls have no faith in us, I know;
And this one, caught with endless trouble,
To-morrow in a pot would bubble,
Or in a stately dish repose –
Small honour, as the Capon knows.

The Falcon the poor creature blamed;
"I am astonished! I'm ashamed!
You scum! you *canaille*! how you act!
You're half an idiot, that's a fact.
I come back to my master's fist,
And hunt for him whate'er he list.

Why, see, he's at the window, there;
You're deaf; he's calling, I declare."
"I know too well," the Fowl replied,
Not caring for the Falcon's pride:
"What does he want to say to me?
The cook has got his knife, I see.

Would *you* attend to such a bait?
Now, let me fly, or I'm too late;
So, cease to mock. Nay, now, good master,
That wheedling voice portends disaster!
Had you seen at the friendly hearth
As many Falcons of good birth
As I've seen Capons put to roast,
You'd not reproach me with vain boast."

The Cat and the Rat

Four animals, of natures various,
Living lives the most precarious,
Together dwelt, and yet apart,
Close to, and e'en within the heart
Of a most ancient pine.
The one was Master Cat, who claws;
Another, Master Rat, who gnaws;
The Weasel third, with waist so fine,
And of a very ancient line.
The fourth was sapient Master Owl,
Whose midnight hoot disturbs the ghoul.
One night, a man about their tree
A snare disposed with secresy;
And Master Cat, at early dawn,
From couch with hope of plunder drawn,
Scarce half awake, fell plump within
The cruelly-invented gin.
Such caterwauling then arose,
That Master Gnaw-cheese hurried round
To see, in fetters safely bound,
The deadliest of his special foes.
Then Master Purrer softly cried,
"Sir Rat, your true benevolence
Is known in all the country wide;
So pray, for pity, take me hence
From this atrocious, strangling snare

In which I've fallen, unaware;
'Tis strange, but true, that you alone,
Of all the Rats I've ever known,
Have won my heart, and, thank the skies!
I've loved you more than both my eyes.
Twas just as I was on my way,
As all devout ones should, to pray,
At early dawn, that I was pent
Within this cursed instrument.
My life is in your hands, my friend;
Pray, with your tooth these shackles rend."
But curtly then replied the Rat,
"Pray, say what I should gain by that?"
"My friendship true, for evermore,"
The Cat replied. "These talons grim
Shall be your guard; the Owl no more
Should watch your nest; the Weasel slim
Shall never make of you his meat.'"
"Not such a fool," replied the Rat,
"Am I as to release a Cat!"
And forthwith sought his snug retreat;
But near the narrow hole he sought
The Weasel watched, perhaps meaning nought.
Still further upward climbed the Rat,

To where the great Owl grimly sat;
At last, by dangers menaced round,
Sir Gnaw-cheese once more seeks the ground,
And, working hard with practised grinder,
Relieves poor Puss from cords that bind her.
  The task is just completed,
    When the ruthless man appears,
And, overwhelmed with equal fears,
The new allies by different paths retreated.
Soon after this adventure
The Cat beheld, one sunny day,
Snug in a place from cats secure,
His friend the Rat, and said, "I pray,
Come, let's embrace, we are friends again.
It gives me, on my word, true pain
To think that one to whom I owe
My life should deem me still his foe!"
"And do you think," replied the Rat,
"That I am ignorant of a Cat?
I know within your bosom lies
The germ of all hypocrisies."

To trust to friendships that rogues feign
Is leaning on a straw, 'tis plain.

The Torrent and the River

With a roar and a dreadful sound,
    The Torrent dashed down the rock.
All fled from its mighty bound;
    And horror followed the shock,
Shaking the fields around.

No Traveller dared essay
    To cross the Torrent, save one,
Who, meeting thieves by the way,
    And, finding all chances gone,
Rode straight through the foam and spray.

No depth! All menace and din!
    The Traveller drew his breath
With courage, and laughed within
    Himself at escape from death;
But the thieves resolved to win.

His path they pursue and keep,
    Till he comes to a River clear,
Peaceful and tranquil as sleep,
    And as far removed from fear:
Its banks are in no way steep.

But pure and glistening sand
    Border the placid wave;
He leaves the dangerous land,
    To find a treacherous grave:
It was deep, you'll understand.

He drinks of the awful Styx,
    For deepest waters are still.
Beware of quiet men's tricks;
    But for noisy men – they will
Battle with words, not sticks.

The Torrent and the River

Education

Cæsar and Laridon, his brother,
Both suckled by the same dear mother,
Sprang from an ancient royal race;
Right hardy in the toiling chase.
Two masters shared the noble brood;
And one the kitchen, one the wood
Made his home. Yet still the same,
They both kept their former name.
Place and custom altered them
In their nature, not in limb.
The one dog purchased by the cook,
Laridon for title took.
His brother to renown soon soars,
Slays by dozens stags and boars.
Soon as Cæsar he was known,
And as wonderful was shown.
But for Laridon none cared,
Or his children – how they fared.
So the Turnspits spread through France –
Vulgar dogs, that toil or dance:
Timid creatures, as one sees
Cæsar's true antipodes.
Time, neglect, and luckless fate
Make a race degenerate;
Wise men's sons turn simpletons;
Cæsars become Laridons.

The two Dogs and the dead Ass

The Virtues must, surely, sisters be,
For that Vices are brothers, we all well know.
And if but to one a man's heart be free,
All the others, like hurricanes, inward blow.
Yet, of course, both of virtues and vices 'tis true
That one heart holds but of either few;
And not more than once in an age we see
The Virtues in one small heart agree.
For if a man be valiant, 'tis sure,
In a thousand cases, he's also rash;
And if he be prudent, the greed for more
Will that respectable virtue dash.
Above all animals beside,
In faithfulness the Dog takes pride;
But, far too oft, for food he craves,
And even dogs are Folly's slaves.

Two Mastiffs, on a certain day,
Beheld a Donkey's carcase floating,
And fain had seized it for their prey,
But baffling winds deceived their gloating.
At length one said, "Your eyes are good,
My friend, so look on yonder flood,
And tell me what is that I see;
If savoury ox or horse it be."
"Of what it is," replied the other,
"What boots it, friend, to make a bother?
For dogs like us, in want of food,
Even a scurvy Ass is good.
The thing that now the most concerns us
Is, how to swim to such a distance,
Against this plaguy wind's resistance.
But, stay! let's quench the thirst that burns us,

By drinking up the river dry;
And when we've quenched our thirst, we'll pass
And gorge us on that savoury Ass."
With haste the Mastiffs now began
To quaff the river as it ran;
But, well-a-day! it came to pass
That, long ere they had reached the Ass,
The twain had long since quenched their thirst,
And, still persisting, nobly burst.
With us weak mortals 'tis the same,
When eager seeking wealth or fame.
What is hopeless seems not so;
So on from ill to ill we go.
A king whose states are amply round,
Will conquer still, to make them square;
And wealthy men, with gold to spare,
Sigh for just fifty thousand pound;
Whilst others, just as foolish, seek
To learn all science, – Hebrew, Greek!
In short, we most of us agree,
'Tis easy work to drain the sea!
A mortal man, to carry out
The projects of his single soul,
Would need four bodies, strong and stout,
And then would not complete the whole.
For, even should his life extend
To twice Methuselah's, depend
Ten thousand years would find him still
Where he began – the total *nil*.

The two Dogs and the dead Ass

Democritus and the Abderanians

How I the base and vulgar hate:
Profane, unjust, and obstinate!
So ever prone, with lip and eye,
To turn the truth to calumny!

The master of great Epicurus
Suffered from this rabble once;
Which shows e'en learning can't secure us
From the malice of the dunce.
By all the people of his town
Was cried, "Democritus is mad!"
But in his own land, well 'tis known,
No prophet credit ever had.
The truth within a nutshell lies:
His friends were fools, – and he was wise.
The error spread to such extent,
That, at length, a deputation,
With letters from Abdera's nation,
To famed Hippocrates was sent,
With humble, earnest hope that he
For madness might find remedy.
"Our fellow-townsman," weeping said
The deputation, "lost his head
Through too much reading. Would that he
Had only read as much as we!
To know how truly he insane is,
He says, for instance, nought more plain is,

Than that this earth is only one
Of million others round the sun;
And all these shining worlds are full
Of people, wise as well as dull.
And, not content with dreaming thus,
With theories strange he puzzles us;
Asserting that his brain consists
Of some queer kind of airy mists.
And, more than this, he says, that though
He measures stars from earth below,
What he himself is he don't know!
Long since, in friendly conversation,
He was the wit of all the nation;
But now alone he'll talk and mumble:
So, great physician, if you can,
Pray come and cure this poor old man."
Hippocrates, by all this jumble,
Was not deceived, but still he went; –
And here we see how accident
Can bring such meetings 'tween ourselves
As scarce could managed be by elves.
Hippocrates arrived, to find
That he whom all men called a fool
Was sage, and wise, and clam, and cool, –
Still searching for the innate mind
In heart and brain of beast and man.
Retired beneath a leafy grove,

Through which a murmuring brooklet ran,
The sage, with patient ardour, strove
The labyrinths of a skull to scan.
Beside him lay full many a scroll
By ancients written; and his soul
Was wrapt in learned thought so wholly,
That scarce he saw his friend advance:
Their greeting was but just a glance; –
For sages right well know the folly
Of idle compliment and word.
So, throwing off all forms absurd,
They spoke, in language large and free,
Of man, his soul and destiny;
And then discussed the secret springs
Which move all bad or holy things.
But 'tis not meet that I rehearse
Such weighty words in humble verse.

From this short story we may see
How much at fault the mob may be;
And this being so, pray tell me why
Some venture to proclaim aloud
That in the clamour of the crowd
We hear the voice of Deity?

The Wolf and the Hunter

O Avarice! thou monster, mad for gain;
Whose mind takes in but one idea of good!
How often shall I use my words in vain?
When shall my tales by thee be understood?
Oh, when will man, with heart so cold,
Still ever heaping gold on gold,
Deaf to the bard as to the wise,
At length from his dull drudgery rise,
And learn how sagely to employ it, –
Or know, in plain truth, to enjoy it?
Towards this course make haste, my friend,
For human life has soon an end.
And yet, again, a volume in one word compressing,
I tell you, wealth is only, when enjoyed, a blessing.
"Well," you reply, "to-morrow 'twill be done!"
My friend, you may not see to-morrow's sun;
Ah! like the Hunter and the Wolf, you'll find
'Tis hard to die, and leave your wealth behind.

A Hunter, having deftly slain
A Stag of ten, beheld a Doe;
So, having taken aim again,
Upon the green sward laid it low.
This booty was sufficient quite
For modest Hunter's appetite;
But, lo! a Boar, of form superb,
Starting from the tangled herb,
Tempted the Archer's greed anew, –

309

The bow was twanged, the arrow flew, –
With futile shears the sister dread
Had frayed his boarship's vital thread.
Full grimly did she now resume
The work at her Tartarean loom,
Nor yet achieved the monster's doom.
Not yet content? – nor ever will be he
Who once has quaffed the cup of victory.
The Boar has just begun to rise,
When, swift, a red-legged partridge flies
Right in the greedy Hunter's view, –
A wretched prize, 'tis very true,
Compared with those already got:
And yet the sportsman takes a shot;
But ere the trigger's pulled, the Boar,
Grown strong for just one effort more,
The Hunter slays, and on him dies:
With thanks, away the partridge flies.

The covetous shall have the best;
The miserly may take the rest. –
A Wolf that, passing by, took note
Of this sad scene, said, "I devote
To Mistress Luck a sumptuous fane.
What! corpses four together slain?
It seems scarce true! But I must be
Prudent midst this satiety,
For such good seldom comes to me."

(This is, of many vain excuses,
The one the miser mostly uses.)
"Enough," the Wolf continued, "here,
To give me for a month good cheer.
Four bodies with four weeks will fit,
But, nathless, I will wait a bit,
And first this Hunter's bowstring chew,
For scent proclaims it catgut true."
Thus saying, on the bow he flings
His hungry form; when, taking wings,
The undischarged bolt quickly flies
Through the Wolf's carcase, and he dies.

And now my text I will repeat –
Wealth, only when enjoyed, is sweet.
Oh, reader, from these gluttons twain
Take warning, ere it be too late.
Through greed was the keen Hunter slain;
Through hoarding up Wolf met his fate.

The Wolf and the Hunter

Book IX

The fraudulent Trustee

Animals I've sung in verse,
Memory's daughters aiding;
Perhaps I should have done far worse,
In other heroes trading.
In my book the dogs sit down
With wolves in conversation;
And beasts dressed up in vest and gown,
All sorts, of every nation,
Reflect each kind of folly duly,
My verse interprets them so truly.
Fools there are, and wise there are,
But my heroes I can't flatter;
For 'tis certain that, by far,
The former ones exceed the latter.
Swindlers I have painted often –
Brutes whom kindness cannot soften;
Tyrants, flatterers, and the crew
Who take your gifts, then bite at you.
In my pages you'll find many
Examples of the utter zany;
But chiefly have I had to do
With those who say what is not true.
The ancient wise man cried aloud,
"All men are liars!" Had he stated
This fact but of the wretched crowd,

E'en then I should have hesitated;
But that we mortals, great and small,
Both good and bad, are liars all,
I should deny at once, of course,
Did I not know the maxim's source.
But he who lies as Æsop lies,
Or, to go a little higher,
As old Homer, is no liar;
For the charming dreams we prize,
With which they have enriched the world,
Are brightest truths in fiction furled.
The works of such should live for ever;
And he who lies like them lies never.
But he who should attempt to lie
As a Fraudulent Trustee did,
A liar is, most certainly,
And should suffer for't as he did.
The story tells us
That, proposing
To journey into foreign lands,
A merchant, in the Persian trade –
In friends all confidence reposing –
Agreement with a neighbour made,
To leave some iron in his hands.
"My metal?" said he, coming back.

"Your metal! 'tis all gone, alack!
A rat has eaten up the lot!
I've scolded all my slaves, God wot!
But, in spite of all control,
A granary floor *will* have a hole."
The merchant opened well his eyes,
And never hinted aught of lies;
But soon he stole his neighbour's child,
And then he asked the rogue to dine.
To which the other answered, wild
With anguish, "Sir, I must decline –
I loved a child – I have but one –
I have! What say I? I have none,
For he is stolen!" Then replies
The Merchant, "With my own two eyes,
On yester eve, at close of day,
I saw your offspring borne away,
With many a struggle, many a howl,
To an old ruin, by an owl."
"An owl," the father cried, "convey
To such a height so big a prey!
My son could kill a dozen such;
For my belief this is too much!"
"I do not that deny," replies
His friend, "yet saw it with these eyes;

And wherefore should you think it strange
That in a land where rats can steal
A ton of iron from a grange,
And owl should seize a boy of ten,
Fly with him to his lofty den,
And of him make a hearty meal?"
The Fraudulent Trustee perceived
Which way the artful story tended,
Gave back the goods, the man received
His child, and so the matter ended.

Between two Travellers, on their road,
Dispute arose, in a strange mode: –
The one a story-teller, such
As oft are met with, who can't touch
On any great or trivial topic,
Without the use – that is, abuse –
Of lenses microscopic.

With them all objects are gigantic,
Small ponds grow huge as the Atlantic.
The present instance said he "knew
A cabbage once that grew so tall,
It topped a lofty garden wall."
"I'm sure," replied his friend, "'tis true,
For I myself a pot have met,
Within which no large church could get."
The first one such a pot derided:
"Softly, my friend," rejoined the second;
"You quite without your host have reckoned;
To boil your cabbage was my pot provided!"

The man of the monstrous pot was a wag,
The man of the iron adroit;
And if ever you meet with a man who'll brag,
Never attempt to stint him a doit,
But match his long bow with your strong bow.

The two Pigeons

Two Pigeons once, as brother brother,
With true affection loved each other;

But one of them, foolishly, tired of home,
Resolved to distant lands to roam.
Then the other one said, with piteous tear,
"What! brother, and would you then leave me here?
Of all the ills that on earth we share,
Absence from loved ones is bitterest woe!
And if to your heart this feeling's strange,
Let the dangers of travel your purpose change,
And, oh, at least for the spring-tide wait!
I heard a crow, on a neighbouring tree,
Just now, predicting an awful fate
For some wretched bird; and I foresee
Falcons and snares awaiting thee.
What more can you want than what you've got –
A friend, a good dwelling, and wholesome cot?"
The other, by these pleadings shaken,
Almost had his whim forsaken;
But still, by restless ardour swayed,
Soon, in soothing tones, he said –
"Weep not, brother, I'll not stay
But for three short days away;
And then, quite satisfied, returning,

Impart to you my travelled learning.
Who stays at home has nought to say;
But I will have such things to tell, –
''Twas there I went,' – 'It thus befel,' –
That you will think that you have been
In every action, every scene."
Thus having said, he bade adieu,
And forth on eager pinion flew;
But ere a dozen miles were past,
The skies with clouds grew overcast;
All drenched with rain, the Pigeon sought
A tree, whose shelter was but nought;
And when, at length, the rain was o'er,
His draggled wings could scarcely soar.
Soon after this, a field espying,
Whereon some grains of corn were lying,
He saw another Pigeon there,
And straight resolved to have his share.
So down he flies, and finds, too late,
The treacherous corn is only there
To tempt poor birds to hapless fate.
As the net was torn and old, however,
With beak, and claw, and fluttering wing,
And by despair's supreme endeavour,
He quickly broke string after string;

And, with the loss of half his plumes,
Joyous, his flight once more resumes.
But cruel fate had yet in store
A sadder evil than before;
For, as our Pigeon slowly flew,
And bits of net behind him drew,
Like felon, just from prison 'scaped,
A hawk his course towards him shaped.
And now the Pigeon's life were ended,
But that, just then, with wings extended,
An eagle on the hawk descended.
Leaving the thieves to fight it out,
With beak and talon, helter-skelter,
The Pigeon 'neath a wall takes shelter;
And now believes, without a doubt,
That for the present time released,
The series of his woes has ceased.
But, lo! a cruel boy of ten
(That age knows not compassion's name),
Whirling his sling, with deadly aim,
Half kills the hapless bird, who then,
With splintered wing, half dead, and lame,
His zeal for travel deeply cursing,
Goes home to seek his brother's nursing.
By hook or by crook he hobbled along,
And arrived at home without further wrong.
Then, united once more, and safe from blows,
The brothers forgot their recent woes.

Oh, lover, happy lovers! never separate, I say,
But by the nearest rivulet your wandering footsteps
stay.
Let each unto the other be a world that's ever fair,
Ever varied in its aspects, ever young and debonair.
Let each be dear to each, and as nothing count the rest.
I myself have sometimes been by a lover's ardour blest,
And then I'd not have changed for any palace here
below,
Or for all that in the heavens in lustrous splendour
glow,
The woods, and lanes, and fields, which were
lightened by the eyes,
Which were gladdened by the feet of that
shepherdess so fair, —
So sweet, and good, and young, to whom, bound
by Cupid's ties, —
Fast bound, I thought, for ever, I first breathed my
oaths in air.
Alas! shall such sweet moments be never more for
me?
Shall my restless soul no more on earth such tender
objects see?
Oh, if I dared to venture on the lover's path again,
Should I still find sweet contentment in Cupid's
broad domain?
Or is my heart grown torpid? – are my aspirations
vain?

The two Pigeons

The Ape and the Leopard

An Ape and a Leopard one day repair –
Money to gain – to a country fair,
And setting up separate booths they vie,
Each with each, in the arts of cajolery.
"Come, see me," cries Leopard, "come, gentlemen
                                                    come,
The price of admission's a very small sum;
To the great in all places my fame is well known,
And should death overtake me, the king on his throne
Would be glad of a robe from my skin;
    For 'tis mottled and wattled,
    And stained and ingrained
With spots and with lines, lines and spots thick and
                                                    thin,
That truly, though modest. I can but declare,
'Tis by far the most wonderful thing in the fair."
This bounce attained its end, and so
The gulls came hurrying to the show;
But, the sight seen, and the cash spent,
They went away in discontent.
Meanwhile the Ape cries – "Come, and see
The sum of versatility!
Yon Leopard boasts, through thick and thin,
A splendid show of outside skin;
But many varied gifts I have
(For which your kind applause I crave)
All safely lodged my brain within.

Your servant I, Monsieur Guffaw,
The noble Bertrand's son-in-law,
Chief monkey to his Holiness
The Pope. I now have come express,
In three huge ships, to have with you
The honour of an interview:
For speaking is my special forte,
And I can dance, and hoops jump through,
And other kinds of tumbling do,
And magic feats perform of every sort;
And for six blancos? no, I say, a sou;
But if with the performance you
Are discontented, at the door
To each his money we'll restore."
    And right was the Ape:
    For the colour and shape
Of fine clothes can but please for awhile,
    Whilst the charms of a brain
    That is witty, remain,
And for ever can soothe and beguile.

    Ah! there's many a one,
    Lord and gentleman's son,
Who holds high estate here below,
    Who to Leopards akin
    Has nought but fine skin
As the sum of his merits to show.

The Acorn and the Gourd

All that Jove does is wise and good,
I need not travel far abroad
To make this maxim understood,
But take example from a Gourd.

Observing once a pumpkin,
Of bulk so huge on stem so small,
"What meant he," cried a bumpkin,
"Great Jove, I mean, who made us all,
By such an act capricious?
If my advice were asked by Heaven,
To yonder oaks the gourds were given,
And 'twould have been judicious;
For sure it is good taste to suit
To monstrous trees a monstrous fruit.
And truly, Tony, had but he
Whom the priests talk of asked of me
Advice on here and there a point,
Things would not be so out of joint.
For why, to take this plain example,
Should not the Acorn here be hung –
For it this tiny stem is ample –
Whilst on the oak the pumpkin swung?
The more I view this sad abortion
Of all the laws of true proportion,
The more I'm sure the Lord of Thunder
Has made a very serious blunder."
Teased by this matter, Tony cries,
"One soon grows weary when one's wise;"
Then dozing 'neath an oak he lies.

Now, as he slept, an Acorn fell
Straight on his nose, and made it swell.
At once awake, he seeks to trace
With eager hand what hurt his face,
And in his beard the Acorn caught,
Discovers what the pain had wrought.
And now, by injured nose induced,
Our friend takes up a different tone –
"I bleed, I bleed!" he makes his moan,
"And all is by this thing produced:
But, oh! if from the tree, instead,
A full-grown Gourd had struck my head!
Ah! Jove, most wise, has made decree
That Acorns only deck the tree,
And now I quite the reason see."

Thus in a better frame of mind
Homeward went our honest hind.

The School-boy, the Pedant, and the nursery Gardener

A Certain Boy, half-spoiled at school –
Your Pedants spoil lads, as a rule;
Ten times a fool, ten times a rogue
They'd made this mischievous young dog. –
A neighbour's flowers and fruits he stole:
A man who struggled, heart and soul,
To raise Pomona's choicest treasure:
In what was bad he had no pleasure.
Each season did its tribute bring,
And Flora's gifts were his in spring.
One day he saw upon a tree
The boy climb up, and recklessly
Spoil half the buds, the promise dear
Of future plenty for the year; –
He even broke the boughs. At last
The Gardener to the school ran fast.
The Master came, with all his train
Of lads. "Of what does he complain?"

The orchard's full of dreadful boys,
Worse than the first, in tricks and noise.
The Pedant, though he meant not to,
Made the first evil double grow.
The Pedant was so eloquent
About the sin and ill intent;
It was a lesson not forgot
By the whole school, an ill-taught lot;
He often cites the Mantuan bard;
At rhetoric toils hot and hard.
So long his speech, the wicked race
Had time enough to spoil the place.
I hate your misplaced eloquence,
Endless, ill-timed, and without sense;
And no fool I detest so bad
As an ill-taught and thievish lad,
Except his Master; yet the best
Of these is a bad neighbour, 'tis confessed.

The Sculptor and the Statue of Jupiter

A Block of marble shone so white,
A Sculptor bought it, and, that night,
Said, "Now, my chisel, let's decree:
God, tank, or table, shall it be?

"We'll have a god – the dream I clasp;
His hand a thunderbolt shall grasp.
Tremble, ye monarchs, ere it's hurled!
Behold the master of the world!"

So well the patient workman wrought
In stone the vision of his thought,
The people cried at last, "Beseech
The gods to grant it power of speech!"

Some even dared the crowd to tell
That, when the chisel's last blow fell,
The Sculptor was the first with dread
To turn away his trembling head.

The ancient poet's not to blame,
For weak man's terror, fear, and shame
The gods invented in each age,
Abhorring human hate and rage.

The sculptor was a child; confess,
His mind, like children's in distress,
Tormented by this ceaseless sorrow,
His doll might angry be to-morrow.

The heart obeys its guide, the mind:
And from this source there flows, we find,
This Pagan error, which we see
Widen to all infinity.

We all embrace some favourite dream,
And follow it down flood and stream.
Pygmalion was in love, 'tis said,
With Venus that himself had made.

Each turns his dream into a truth,
And tries to fancy it all sooth.
Ice to the facts before his face,
But burning falsehood to embrace.

The Mouse metamorphosed into a Girl

A Mouse from the beak of an owl fell down,
A Brahmin lifted it up, half dead:
Tenderly nursed it, and tamed it, and fed.
I could not have done such an act, I own;
But every land has its own conceit:
With a Mouse I'd rather not sit at meat.
But Brahmins regard a flea as a friend,
For they think that the soul of a king may descend
To some beast, or insect, or dog, or mite, –
Pythagoras taught them this law erudite.
Thus believing, the Brahmin a sorcerer prayed
That the Mouse might resume some more elegant
dress.
The wise man consented, and, truth to confess,
Performed his task well, for the Mouse became Maid,–
Ah! a Maid of fifteen – such an elegant creature,
Of a form so genteel, of such exquisite feature,
That if Paris had met her, that amorous boy
Would have risked, to possess her, full many a Troy.
Surprised at the sight of a being so fair,
The Brahmin said, "Darling, you've but to declare
Whom you'll have for a husband, for none will refuse
Such a beautiful bride; – you have only to choose."
Then the Maiden replied, "I confess that I long

For a husband that's valiant, and noble, and strong."
Then the Brahmin knelt down, and addressing the Sun,
Cried, "Noblest of living things, you are the one!"
But the Lord of the Daylight replied, "'Tis not true
That I am so strong; for the Cloud you see yonder,
Piled high with the rain, and the hail, and the thunder,
Could hide me at once, if he chose, from your view."
To the Cloud, then, appealing, the Brahmin declared
That with him, Lord of Storms, his child's fate
should be shared.
"No, No!" said the dark Cloud; "it never can be,
For at each breath of wind I am driven to flee.
If you'd have for a son-in-law somebody strong,
Your Maid to the North Wind should fairly belong."
Disgusted with constant refusals like these,
The Brahmin appealed to the wild, roving Breeze;
And the Breeze was quite willing to wed the fair
Maid,
But a Mountain Top huge his love's pilgrimage
The ball, at this game of "a lover to find," [stayed.
Now passed to the Hill, but he quickly declined;
"For," said he, "with the Rat I'm not friends, and,
I know,
If I took the fair Maid, he would gnaw at me so."

At the mention of Rat, the fair Maiden, with glee,
Cried, "'Tis Rat, and Rat only, my husband shall be!"
See a Girl for a Rat now Apollo forsaking!
It was one of those strokes which Love glories in
                                                    making.
And, 'twixt you and me, such strange instances are,
'Mongst girls that we know of, more frequent than
                                                    rare.
With men and with beasts it is ever the same:
They still show the trace of the place whence they
                                                    came;
And this fable may aid us to prove it; but yet,
On a nearer inspection, some sophistry's met
In its traits; for, to trust to this fanciful story,
Any spouse were more good than the Sun in his glory.

But, what! shall I say that a giant is less
Than a flea, because fleas can a giant distress?
The Rat, if this rule must be strictly obeyed,
Of his wife to the Cat would a present have made:
And the Cat to the Dog, and the Dog to the Bear;
Till, at length, by a sort of a high-winding stair,
The story had brought us where first 'twas begun,
And the beautiful Maid would have married the Sun.
But let us return to the Metempsychosis
The truth of which, firstly, this fable supposes.
It seems to me plain that the fable itself
The system decidedly puts on the shelf.
According to Brahmin law, animals all
That inhabit the earth, be they mighty or small, –
Be they men, mice, or wolves, or e'en creatures
                                            more coarse, –
Their souls have derived from one general source;
And vary, in physical actions, just so
As the form of their organs may force them to do.
And if this be the case, then, how came it that one
Of so fine-formed a frame did not wed with the Sun?
Whereas, as we know, to a Rat she devoted
The charms on which many a king would have doated.

All things considered, I'll declare
That girl and mouse souls different are.
We must our destiny fulfil,
As ordered by the sovereign will.
Appeal to magic, – it is all in vain;
The soul, once born, will still the same remain.

The Madman who sold Wisdom

Never get in a Madman's reach:
Ye wise men, listen to my speech.
It's my advice – or right or wrong –
To flee from such crazed folk headlong;
In courts you often see them stalk,
The prince smiles at them in his walk;
To rogue and fool, and the buffoon,
They serve for jokes from morn to noon. –
A Madman once, in market-place,
Said he sold Wisdom. The dolts race
To buy the treasure. What fun is his,
Watching the silly people's phizzes,
When for their money they obtain
A blow that gives their red ears pain,
And forty yards of common thread.
Some were indignant; they, instead
Of pity, only mockery got.
The best way was to bear one's lot,
And walk off laughing; or else go
Home, and not talk about the blow.
To ask the meaning of all this
Was to secure a wise man's hiss;
There is no reason in such folks.
'Tis chance begets such crazy jokes,
And yet the thread it was mysterious.
One of the dupes who took it serious
Went to consult a sage he knew,
Who replied thus at the first view: –
"These hieroglyphics I can see;
People of sense infallibly
Between themselves and madmen place
At least some fathoms of this lace;
Or else they will a buffet gain,
And never much redress obtain.
You are not gulled; a crazy fool
Has sold you wisdom from his school."

The Madman who sold Wisdom

The Oyster and its Claimants

Two travellers discovered on the beach
An Oyster, carried thither by the sea.

'Twas eyed with equal greediness by each;
    Then came the question whose was it to be.
One, stooping down to pounce upon the prize,
    Was thrust away before his hand could snatch it.
"Not quite so quickly," his companion cries;
    "If *you've* a claim here, *I've* a claim to match it;
The first that saw it has the better right
    To its possession; come, you can't deny it."
"Well," said his friend, "my orbs are pretty bright,
    And I, upon my life, was first to spy it."
"You? Not at all; or, if you *did* perceive it,
    "I *smelt* it long before it was in view;

But here's a lawyer coming – let us leave it
    To him to arbitrate between the two."
The lawyer listens with a stolid face,
    Arrives at his decision in a minute;
And, as the shortest way to end the case,
    Opens the shell and eats the fish within it.
The rivals look upon him with dismay: –
    "This Court," says he, "awards you each a shell;
You've neither of you any costs to pay,
    And so be happy. Go in peace. Farewell!"

How often, when causes to trial are brought,
Does the lawyer get pelf and the client get naught!
The former will pocket his fees with a sneer,
While the latter sneaks off with a flea in his ear.

The Oyster and its Claimants

The Wolf and the starved Dog

Once on a time, a little Carp to man
Preached all in vain; they put him in the pan.
And I repeat, 'tis foolish to let slip
The glass that's full, and half way to the lip,
In hopes of better wine. The fish was wrong;
The fisherman was right, his reason strong.
One speaks out boldly when a life's to save;
It needs some eloquence King Death to waive;
But still I hold I'm right, and don't demur,
If from my former text I do not stir.
A Wolf, less wise than our good fisherman,
Meeting a Dog outside the village, ran
To bear him off. The poor Dog pleaded hard
That he was thin, and not worth his regard.
"My lord, I shall not please you, that is pat;

Wait till the marriage, I shall then grow fat
And quite myself – when master's daughter's wed."
The Wolf believed all that the terrier said.
The day expired; he came with faith to see
If good had come from this festivity.
To Wolf without the Dog spoke through the gate:
"Friend, I am coming, if you'll only wait;
The porter of our lodge is coming, too,
We'll soon be ready, sir, to wait on you."
The porter was a mastiff, you must know,
Ready to crunch up wolves, and at one blow.
The caller paused: "Your servant I remain,"
He said, and ran and sought the wood again;
Swift, but not clever: the remark was made,
"This Wolf was not a master of his trade."

"Not too much"

I find in no one race or nation
Of men what I call moderation;
Both animals and plants do err
In this respect, I must aver.
Nature's great Master wished that we
Should guard the golden mean, you see;
But do we? – No; and once more, No!
Whether to good or ill we go.
The corn that Ceres from her hand
Spreads lavish o'er the fertile land,
Too richly grows, and drains the ground,
Luxuriant, and without a bound;
So that from rank and crowded grain
All nourishment the deep roots drain;
The trees spread likewise heedlessly
To check the corn. God graciously
Gives us the sheep to check ill growth;
Amid the corn they, nothing loath,

Plunge headlong, and so, ruthless, spoil
The slow result of peasants' toil.
Then Heaven sends the wolf to thin
The sheep – they gobble kith and kin –
If they spare one 'tis not their fault,
They're but too ready to assault;
Then man the speedy punishment
Unto the cruel wolves is sent.
Next man – far worst of all abuses –
The power Divine he rashly uses.
Man, of all animals yet known,
Is more disposed to this, I own;
Little or great, unto excess
We carry all things, I confess;
No soul that lives but errs, I see,
In this respect continually,
The good text, "Not too much," is met
Often, but never practised yet.

The wax Candle

From heaven the Bees came down, they say,
And on Hymettus' top, one day,
Settled, and from sweet Zephyr's flowers
Stole all the treasures and strange powers;
And when th'ambrosia from each field,
Long in their store-rooms close concealed,
Was, to speak simple French, all taken,
And the mere empty comb forsaken,
Many Wax Tapers, from it made,
Were sold by those to whom that trade
Belongs. One of these Candles, long and thick,
Seeing clay hardened into brick
By fire, made to endure for aye,
Like an Empedocles, to die,
Resolved to perish in the flame.
A foolish martyr, seeking fame,
He leaped in headlong. Reasoning vain:
Small wisdom in his empty brain.
No human being's like another:
One cannot argue from one's brother.
Empedocles burnt up like paper;
Yet wasn't madder than this Taper.

Jupiter and the Traveller

The gods our perils would make wealthy,
If we our vows remembered, when once made.
But, dangers passed, and we, all safe and healthy,
Forget the promises on altars laid;
We only think of what we owe to men.
Jove, says the atheist, is a creditor
Who never sends out bailiffs; if so, then
What is the thunder meant as warning for?
A Passenger, in tempest tossed and rolled,
To Jupiter a hundred oxen offered.
He hadn't one; had he been only bold,
A hundred elephants he would have proffered:
They'd cost him not a single farthing more.
Suddenly mounted unto great Jove's nose
The scent of beef bones burnt upon the shore.
"Accept my promised vow," the rascal crows;
"'Tis ox you smell: the smoke is all for thee:
Now we are quits." Jove smiled a bitter smile;
But, some days after, sent a dream, to be
The recompense of that man's wicked guile.
The dream informed him where a treasure lay:
The man ran to it, like a moth to flame.

Some robbers seized him. Having nought to pay,
He promised them at once, if they but came
Where he'd a hundred talents of good gold.
The place, far off, pleased not the wary thieves;
And one man said, "My comrade, I am told
You mock us; and he dies, whoe'er deceives.
Go and take Pluto, for an offering,
Your hundred talents: they will please the king."

Jupiter and the Traveller

The Cat and the Fox

The Fox and Cat, two saints indeed,
To make a pilgrimage agreed:

Two artful hypocrites they were, –
Soft-footed, sly, and smooth, and fair.
Full many a fowl, and many a cheese,
Made up for loss of time and ease.
The road was long, and weary too:
To shorten it, to talk they flew.
For argument drives sleep away,
And helps a journey on, they say.
The Fox to the Cat says, "My friend,
To be so clever you pretend;
Say what am I? I've in this sack
A hundred tricks." "Well, on my back,"
The other, very timid, said,
"I've only one, I'm quite afraid;
But that, I hold, is worth a dozen,
My enemies to cheat and cozen."
Then the dispute began anew,
With "So say I!" and "I tell you!"
Till, suddenly, some hounds in sight

Silenced them soon, as it well might.
The Cat cries, "Search your bag, my friend,
Or you are lost, you may depend:
Choose out your choicest stratagem!"
Puss climbed a tree, and baffled them.
The Fox a hundred burrows sought:
Turned, dodged, and doubled, as he thought,
To put the terriers at fault,
And shun their rough and rude assault.
In every place he tried for shelter,
But begged it vainly; helter skelter,
The hounds were on the treacherous scent,
That still betrayed, where'er he went.
At last, as from a hole he started,
Two swift dogs on poor Reynard darted;
Then came up all the yelping crew,
And at his throat at once they flew.

Too many schemes spoil everything,
We lose our time in settling.
Have only one, as wise man should:
But let that one be sound and good.

The Cat and the Fox

The Husband, the Wife, and the Robber

A Husband, loving very tenderly –
Most tenderly – his wife, was treated ill
By her; – her coldness caused him misery.
No look, no glance, no, not a friendly word, –
Not e'en a smile, such as she gave her bird, –
But cold looks, frowns, and peevish answers, still.

He did not Venus nor yet Hymen curse,
Nor blame his destiny and cruel lot,
Yet daily grew the evil worse and worse:
Although he loved her every hour the more.
It is so now, and has been so of yore.
In fact, he was a Husband, was he not?

One night, as he lay moaning in his sleep,
A Robber entered; and, struck dumb with fear,
The fretful Wife, too frightened e'en to weep,
Sprang to her Husband's arms, and, sheltered there,
Defied all sorrow, trouble, danger near,
As her heart softened, and burst forth the tear.

"Friend Robber," said the Husband, "but for thee
I had not known this boundless happiness.
Take all I have, – I give thee liberty;
Take house and all, to prove my gratitude."
Thieves with much modesty are not endued;
The Robber took sufficient, I confess.

From this I argue that fear is so strong,
It conquers hatred, and love, too, sometimes.
Yet love has triumphed over passion's throng:
Witness the lover, who his house burnt down,
So he might win Hope's brightest laurel crown,
By rescuing her, the lady he'd loved long,
And so secure her heart. I like the story:

It stikes my fancy very pleasantly;
It is so Spanish in its tone. I glory
In love, so chivalrous and mettlesome,
And hold it grand (so will all times to come).
'Twas not by any means insanity.

The two men and the Treasure

A Man of cash and credit shorn
  (The Devil only in his purse),
Resolved to hang himself one morn,
  Since death by hunger might be worse:

A kind of death which pleases not
  Those curious in their final taste.
A rope and nail he quickly got,
  And fixed them to a wall in haste.

The wall was weak and very old,
  With the man's weight it crumbling fell;
When out there came a stream of gold,
  The Treasure that he loved so well.

He did not stay to count, but ran;
  Pale Penury no more he feared.

When in the miser came – poor man!
  To find his wealth had disappeared.

"Gold gone! This cord's my only wealth!"
  He cried; "now I have lost all hope:"
And so straightway he hanged himself.
  How changed the fortunes of that rope!

The miser saves his wealth for those
  Who may be prudent, may be thieves;
Into the grave perhaps it goes:
  Who knows the changes Fortune weaves?

For Lady Fortune mocks outright
  At human nature's dying pangs;
And if by you or me made tight
  The rope, she laughs that some one hangs!

The Monkey and the Cat

Bertrand and Raton – a Monkey and Cat –
Were messmates in mischief, with roguery fat;
There was nothing they feared, there was nothing
they spared,
And whatever they plundered they usually shared.
If anything close by was stealable, they
Would never go foraging out of their way.
Bertrand stole everything Raton to please,
And Raton cared less for the mice than the cheese.
One day at the fire, when all clear was the coast,
The pair were both spying some chesnuts at roast:
To steal a good meal is its pleasure to double;
Besides, it would bring the cook's man into trouble.
Says Bertrand to Raton, "My brother, you see,
Fate's given a moment of glory to thee;

Get those chesnuts, and quickly, my brave one, I pray,
The gods have vouchsafed us a dinner to-day."
And so to snatch chesnuts poor Raton agreed,
And at once set to work on the dangerous deed.
With gingerly touch he the cinders withdrew,
And snatched the hot prizes, first one, and then two.
He has pilfered quite half, but has not eaten one;
The eating his comrade, Bertrand, has done.
A scullion comes – there's adieu to the theft –
And Raton is empty and querulous left.

Your nobles are much in a similar case,
Who as flatterers dangerous service embrace;
And to gratify kings, fingers often will burn,
Then homeward, though wiser, still poorer return.

The Monkey and the Cat

The Kite and the Nightingale

A daring thief, a Kite by name,
Spread dire alarm o'er hill and dale.
E'en little children cried, "For shame!"
    When he pounced on a Nightingale.
The bird of Spring for life prayed well –
    "I'm fit for songs, and not for eating;
Oh, hear my notes, and I will tell
    My tale of Tyreus, still repeating."

"Tyreus! is that good food?" then said
    The Kite. "No, no;" was the reply;
"He was a mighty king, who made
    His love to me, with vow and sigh.
"His cruel love was strong: too strong!
    'Twas mad – 'twas criminal: now, sire,
Let me transport you with my song;
    A song so sweet you must admire."

Not having eaten all the day,
    The Kite had other views of things.
Thus – "What's the use of music, pray?
    I, too, can talk of mighty kings.
"When you take kings – or kings take you –
    Sing to them and their pretty dears;
I'm hungry, and know what to do –
    An empty stomach has no ears."

The Shepherd and his Flock

"Alas! I see another one
Of my poor foolish flock is gone!
The wolf, relentless, day by day,
Makes still another sheep his prey.
In vain I count them, oft and oft –
Ten times a hundred; they're so soft,
That they have let my Bob be torn
By wolfish jaws. Ah! me, forlorn!
My darling Bob would follow me,
In town or in the country, up and down,
O'er all the world, with tread for tread,
If I but showed a bit of bread.
A furlong off my step he knew,
And to my piping time kept true.
Alas! poor Bobby!" When, at last,
This funeral discourse had past,
And Robin's fame was duly sounded,
The Shepherd, by his flock surrounded,
Addressed them all, ram, lamb, and sheep,
And said, that if they'd only keep
United, never wolf would dare
Their wolly-coated throats to tear.
The flock declared, with solemn bleat,
They all their master's views would meet,
Form ever one united band,
And chase Sir Wolf from out the land.
Delighted at their brave reply,
Guillot regaled them sumptuously.

But, sad to say, before the night,
There happened a disaster new.
A horrid wolf appeared in sight,
And off the timid creatures flew.
In truth 'twas a mere shadow, but
The ant's a wolf in Lilliput.

Bad soldiers you in vain address;
Heroic aims they all profess;
But let the slightest danger show,
In spite of generals, off they go.

Book X

The two Rats, the Fox, and the Egg
To Madame de la Sablière

Iris, it were easy, quite,
Verses in your praise to write,
Were't not that, scornful, you refuse
The plaintive homage of my muse,
In that unlike your sisters fair,
Who any weight of praise can bear:
Most women doat on flattery's lies,
Nor are they, on this point, unwise;
For, if it be a crime, 'tis one
That gods and monarchs fail to shun.
That nectar which, the poets say,
Is quaffed by him who holds the sway
O'er thunders, and which kings on earth
Get drunk on, from their earliest birth,
Is flattery, Iris, flattery – such
As you 'll not even deign to touch.
No, Iris! you have rich resources
In genuine wit, and wise discourses, –
Sometimes half earnest, sometimes gay;
The world believes it not they say:
Let the poor world think what it may.
In conversation, I maintain
That truth and jokes are equal gain.

Pure science well may be the stay
Of friendly converse; but the ray
Of mirth should, ever and anon,
Electric, light friends' union.
Discourse, when rightly comprehended,
Is with a thousand graces blended,
And much resembles gardens sweet,
Where Flora's various beauties meet;
And where the bees search every bloom,
And from each bush bring honey home.
Allowing this to be so, let
Some theories in my tales be met:
Theories philosophic, new,
Engaging, subtle; have not you
Heard speak of them? Their holders say
That animals are mere machines,
And move but by mechanic means;
That, move or gambol as they may,
They move but blindly, have no soul,
No feeling heart, no self-control;
But are like watches, which, set going,
Work on, without their object knowing.
If we should open one of these,

What is't the eye within them sees?
A score of tiny wheels we find;
The first is moved, then, close behind,
A second follows, then a third,
And so on, till the hour is heard.
To hark to these philosophers,
The heart is such; some object stirs
A certain nerve, and straight, again,
A fellow-nerve endures the strain;
And so on, till the sense it reaches,
And some deep vital lesson teaches.
"But how's it done?" These theorists cry,
'Tis done by pure necessity;
That neither will nor even passion
Assist in it, in any fashion.
That, moved by some inherent force,
The beast is sent to run the course
Of love and grief, joy, pain, and hate,
Or any other varied state.
A watch may be a watch, and go,
Compelled by springs; but 'tis not so
With us; – and here 'twere wise to ask
Descartes to aid us in our task, –

Descartes, who, in the times of eld,
Had for a deity been held;
And who, between mere men and spirits,
Holds such a place, by special merits,
As 'twixt man and oyster has
That patient animal, the ass.
He reasons thus, and boldly says,
"Of all the animals that dwell
On this round world, I know, full well,
My brain alone has reason's rays."

Now, Iris, you will recollect,
'Twas taught us by that older science,
On which we used to have reliance,
That when beasts think, they don't reflect.
Descartes goes farther, and maintains
That beasts are quite devoid of brains.
This you believe with ease, and so
Can I, until to woods I go,
Just when, perchance, some motley crew,
With dogs and horns, a stag pursue.
In vain it doubles, and confounds,
With many a devious turn, the hounds.

At length this ancient stag of ten,
Discovering all its efforts vain,
And almost wholly worn and spent,
Drives by main force, from covert near,
Athwart the dogs, some younger deer,
To tempt them off, by fresher scent.
What reasoning here the beast displays!
Its backward tracks on beaten ways,
Its numerous schemes its scent to smother,
And skill, at length, to thrust another
On danger almost at its feet,
For some great party chief were meet;
And worthy of some better fate
Than death from dogs insatiate.

'Tis thus the red-legged partridge, sprung
By pointer, strives to save her young,
As yet unfledged. With piteous cries,
And lagging wing, she feigns to rise,
Runs on, then halts, then hurries on again,
And dog and hunter tempts across the plain;
But when her nest is far enough behind,
She laughs at both, and skims along the wind.
'Tis said that beings have been found,

In distant lands, in northern climes,
Who still in ignorance profound
Are steeped, as in primeval times.
But only of the men I speak,
For there four-footed creatures break
The force of streams by dams and ridges,
And join opposing banks by bridges:
Beams morticed well with beams, their toil
Resists the stream's attempt to spoil;
Each labourer with the other vies
And old ones guide young energies
Chief engineers the whole survey,
And point out aught that goes astray.
Pluto's well-ordered state could never
Have vied with these amphibians clever.
In snows they build their houses high,
And pass o'er pools on bridges dry:
Such is their prudence, art, and skill;
Whilst men like us around them still,
If they, perchance, should have the whim
A distant shore to reach, must swim.

Now, spite of all, this evidence
Convinces me of beavers' sense.

But still, my point to make more clear,
I will a story here relate,
Which but lately met my ear
From lips of one who rules in state:
A king, I mean, and one whose glory
Soars high on wings of victory –
The Polish prince, whose name alone
Spreads terror round the Turkish throne.
That kings can lie not is well known:
He says, then, that his frontiers wide
Are edged by wilds where beasts reside,
Who warfare wage inveterate,
And to their sons transmit their hate.
"These beasts are fox-like," says the king,
And to their wars such art they bring,
That neither this nor any age
Has seen men with like skill engage.
All pickets, sentinels, and spies,
With ambuscades and treacheries,
That she who from Styx's entrails came,
And unto heroes gives their fame,
Invented has, for man's perdition,
These beasts employ, with erudition.
To sing their battles we should have

Homer restored us, from the grave;
And, oh! that he who Epicurus
Rivals once more could re-assure us
That, whatever beasts may do,
Is to mechanic means but due;
That all their minds corporeal are;
That building houses, making war,
They are but agents, weak and blind,
Of some mere watchspring in the mind.
The object which their sense attacks,
Returning, fills its former tracks,
And straightway, in their bestial pates,
The image seen before creates,
Without that thought, or sense, or soul
Have o'er the thing the least control.
But men a different station fill,
And, scorning instinct, use their will.
I speak, I walk, and feel within
Something to God-like power akin.
Distinct from all my flesh and bone,
It lives a life that's all its own,
Yet o'er my flesh it rules alone.
But how can soul be understood
By what is merely flesh and blood?

There lies the point. The tool by hand is guided;
Who guides the hand has not yet been decided.
Ah! what is that strange power which wings
The planets on their heavenly way?
Doth each some angel lord obey?
And are my spirit's secret springs
Moved and controlled the selfsame way?
My soul obeys some influence;
I know not what it is, nor whence.
That secret must forever lie
Hid by God's awful majesty.
Descartes knew just as much as I:
In other things he may supplant
All men; he's here as ignorant.
But, Iris, this, at least, I know, –
That no such lofty souls endow
The beasts of whom I've made example: –
Of soul, man only is the temple.
Yet must we to the beasts accord
Some sense the plant-world can 't afford;
And even plants have humble lives.
But let me add one story still;
And let me know how much your skill
Of moral from its facts derives.

Two Rats, seeking something to eat, found an Egg:
For such folks, to have something to eat is sufficient;

The two Rats, the Fox, and the Egg

And seldom or never you'll find that they beg
Of the gods turtle soup, or a French cook proficient.
Full of appetite, nimbly they sat down to eat,
And soon from the shell would have drawn out the meat,
When a Fox in the distance appeared, to molest them,
And a question arose, which most greatly distress'd them,–
No other, as you may suppose, but the way
The Egg from Sir Reynard's keen snout to convey.
To drag it behind them, or roll it on floor,
To pack it behind them, or shove it before,
Were the plans tried in turn, but were all tried in vain.
When at length the old mother of arts made it plain
That, if one on his back held the Egg in his paw,
The other from danger could readily draw.
The plan was successful, in spite of some jolting;
And we leave the two sages their pleasant meal bolting.
Who shall, after this, declare
That beasts devoid of reason are?
For my part, I'll to beasts allow
The sense that dwells in childhood's brow.
Reason, from childhood's earliest years,
In all its acts and ways appéars;
And so it seems to me quite plain
That without soul there may be brain.
I give to beasts a sort of mind,
Compared to ours, a league behind.

Some matter I would subtilise,
Some matter hard to analyse,
Some atom's essence, light's extract;
Fire, subtlest of all things; in fact,
The flames that out of wood arise
Enable us to form some thought
Of what the soul is. Silver lies
Involved in lead. Beasts' brains are wrought
So that they think and judge; – no more.
They judge imperfectly. 'Tis sure
No ape could ever argue. Then
Above all beasts I'll place us men;
For to us men a double treasure
Belongs – that sense which, in some measure,
To all things living here below,
The wise and foolish, high and low,
Is common; and that holier spirit
Which men, with seraphim, inherit.
And, oh! this loftier soul can fly
Through all the wondrous realms of sky:
On smallest point can lie at ease;
And though commenced shall never cease.
Things strange, but true. In infancy
This soul must dim and feeble be;
But ripening years its frame develop,
And then it bursts the gross envelope
Which still in fetters always binds,
In men and beasts, the lower minds.

The Man and the Snake

A man once saw a Snake, and said,
"Thou wretched thing, I'll strike thee dead –
'Tis for the general good!"
And straight the wicked thing
(By *wicked,* be it understood,
I mean not Man, but wretch with sting;
For some my meaning might mistake),
Well, this base and atrocious Snake
   Was placed in sack,
   And doomed, alack!
To death without the aid of jury!
But yet the Man, despite his fury,
To show that he with justice acted,
His reasons in these words compacted: –
"Oh, symbol of all that is base,
'Twere a crome to spare one of thy race;
For mercy to those that are bad
Can from foolish ones only be had;
And no more shall thy sting or thy teeth,
Oh, thou villanous Snake, find their sheath!"
   The Serpent, thus addressed,
   His counter views expressed,
   And briefly made reply: –

"O Man! if all must die
Who graceless are, there's none
Who would not be undone.
Yourself shall be the judge; I'll take
From you excuse for me, the Snake.
My life is in your hands, I know,
But ponder ere you strike the blow,
And see now what you justice call
Is based on vices great and small.
Your pleasure and convenience
You'll satisfy at my expense;
But, pray, think not that I am rude,
If, dying, I this statement make –
That Man, and not the Snake,
The symbol is of all ingratitude."
These words the angry Man surprise,
He starts aside, and then replies –
"Your words are nonsense, and to me
Belongs of right your fate's decree;
But, nathless, let us have resort
Unto some independent court."
The Snake assented; and a Cow
That stood hard by, appealed to, said –

"The case is plain; I can't see how
The thing should puzzle any head:
The Snake is right, I'll frankly say;
For yonder Man, for many a day,
With milk and curd I've amply fed,
And long ere this his child were dead,
If my rich food his pining son
Had rescued not from Acheron.
And now that I am old and dry,
He leaves me, wanting grass, to die;
Sure, had a Serpent been my master,
It could have been no worse disaster."
Thus saying, with an awkward bow,
Walked off, or rather limped, the Cow.
The Man, aghast at this decree,
Exclaimed, "O Snake! it cannot be;
The Cow is doting. Let us place
Before this Ox our mutual case."
The Snake assents, and heavily
The Ox walks up, and by-and-by,
Still ruminating, makes reply
To this effect – "That, after years
Of painful toil and weariness,
That Ceres' wealth Man might possess
(And here the Ox burst into tears),
His sole reward had been the goad,
When panting with some weighty load;
And, what was worse, his owner thought

He – Ox – was honoured, being bought
By cruel butcher, to be flayed,
And as a prize beast then displayed!
The Man declared the Ox a liar,
And said, "Yon Oak-tree shall be trier."
The tree, appealed to, made a case
Redounding unto Man's disgrace;
Told how he sheltered Man from rain,
Told how he garnished hill and plain,
Told how he gave Man flowers and fruits,
And how that, when Man's will it suits,
He cuts him down and burns his roots!

The Man, convinced against his will,
Resolved to have his vengeance still;
So took the Serpent, bag and all,
And banged it up against the wall,
Until the wretched Serpent died,
And human wrath was satisfied.

It is ever thus with the rich and great,
Truth and reason they always hate;
They think that all things here below
Solely for their convenience grow;
And if any this simple truth denies,
They call him a sulky growler of lies;
And this being so, when you wish to teach
The truth to such people, keep out of their reach.

The Tortoise and the two Ducks

A Tortoise once, with an empty head,
Grown sick of her safe but monotonous home,
Resolved on some distant shore to tread; –
It is ever the cripple that loves to roam.
Two Ducks, to whom our friend repaired
To gossip o'er her bold intent,
Their full approval straight declared;
And, pointing to the firmament,
Said, "By that road – 'tis broad and ample –
We'll seek Columbia's mighty range,
See peoples, laws, and manners strange;
Ulysses shall be our example."
(Ulysses would have been astounded
At being with this scheme confounded.)
The Tortoise liking much this plan,
Straightway the friendly Ducks began
To see how one for flight unfitted
Might through the realms of air be flitted
At length within her jaws they fitted
A trusty stick, and seizing each an end,
With many a warning cry – "Hold fast! hold fast!"
Bore up to heaven their adventurous friend.
The people wondered as the cortége passed,
And truly it was droll to see
A Tortoise and her house in the Ducks' company.
"A miracle!" the wondering mob surprises:
"Behold, on clouds the great Queen Tortoise rises!"
"A queen!" the Tortoise answered; "yes, forsooth;
Make no mistake – I am – in honest truth."
Alas! why did she speak? She was a chattering dunce:
For as her jaws unclose, the stick slips out at once,
And down amidst the gaping crowds she sank,
A wretched victim to her claims to rank.

Self-pride, a love of idle speaking,
And wish to be for ever seeking
A power that Nature ne'er intended,
Are follies close allied, and from one stock descended.

Book X, Fable III

The Cormorant and the Fishes

Through all the country far and wide,
In pools and rivers incessantly diving,
A Cormorant greedy his table supplied,
On their finny inhabitants so daintily thriving.
　　But at length there came a day
　　When his strength gave way,
And the Cormorant, having to fish for himself,
Unskilled to use nets which we mortals employ,
The fish for our own selfish use to decoy,
Began soon to starve; with no crumb on the shelf,
What could he do now? – Necessity, mother,
Who teaches us more than we learn when at school,
Advised the poor bird to go down to a pool,
And addressing a Cray-fish, to say to him –" Brother,
Go tell your friends a tale of coming sorrow:
Your master drains this pool a week to-morrow!"
The Cray-fish hurried off without delay,
And soon the pool was quivering with dismay:
Much trouble, much debate. At length was sent
A deputation to the Cormorant.
"Most lordly web-foot! are you sure th'event
Will be as you have stated? If so, grant
Your kind advice in this our present need!"
The sly bird answered – "Change your home with speed."

"But how do that?" "Oh! that shall be my care:
For one by one I'll take you to my home,
A most impenetrable, secret lair,
Where never foe of finny tribe has come;
A deep, wide pool, of nature's best,
In which your race may safely rest."
The fish believed this friendly speech,
And soon were borne, each after each,
Down to a little shallow, cribbed, confined,
In which the greedy bird could choose them to his mind.
   And there they learnt, although too late,
    To trust no bills insatiate.
But, after all, it don't much matter –
A Cormorant's throat or human platter –
Whether a wolf or man digest me,
Doesn't seem really to molest me;
And whether one's eaten to-day or to-morrow
Should scarcely be any occasion for sorrow.

The Cormorant and the Fishes

The Miser and his Friend

A Miser once who'd got much money,
Was puzzled how to hide that honey;
For ignorance and love of gain
Being ever sisters twain,
Had left him at a total loss
Where to secrete his golden dross;
And why the Miser was so hot to find
A place of safety for his hoarded pelf,
Was simply the great fear that filled his mind,
That some day he should spend and rob himself:
Yes, rob himself by gathering pleasure
From the usage of his treasure.
Poor Miser! how I pity your mistake!
Wealth is not wealth unless we use it,
And when we do not we abuse it.
Why keep money till the sense
Of pleasure dies in impotence?
To gather gold alone is wretched slaving;
To have to watch it makes it not worth having.
However this may be, our Miser might
Have found some trusty banker for his gold;
But it seemed better, to his purblind sight,

To give it to the depths of earth to hold.
So with a comrade's aid
It soon beneath the turf was laid;
But when a little time was past,
Our Miser going to re-visit
His buried treasure, found a huge deficit.
At first despair oppressed him; but at last
He hurried to his comrade, and he said —
"To-morrow I shall want your help again;
Some bags of gold still in my house remain,
And they had better with the rest be laid."
The comrade immediately hurried away,
And returned all the gold he had taken,
Intending to grasp the whole lot the next day;
But in this he was somewhat mistaken;
For the Miser grown wise by the loss of his store,
Resolved 'neath the earth to conceal it no more,
But to use and enjoy it; and thus the poor thief,
By being too clever, came headlong to grief.
   In my belief there is no ill in
   Playing the rascal to a villain.

The Wolf and the Peasants

A conscientious Wolf one day
(If conscientious Wolves there be),
Lamenting he was beast of prey,
Though such but by necessity,
Exclaimed – "I'm dreaded far and near,
To all a thing of hate and fear;
Dogs, hunters, and peasants combine to pursue me,
And weary out Jove with their prayers to undo me:
In England long since a price paid for my head,
Has caused the whole race to be utterly dead.
I'm an object of wrath to each ignorant squire,
Who orders his people to hunt me and kill;
And if a child cries, all that mothers require
Is to mention my name to make it be still.
And why this universal spite,
In all the country round,
Which never leaves the Wolf at rest?
Because, perchance, by hunger prest,
To satisfy my appetite,
I've eaten scurvy sheep, or ass, or mangy hound.
Ah! well, henceforth I'll eat no living thing,
But feed on herbs, and water from the spring;
Or starve and die – a cruel, cruel fate –
Sooner than be a thing of universal hate."
Saying these words, a pleasant savour drew

Our wolf's attention to some shepherds near,
Feasting on what his wolfish instinct knew
Had once been lambkin, to some mother dear.
"Ah, ah!" he exclaimed, "this is strange, by my troth;
I'm reproaching myself for each lamb that I've slain,
Whilst the shepherds and sheep-dogs themselves are
                                        not loth
To regale on roast lamb is abundantly plain;
And shall I, then, a Wolf, feed on nothing but grass?
No, not if I know it! The day shall not pass
Till a lambkin has gone down my cavernous jaws,
Without waiting for any of cookery's laws.
A lamb, did I say? I should just think so, rather;
Aye, the mother that bore him, and also his father."
Well, the Wolf was right; for as long as we feed
On animals' flesh, it is surely unjust
That we should endeavour to make them recede
To the primitive food of a root or a crust.
And beasts of prey, we should always remember,
Know not the use of spit or ember.

    Shepherds, shepherds! trust to me;
    The Wolf a hermit ne'er can be.
    And sure the Wolf is only wrong
    When he is weak and you are strong.

The Swallow and the Spider

"O Jupiter! who from thy regal brow
Drew forth Minerva, my old enemy,
List to the prayer of a poor Spider now;
  Listen, I pray to thee.
Progne here and there, all day, and everywhere,
Ever skimming, flitting, fifty times a day,
Passes by me sitting in my trimly woven lair;
Passes by me impudent, and bears away my prey:
Yes, swallows up the flies that are crowding to my net,
Which with skilful patience 'tween the laurel boughs
                                        I've set."
Thus the Spider, who of yore so artistically wove,
But now reduced in rank to the state of humble spinner,
Regarding every fly as hers of right for dinner,
Complained in noisy accents unto all-deciding Jove.

Past the luckless Spider's door,
  And with pitiless delight,
Bearing to her brood incessantly the food,
Which the clamorous little gluttons demanded more
                                        and more.
But sad it is to tell! still worse was yet to come,
  For the Swallow, skimming, flitting,
  Spied the Spider sadly sitting,
And snatched her hanging helpless from her once
                                        well-ordered home.

In this world here below, it is Jupiter's plan
Two tables to spread for two different classes;
At the one feasts the skilful, strong, vigilant man,
At t'other starve feeble and ignorant masses.

The Partridge and the Fowls

Once to a red-legged Partridge it befell
Amongst a lot of fighting Cocks to dwell.
Now, as the latter are a gallant race,
Fighting with pleasure for a dame's embrance,
The Partridge hoped that she would treated be,
By these brave birds, with hospitality.
But soon, alas! her hopes were cross'd,
For oft, by angry passions toss'd,
Her fiery hosts, with spur and beak,
Would tear plumage, brown and sleek.
At first, this grieved the Partridge much;
But when, as soon she did, she saw her foes
Inflicting on each other equal woes,
She ceased to blame them; "For," said she, "they're
                                                such
As Jupiter has made them; and we know
That he has planted many various creatures here below:
The Partridge mild; the Game-cock, rude and wild.
If I could be as I would be,
I'd pass my life in gentle company.
But what avails these vain regrets?
The master here takes Partridge in nets,
And forces them to live with Fowls. We owe
To man, and not to Nature, all our woe."

The Dog whose Ears were cut

"What have I done, I should like to know,
That my master should make me a public show?
Amongst other dogs I can never now go!
   Oh, kings of animals, human race!
   Tyrants, authors of my disgrace!
I wish some demon would treat you the same!"
Thus a young Dog reflected, mad with pain,
As they cropped his long ears, but his cries were in vain,
And he thought himself lost; but he found, one fine day,
That his loss was a gain, for, by nature endowed
With a combative spirit, in many a fray
He saw that to cropping his long ears he owed
Avoidance of many a subject for tears, —
Rough dogs, when they fight, bite their enemies' ears:
For hostile mastiffs his were best of all.
'Tis easy to defend one opening in a wall;
Armed with a collar, and with ears but small,
Our young Dog meets his foes, fights, and defeats them all.

The Shepherd and the King

Our lives are spoiled by demons twain;
Turn in, turn out; by each, in season;
By each with reckless force is slain
That which we mortals call our *reason*.
And if you ask their name and state,
I'll name god Love, the potentate,
For one; and for the other,
I'll name Ambition, Love's half-brother,
Who, not seldom, Love defeats,
And reigns within his choicest seats.
All this I soon could prove; but now
That which I wish to tell is how
A Shepherd by a King was sent for,
And what this royal deed was meant for.
The tale belongs to distant ages,
And not to those which fill these pages.
A numerous flock that filled the plain,
And brought the owner heaps of gain,
Through Shepherd's care and industry,
Once met a sapient's Monarch's eye.
Pleased with such skill and thrift, he said,
"Good Shepherd, to rule men thou'rt bred;
Leave now thy sheep. Come, follow me;
Accept my widest satrapy.
And so our Shepherd, who before
Had scarce had friend but hermit poor,
And very seldom had in view

Aught but his sheep and wolf or two,
Was with a viceroy's sceptre graced;
Nor was he by this change misplaced,
For Nature had endowed his mind
With funds of great good sense;
And how to govern human kind
He amply learned from thence.
Ere many days had passed away,
His former friend, the hermit,
Came running quickly, crying – "Say,
'Tis dream-work, or as truth affirm it,
That you are now beloved of kings,
And deal yourself in regal things.
Oh, kings mistrust; their favour goes
Like snow on water; thousand woes
Fall ever on the luckless wight
Who basks a time in kingly might.
You know not to what precipice
You haste. Come back; take my advice."
The other smiled; on which the man
Of sacred life, continuing, said –
"Alas! already I can scan
How far astray your wits have fled;
Your foolish conduct calls to mind
The story of the traveller blind,
Who sees a snake benumbed with cold;
The creature frosts so numb and nip,
He lies like some old leathern whip;
His own just lost, the man takes hold,
And waves the reptile in his joy,
When one who passes by that way
Cries – 'Heavens! throw that snake away,
Or quickly 'twill your life destroy.'

'No snake; but a good whip,' replied the other.
'No whip; but snake,' replied the stranger;
'And, pray, should I thus make a pother
Unless I saw your woful danger?
And will you really keep that thing,
With fangs so sharp, and deadly sting?'
'Of course, I shall; my whip was lost,
And this will save another's cost.
You speak from envy – sir, good-bye.'
The snake, now brandished wide and high,
Grew warm and warmer gradually,
And, stinging, caused the fool to die.
But, as for you, my satrap friend,
You hasten to a bitterer end."
"What! worse than death?" the satrap cried.
"Ah! worse than death," the sage replied.
And, in due time, the hermit's word
Was proved with truth in due accord;
For all the pests that haunt a Court,
By hint and wink, and false report,
Soon made the satrap's virtuous skill
Seem to his royal master ill.
Cabals arose on every side;
Defeated suitors loudly cried,
"With what belonged to us he built that palace wide."
The Monarch fain would see this wealth,
And thither stole one day by stealth,
But nought within it met his eyes
Save modest mediocrities,
And praises of the joys that lie
In loneliness and poverty.
"His wealth, then," cried the pests, "consists
In diamonds, pearls, and amethysts;

In yonder chest with locks his hoard,
The ransom of a king, is stored!"
The Monarch, with his own white hands,
Throws back the wooden lid – and mute
Each base calumnious courtier stands;
For in that oaken chest is nought
But cap and jacket, roughly wrought,
A simple cloak, a shepherd's flute.
"Ah! much-loved treasures;" then exclaims
The Shepherd; "you are dear, indeed,
For never did you rouse the greed
Or malice of my fellow-men,
And you your master now reclaims;
Let's leave this palace, ne'er again
To enter, save in airy vision.
Monarch! pardon this decision;
When I mounted Fortune's height,
A fate untimely met my sight;
But who, alas! is quite so wise,
As not sometimes to wish to rise?"

The Shepherd and the King

The Fish and the Shepherd who played on the Clarionet

Tircis, for his loved Anette
Playing on the Clarionet,
Poured forth strains of music, such
As the very dead might touch: –
Played and sang beside a stream
Which through the meadows flowed like some
delicious dream.
Meanwhile, Annette, demure and pretty,
With rod and line, on fishes bent,
Stood, listening unto Tircis' ditty,
Which failed to lure them from their element.
Still Tircis sang, "Come, come, ye fishes, come:
Come from the cool depths of your watery home;
Forsake your naiad, and see one more fair:
Surrender all your lives to Annette's care!
    She is gentle, she is kind;
    In her keeping you will find
Your lives more safe than down below.
    Safe in a crystal pool, no want you'll know.
    And should you in her keeping die,
    Your fate I'd suffer willingly."
  Now this song was well sung, and the instrument's
strains
Were deliciously sweet, but, in spite of his pains,
The fishes avoided the charmer's keen hook.
Then Tircis lost patience, and hastily took
A net called a trammel, and, sweeping the stream,
Placed at Annette's disposal trout, greyling, and bream.
    Oh, shepherds of men, and not of sheep;
    Kings, who think you can safely keep
    Your subjects in order by rule of right,
    Attend to my counsel, and spread out your nets,
    Before the time comes for forlorn regrets,
    And let them cringe, under the rule of might.

The Fish and the Shepherd who played on the Clarionet

The two Parrots, the Monarch, and his Son

A Parrot and his child, 'tis said,
On royal dishes daily fed,
Having the affections won
Of a monarch and his son.
An equal age made either pair
Affection for each other bear.
The fathers gravely loved each other;
And their chicks, though wild and young,
At school or play, together clung,
As fondest brother unto brother.
That a parroquet thus by the son of a king
Should be loved, need we say, was a wonderful thing.
Now the fates had endowed this young heir to the throne
With a love for all creatures that he called his own;
And a Sparrow, by arts which caused prudes to despise her,
Had contrived how to make this great Monarch's son prize her.
　　And so it chanced, alack! one day,
　　That the rivals twain, at play,
　　Fell into a desperate rage;
　　And the youthful Parrot, stung
　　By some taunt the Sparrow flung,

Attacked, and sent her dying to her cage.
And then the Prince, with equal fury seized,
The slayer snatched, and in a death-grip squeezed.
   Soon to the Parrot-father's ears
The tidings came, and then the air
Was tortured by his wild despair;
But nought availed, or moans or tears,
For his child was lying still –
Inanimate, with voiceless bill.
Then from his woe the bird awoke,
And, with a cruel, double stroke,
Tore out the wretched Prince's eyes.
This done, unto a pine he flies,
And on its topmost branch he knows
What joy from satiate vengeance flows.
Runs, then, the King to him, and cries,
"Come down, my friend, our tears are vain;
In love let's bury woe and hate.
This wretchedness, 'tis very plain,
Comes from my son; or, rather, Fate
Had long since writ her stern decree,

Your son should die, and mine not see,
And that we parents twain should live disconsolate."
On this the father bird replied –
"Too great a wrong us twain divide;
Nor can I think he'll smother hate,
Who heathenishly speaks of Fate.
But whether it be Providence
Or Fate that rules our lives, I'm sure
That I will never move from hence
Till tempted by some wood secure.
I know that in a kingly breast
Vengeance for a time may rest;
But kings are also like the gods,
And, soon or late, you feel their rods.

I can scarcely trust you far,
Though sincere you think you are;
But you are losing time below,
For with my will I'll never go.
And trust me, hate, like love, is best
By absence lullabied to rest."

The Lioness and She-Bear

A mother Lion had lost her young:
A hunter had stolen her cub away;
And from the dawn, when the gay birds sung,
All through the shadeless hours of day,
She filled the forest with huge dismay;
Nor did the night, with its silent charms,
Still the voices of this childless mother's alarms.
At length a She-Bear rose, and said,
"Do you ever think of the children dead,
By your paws and jaws so cruelly slain?
Yet their mothers silent still remain;
And why not you?" The beast replied,
"My child is lost, perhaps has died;
And nothing for me now is left
But a life of hope bereft."
"And what condemns you to this wretched fate?"
"Fate!" echoed then the beast disconsolate.
From since the time the world a world became,
All living things have thought or said the same.
You wretched mortals, who bewail
That over you Tate's darkest cloud is thrown,
Just think of Hecuba's sad tale,
Then thank the gods that it is not your own.

The two Adventurers and the Talisman

I have never heard or read
In annals true or fabled story,
That paths of pleasure ever led
Mortal heroes unto glory;
And in proof of this one sees
The labours twelve of Hercules.
However, once, by Talisman
Induced, a knight conceived the plan
Of mounting horse and couching lance,
And seeking lands of fair romance,
Accompanied by one he knew.
After a time there came in view
A post upon the public way,
On which was writ – "A moment stay,
 Adventurous knight. If you would see
That which no knight has seen before,
Venture across yon torrent's roar,
And from the root of yonder tree
Yon elephant's huge head of stone
Raise up, and, without resting, bear
To yonder mountain's crest, which proudly stands alone."

Now of these knights one was of those
Who shudder at your swashing blows.
"The torrent's deep and broad," he cried;
"And if we reach the other side?
Why climb unto a mountain's crest,
With a stone elephant opprest?
'Tis true the artist may have wrought
His work on such a scale, a man
Might bear it for a yard, then rest;
But tell me not that mortal can
Bear it to yonder mountain's top,
Not daring once for breath to stay.
Perhaps this mystic head is naught
But such as one might bear away;
And if the latter be the truth,
Success were honour small, in sooth.
The whole thing is so plain a trick,
I'll leave it. Come, my friend, be quick."
This wise man having passed along,
The other crossed his breast, and made
A dash across the torrent strong,
And found beneath the tree the beast's head laid.
He raised it, and, with breathless stride,
He bore it to the mountain's brow,
And there, upon a terrace wide,
Gazed on a city fair that stretched below.
"Umph!" cried the elephant, and then
Forth swarmed a host of armed men.
All other errant knights but this
Would now have shown some cowardice;

The two Adventurers and the Talisman

But he, so far from turning back,
Couched lance in rest, and spurred to the attack.
But what the hero's great surprise,
When all the crowd, with joyful cries,
Proclaimed him monarch, in the place
Of one just dead! With modest grace
The knight declared he was not fit
A crown to wear, and then took it.
Sixtus the Pope once said so, too;
(And is it, then, so bad a thing
To be a pope, or be a king?)
But Sixtus said what was not true.

Blind fortune to blind courage is a friend;
And often he will gain his end
Who rashly acts; whilst he who tarries,
By prudence quite deceived, miscarries.

The Rabbits
To the Duke de Rochefoucauld

I have often said, on seeing
How men like animals seem to act,
That the lord of the earth, a poor frail being,
Is not much better, in fact,
Than the beasts whom he rules; and that Nature
Has given to each living creature
A sense of morality's force,
That its origin owes to the one same source.
At that witching hour when day
In the brown of the eve melts away,
Or at that when the long-brooding night
Has just lifted its pinions for flight,
I climb up some tree, at the edge of a wood,
And there, like a Jove, so wise and so good,
I startle with fear
Some young Rabbits gambolling near.

Then the nation of Rabbits,
Which, in tune with its habits,
With eyes and ears both open wide,
Played and browsed on the woodland side,
Perfuming its banquets with odours of thyme,
With a hurry and scurry,
Tails turned in a hurry,

Seeks its earth-sheltered burrows (thieves flying from
crime.)
But five minutes, or so,
Have not vanished, when, lo!
More gay than before,
On the fragrant green floor,
A rollicking band,
The Rabbits are there, again, under my hand!
Ah! do we not in this perceive
A picture of the race of men
Who, shipwrecked once, will still again
The safety of the harbour leave,
Risking fresh shipwreck from the selfsame wind?
True Rabbits! They, to fortune blind,
Entrust their wealth, and all their store!
And of this truth take one example more.

When stranger dogs pass through some place
Where they do not of wont reside,
The native dogs at once give chase,
With hungry jaws, all opening wide
(Fearing that the intruders may
Snatch the true owner's food away),
And never weary till th'intruders

Are safely driven from their borders.
Just so with those whom gracious fates
Have made the governors of states;
And those whom many artful plans
Have made much-favoured courtesans;
And merchants; men of any kind;
In all you'll find this jealous mind.
Each one, in his several place,
To the intruder grants no grace.
Your fine coquettes and authors are
Precisely of this character.
Woe to the unknown writer who
Dares publish something bright and new!
Poets forgive you any crime,
If you'll not rival them in rhyme.
A thousand instances of this
I might recite; but well I wis
That works should never be too long.
Moreover, you should always show

You think your readers wise, you know;
So now I'll close this song.

Ah! you, to whom I owe so much;
Whose greatness, and whose modesty
Are in exact equality;
Who cannot bear that men should touch
With praiseful tongues your well-earned fame,
Who still will blush with needless shame;
You, who scarcely have allowed
That I should make my verses proud,
And from critics and from time
Protect my insufficient rhyme,
By heading them with one of those
Great names which make our nation's pride,
Our France, whose annals long disclose
More famous names than all the world beside;
Oh, let me tell the universe
That you gave me this subject for my verse.

The Rabbits

The Merchant, the Nobleman, the Shepherd, and the King's Son

A Merchant, Shepherd, Lord, and a King's Son,
Adventuring to a distant land,
By waves and shipwrecks utterly undone,
Found themselves beggars on a foreign strand.
It matters not to tell at large
What chance had joined them in an equal fate;
But, one day, sitting on a fountain's marge,
They counsel took, disconsolate.
The Prince confessed, with many a bitter sigh,
The ills that fall on those who sit on high.
The Shepherd thought it best to throw
All thoughts of former ills afar; –
"Laments," he said, "no medicines are;
So let us use the arts we know,
And work, and earn the means to take us back to Rome."
But what is this? Can prudent language come
From Shepherd's mouth? and is it not, then, true
That they alone are wise whose blood is blue?

Surely sheep and shepherd are,
As far as thought goes, on a par?
However, wrecked on shores American,
Without a choice, the three approved this plan.
The Merchant cried that they should keep a school;
Himself arithmetic would teach by rule,
For monthly pay. "And I," the Prince exclaimed,
"Will teach how proper laws for states are framed."
The Noble said, "And I intend to try
For pupils in the art of Heraldry." –
As though such wretched stuff could have
A home beyond the Atlantic wave!
Then cried the Shepherd, "Worth all praise
Are your intentions; but, remark, the week
Has many days. Now, where a meal to seek
I am somewhat in the dark.
Your prospects of success are good,
But I am pining, now, for food;

Tell me therefore, comrades, pray,
Whence comes to-morrow's meal, and whence the meal to-day?
You seem in your resources rich;
But food to-day's a subject which
So presses, that I really must
Decline to put in you my trust."
This said, the Shepherd in a neighbouring wood
Collected fagots, which he sold for food,
And shared it kindly with his clever friends,
Before their talents had attained their ends,
Or, by long fasting, they were forced to go
And air their talents in the world below.
From this adventure we, I think, may learn
That for life's daily needs much learning is not wanted;
But that to every man the power to earn
Food by his labour has been freely granted.

Book XI

The Lion

Through spoil and plunder, wealthy grown,
A Leopard once claimed as his own,
In meadows broad, and forests deep,
Full many a steer, and stag, and sheep.
At length, upon some luckless morn,
Not far away, a Lion born,
Received, as usual is with great ones,
The compliments well known as state ones.
But this once done, King Leopard said
To Mr. Fox, his vizier keen,
"I know you suffer from the spleen,
Because this Lion-whelp is bred.
But why be fearful, since his father
Is in death's keeping? Pity, rather,
This orphan child, disconsolate,
For he will have a lucky fate,
If he, instead of seeking strife,
Can but contrive to save his life."
The Fox replied, "For orphans such
My pity is not over much.
In fact, two things alone remain, –
His friendship by some means to gain,
Or else to kill him, ere he grows
Too strong for all the world t' oppose.
His horoscope I've duly cast,
And find that he will ever be
To us the bitterest enemy,
But to allies he will cling fast.

The Lion

So, now, decide: become his friend,
Or straightway of him make an end."
But argued thus the Fox in vain:
The Leopard slept, with all his train,
Until the Lion's whelp, full grown,
Spread havoc, and made all his own.
Then Mr. Fox, with careworn brow,
Appealed to, said, "'Tis useless, now,
To think of meeting force by force:
Suppose to friends you had recourse,
They would but eat up all your store,
And Master Lion does no more.
But, sire, remember that the Lion
Has got three friends he can rely on,
Who ask for neither pay nor food, –
Strength, Vigilance, and Fortitude.

So, send him now a sheep or two;
If that won't answer, lambs a few;
And if he's not content with that,
A heifer add, both large and fat;
For by this means, perchance, you may
Save something from this beast of prey."
Thus spoke the Fox; but to his master
Th'advice seemed ill; and thence disaster
Spread over all the country round;
For still, combine as might the states,
Republics, cities, potentates,
They still the Lion master found.
If you would now the moral know,
Just to this brief advice attend: –
If you have let a Lion grow,
Take care that he becomes your friend,

The Gods and Instructors of Jupiter's Son

Jupiter youthful, once on a time,
Thought it no crime
To bring up his son as the mortal ones do;
And straightway this godlike one, given to jollity,
   Love's sweet frivolity,
Thought it no harm maiden's favour to sue,
   For in him love and reason,
   Skipping over a season,
Long ere the usual time, taught him to woo.
   Flora was first to set
   His poor young heart in fret;
   And with sighs and tears tender,
   Forgetting no lover's trick,
   This roguish young hero quick
   Made her surrender.
   And shortly it was evident
   That, thanks to his supreme descent,
   All other god-born children were
   Surpassed by Jupiter's young heir;
But Jupiter, rather dissatisfied
   (In his pride),
Assembling his council, one thunderous day,
Said, "I've hitherto ruled all this universe wide
Alone; but I feel, now, the weight of my sway,
And would fain to my child give some power away.

He's blood of my blood, and already, afar,
His altars are worshipped in many a star;
But before I entrust him with sovereign place,
I should like him to grow, both in knowledge and
grace."
 Thus the God of Thunder spoke,
 And then, with one acclaim sonorous,
 A shout of praise, in tuneful chorus,
 The echoes deep of heaven awoke.
 When silence was at length restored,
 Mars, God of War, took up the word,
 And said, "I will myself impart
 To this young prodigy the art
 Through which this realm so vast has grown,
And those who mortal were are now as godlike known."
 Then Apollo, tunefully,
 Murmured, "He shall learn from me
 All that sweet and mystic lies

In music's deepest harmonies."
Next Hercules, with eyes of flame,
Exclaimed, "I'll teach him how to tame
The monsters that invade the breast,
The vain temptations that infest
The heart's recesses; yes, I'll teach
Your offspring how with toil to reach
Heights and honours that alone
Are to steadfast virtue known."
When all had spoken, with an air of scorn
Smiled, in reply, the child of Venus born:
 "Leave," he said, "the boy alone to me,
 And all that he can be he'll be."

And speaking thus, well spoke god Cupid;
 For there's nought on earth more plain
That he is not wholly stupid
Who, loving well, does all things gain.

The Farmer, the Dog, and the Fox

The Wolf and the Fox are neighbours strange,
And within their reach I'd not build my grange.
One of the latter had long espied
The fowls of a Farmer; but though he tried
Each art of his cunning, the hens were still
Safe from the jaws of the midnight ranger.
Perplex'd as he was 'twixt his hungry will
And the wholesome dread of impending danger,
"Alas!" he cried, "it is fine, forsooth,
That wretches like these should mock me.
I come and I go, and I whet my tooth,
And with brilliant schemes I stock me;
And all this time that horrible lout,
The Farmer, makes money, week in, week out,
Of chicken and capon, or roasts or boils;
Whilst I, who surpass him in wit and sense,
Would be glad if I could but carry from hence.
The toughest old hen, as reward for my toils.
By the gods above and the gods below,
Omnipotent Jove! I should like to know,
And I will know, too, why you made me a Fox
To suffer such troubles and impudent mocks."
So breathing his vengeance, Sir Sly Fox chose
A night when the world was bathed in repose;
When the Farmer, his servants, and even his dogs,
Cocks, chickens, and hens slept as sound as logs.

Now the Farmer himself, with a folly extreme,
Had left the door open ere he went to dream;
And the consequence was, that the Fox entered in it,
And its feathered inhabitants slew in a minute.
With the morrow's new-born sun,
All the slaughter that was done
Struck the eye with huge dismay,
And almost made the sun avert his rising ray.
'Twas a parallel, in fact,
With Apollo's direful act,
When, with Atreus' son enraged,
With the Greeks such war he waged,
That great hillocks of the slain
Lay heaped high upon the plain.
Not unlike the ghastly scene
When great Ajax, filled with spleen,
Flocks of sheep and herds of oxen madly slew,
Dreaming that he smote the crew
Who, with famed Ulysses wise,
Had deprived him of his prize.
Then the Fox, whom none could parry,
Having seized on what he might,
Thought it quite unwise to tarry,
And discreetly took to flight.
Now when the Master rose, be sure
Against his men and dogs he swore,

For 'tis a common trick of masters
Others to blame for their disasters.
"Oh, wretched Dog!" he shouted forth;
"O Dog! for drowning only worth,
Why barked you not to let us know?"
"Master," the Dog replied, "I trow,
Master and Farmer, 'tis not fair
That I your anger now should share.
The fowls are yours, and yours the gain;
Then why should I, sir, suffer pain,
Because you leave your fowls exposed
To any thief that way disposed?"
Such reasoning, we must all admit,
For a mere Dog, was fraught with wit;
But, on the other hand, 'tis sure
That masters can't such wit endure,
As Carlo found, when soundly whipped
For words of sense unwisely slipped.

Now, fathers all, whoe'er you be
(I am not at that high degree),
When you would sleep, trust none of those
Around you, but your own doors close.
He who would have a thing well done
Should trust unto himself alone.

The Dream of an Inhabitant of Mogul

Once on a time, in slumber wrapt,
A certain peasant had a vision
Of a great Vizier, calmly lapt
In endless joys of fields Elysian;
Then straightway in a moment's space
The dreamer sees another place,
Wherein a Hermit bathed in fire
Endures such torments as inspire
Even those who share his fate
With sympathy compassionate.
Unusual this; indeed, so curious,
It seemed as though the dreams were spurious,
And to the dreamer so surprising,
That straight he woke, and fell surmising
His dreams were ill, as some aver.
But soon a wise Interpreter,
Consulted, said, "Be not perplexed,
For if to me some skill is given
To understand a secret text,
These dreams are messages from heaven,
And mean, "On earth, whene'er he could,
The Vizier sought sweet solitude;
Whereas the Hermit, day by day,
To courts of viziers made his way."
Now, if to this I dare to add,
I'd praise the pleasures to be had
Deep in the bosom of retreat;

Pleasures heavenly, pure, and sweet.
O Solitude! I know your charms!
O Night! I ever in your breast,
Far, far from all the world's alarms,
By balmy air would still be blest;
Oh, who will bear me to your shades?
When shall the Nine, the heavenly maids,
Far from cities, far from towns,
Far from human smiles and frowns,
Wholly employ my tranquil hours,
And teach me how the mystic powers
Aloft, unseen by human eyes,
Mysterious, hold their mighty sway?
And how the planets, night and day,
Fashion and rule our destinies?
But if for such pursuits as these
I am not born, at least among
The groves I'll wander, and in song
Describe the woods, the streams, the trees.
No golden threads shall weave my fate;
'Neath no rich silk I'll lie in state;
And surely yet my eyes shall close
In no less deep and sweet repose.
To Solitude fresh vows I'll pay;
And when, at length, the fatal day
Shall place me in the arms of death,
As calm I've lived, so calm I'll yield my breath.

The Lion, the Ape, and the two Asses

A young King Lion, desirous to shape
By morality's laws his government,
On one fine morning, prudently sent
For that clever old master of arts, the Ape;
And the statesman, consulted, sagely replied,
"O King, hold this maxim as your very best guide –
Let your own self-will to the good of the state
Be in all cases subordinate;
For 'tis simply neglect of this wholesome rule
That so oft makes us animals play the fool.

It is not in one day, or even in two,
That this evil self-love you'll contrive to subdue;
But should you succeed, oh, my monarch august,
You will never be foolish, and seldom unjust."
"Give me examples," replied the King,
"Of both the one and the other thing."
"Each species has its vanity,"

The Ape said very seriously;
"As, for instance, my own; for the lawyers call
All but themselves mean, base, and small.
But, on the other hand, self-esteem
Leads us to laud our deeds to the sky,
As, by doing this, we fondly deem
That our own position is raised as high.
And now I deduce, from what I have said,
That much so-called talent is mere grimace –
A trick which, as wise men know, has led
Many an idiot to power and place.

"Whilst following close, but the other day,
The steps of two Asses, who foolishly
Fed each other with flattery,
I heard the one to the other say,
'Is it not, sir, a shame and disgrace
That the tribe of mankind, that perfect race,

Should profane our dignified name, by denoting
As asses all those that are stupid or doting?
And even has ventured such lengths as to say,
That, when mortals speak nonsense, they utter a bray!
'Tis pleasant, forsooth, to perceive how mankind
Dream they're above us, and yet are so blind.
No, no, let their orators silent remain,
For they are the brayers, and fools in grain;
But with man let us cease one another to bother:
'Tis enough that we quite comprehend one another.
I will only here add that you have but to speak,
To make larks seem hoarse, and the blackbird to
squeak.'

These qualities, sir,' then the other replied,
'In yourself, in the fullest perfection, reside.'
And, having thus spattered each other with praise,
They trot far and wide to repeat the same craze;
Each fondly in hope, like a couple of crows,

That a caw shall come back for the caw he bestows.
But this trait is not asinine only, I own,
For I myself many great people have known
Who would gladly, instead of my-lording each other,
Have saic, each to each, 'My Imperial Brother!'
But I've spoken too long, and will only request
That this secret be hid in your Majesty's breast:
Since your Majestiy wished me some trait to divulge,
Which would show him how those who in self-love
indulge
Become objects of scorn; it would take me too long
To show also, now, how it leads to worse wrong."
    Thus spoke the Monkey false by nature;
    But it has still in doubt remained
    If he the other point explained;
    Your Monkey is a knowing creature,
    And knows it is not fortunate
    To be too truthful with the great.

The Wolf and the Fox

Why to the Fox does Æsop ever
Give the palm of being clever?
I the reason oft have sought,
Without of reason finding aught.
When the Wolf's engaged in strife,
To save his own or take a life,
The Fox can do no more than he,
Or half as much, and so I might
With Master Æsop disagree.
But there's a case has come to light,
In which 'tis fair I should admit
The Fox displayed the greater wit.
On one fine night it so befell
That Reynard, looking down a well,
The moon's full silver circle sees,
And takes it for a lordly cheese.
Two pails, above the well suspended,
To draw the water were intended;
And into that which higher hung,
Good Master Reynard, famished, sprung.
Down swift he went, and, to his woe,
Found out his sad mistake below.
He saw his death before his eyes;
For he could never hope to rise,
Unless some other famished thing,

Enticed by Dian's silver face,
Into the other pail should spring,
And then, by sinking, take his place.
Two days passed on without a visit
From any creature; and, meanwhile,
Old Time had made a huge deficit
In Mistress Moon's well-rounded smile.
But, just as all seemed lost, at last
A hungry Wolf the well's mouth past;
To whom the Fox, with joyous hail,
Cried, "Mister Wolf, with me regale;
This glorious cheese you here behold,
From Fauna's hands received its mould,
Of milk which heifer Io gave.
If Jupiter were lying ill,
I think the god himself would crave
Of this delicious cheese to have his fill.
I've eaten my share, as you plainly may see,
But enough still remains both for you and for me;
So, enter that pail, placed expressly for you."
Now, whether this story was told well, or not,
The Wolf, like a fool, took it all in as true,
And into the bucket with eagerness got;
When, outweighed, of course, Master Reynard got up,
And the other remained, on the moonshine to sup.

And yet, why blame the luckless beast?
For, tempted by some phantom feast,
   As easily deceived,
That which he hopes, or that he fears,
In either of the hemispheres,
   Is by each man believed.

The Peasant of the Danube

To judge by appearances only is wrong,
The maxim is true, if not very new,
And by means of a mouse I have taught it in song;
But to prove it at present I'll change my note,
And with Æsop and Socrates, also, I'll quote
A boor whom Marcus Aurelius drew,
And left us a portrait both faithful and true.
The first are old friends; but the other, unknown,
Is sufficiently well in this miniature shown.
    His chin was clothed with a mighty beard,
    And all his body so thickly furred,
    That much he resembled a grizzly bear –
    One that had never known mother's care;
'Neath eyebrows shaggy, two piercing eyes
Glared in a way more fierce than wise;
Whilst ill-shaped lips and a crooked nose,
The sum of his facial beauties close.
A girdle of goat-skin formed his dress,
With small shells studded for comeliness.
This sturdy youth, at a time when Rome
Spoiled many a race of its native home,
Was sent as a sort of deputation,
By Danubian towns, to the Roman nation.
Arriving after toilsome travels,
The rustic thus his tale unravels:
"O Romans! and you, reverend sires,
Who sit to list to my desires,
First, let me pray the gods, that they
May teach me what I ought to say,
And so direct my ignorant tongue,
That it may utter nothing wrong!

The Peasant of the Danube

Without their intervention must
Be all things evil, all unjust.
Unless through them we plead our cause,
'Tis sure we violate their laws.
In witness of this truth perceive
How Roman avarice makes us grieve;
For 'tis not by its arms that Rome
Has robbed us both of peace and home;
'Tis we ourselves, ill ways pursuing,
Have worked at length our own undoing.
Then, Romans, fear that Heaven, in time,
To *you* may send the wage of crime,
And justice, in *our* vengeful hands
Placing its destructive brands,
Hurl swift o'er you the endless waves
Of war, and make you fettered slaves!
Why, why should we be slaves to you?
What is't that you can better do
Than the poor tribes you scourge with war?
Why trouble lives that tranquil are?

Before you came we fed in peace
Our flocks and reaped our fields' increase.
What to the Germans have you taught?
Courageous they and quick of thought,
Had avarice been their only aim,
They might have played a different game,
And now have held the world in chains;
But, ah! believe me, they would not
Have scourged your race with needless pains,
Had victory been now their lot.
The cruelties by your prefects wrought
Can scarce be ever borne in thought;
Us e'en your Roman altars scare,
For your god's eyes are everywhere.
The gods, alas! 'Tis thanks to you
That nought but horror meets their view,
That they themselves are scoffed and jeered at,
And all but avarice is sneered at.
Of all the cruel men you sent
To rule our towns, not one's content.

They seize our lands, they make us toil,
And e'en our little huts they spoil.
Oh, call them back. Our boors refuse
To till the fields for others' use.
We quit our homes, and to the mountains fly,
No tender wife now bears us company;
With wolves and bears we pass our lives away,
For who would children rear for Rome to slay?
And, oh! the terrors of your prefects bring
One added horror; for a hateful thing,
Unknown before, has now spread far and wide
Throughout our native land – Infanticide!
Call back your men, or else the German race
From day to day in vice will grow apace.
But why should I come here to make appeal?
The self-same vices spoil your commonweal:
At Rome, as on the Danube's banks, the way

To gain a scrap of justice is to pay.
I know my words are rude, and only wait
Humbly to suffer candour's usual fate."
The half wild peasant paused, and all,
Astonished that such words could fall
From lips uncouth, and that such sense,
Large-heartedness, and eloquence,
Could dwell within a savage man,
Proclaimed him a Patrician.
The Danube's prefects were recalled,
And others in their place installed.
And more than this, the Senate made
A copy of the Peasant's speech,
All future orators to teach
How to tell truth, convince, persuade.
But sad to tell, not long at Rome
Had eloquence like this its home.

The old Man and the three young Men

An Old Man, planting a tree, was met
By three joyous youths of the village near,
Who cried, "It is dotage a tree to set
At your years, sir, for it will not bear,
Unless you reach Methuselah's age:
To build a tomb were much more sage;
But why, in any case, burden your days
With care for other people's enjoyment?
'Tis for *you* to repent of your evil ways:
To care for the future is *our* employment!"
Then the aged man replies –
"All slowly grows, but quickly dies.
It matters not if then or now
You die or I; we all must bow,
Soon, soon, before the destinies.
And tell me which of you, I pray,
Is sure to see another day?
Or whether e'en the youngest shall
Survive this moment's interval?
My great grandchildren, ages hence,
Shall bless this tree's benevolence.

And if you seek to make it plain
That pleasing others is no gain,
I, for my part, truly say
I taste this tree's ripe fruit to-day,
And hope to do so often yet.
Nor should I be surprised to see –
Though, truly, with sincere regret –
The sunrise gild your tombstones three."
These words were stern but bitter truths:
For one of these adventurous youths,
Intent to seek a distant land,
Was drowned, just as he left the strand;
The second, filled with martial zeal,
Bore weapons for the common weal,
And in a battle met the lot
Of falling by a random shot.

The third one from a tree-top fell,
And broke his neck. – The Old Sage, then,
Weeping for the three Young Men,
Upon their tomb wrote what I tell.

The old Man and the three young Men

The Owl and the Mice

Whene'er you have a tale to tell,
Ne'er call it marvellous yourself,
If you would have it go down well,
For, if you do, some spiteful elf
Will scorn it; but for once I'll vow
The tale that I shall tell you now
Is marvellous, and though like fable,
May be received as veritable.
So old a forest pine had grown,
At last 'twas marked to be cut down.
Within its branches' dark retreat
An Owl had made its gloomy seat –
The bird that Atropos thought meet
Its cry of vengeance to repeat.
Deep in this pine-tree's stem, time-worn,
With other living things forlorn,
Lived swarms of Mice, who had no toes;
But never Mice were fat as those,
For Master Owl, who'd snipped and torn,
Day after day fed them on corn.
The wise bird reasoned thus: "I've oft
Caught and stored Mice within my croft,
Which ran away, and 'scaped my claws;
One remedy is, I'll cut their paws,
And eat them slowly at my ease –
Now one of those, now one of these.

To eat them all at once were blameful,
And my digestion is so shameful."
You see the Owl was, in his way,
As wise as we; so, day by day,
His Mice had fit and due provision.
Yet, after this, some rash Cartesian
Is obstinate enough to swear
That Owls but mechnism are.
But how, then, could this night-bird find
This craftily-contrived device,
The nibbling of the paws of mice,
Were he not furnished with a mind?

See how he argued craftily:
"Whene'er I catch these Mice, they flee;
And so the only way to save them
Is at one huge meal to brave them.
But that I cannot do; besides,
The wise man for bad days provides.
But how to keep them within reach?
Why, neatly bite the paws from each."
Now, could there, gentle reader mine,
Be human reasoning more fine?

Could Aristotle's self have wrought
A closer chain of argued thought?

The Owl and the Mice

Book XII

The Companions of Ulysses
To the Duke of Burgundy

O Prince! to whom the immortals give
Their care, and power, and grace, permit
My verse may on your shrine still live,
By burning there, though void of wit.
I know 'tis late; but let my muse
Plead years and duns for her excuse.
My soul is faint, and not like yours,
Which as an eagle proudly soars.
The hero from whose veins you drew
This brilliant soul, is e'en like you,
In martial fields; 'tis not his fault
His steps at victory's archway halt:
Some god retains him; the same king
Who once the Rhine with victory's wing
Swept over in one month, they say.
Then speed was right; but now, delay.
But I must pause. The Loves and Smiles
Detest the verse that runs to miles:
And of the Loves and Smiles your court
Is, all men know, the chief resort.
But other gods its precincts grace:
Good Sense and Reason there have place;

And I must beg that you will seek
Of these a story from the Greek,
Of certain men, who yielding up
Their souls to Folly's poisoned cup,
From men to beasts were quickly changed,
And in brute forms the forest ranged.

After ten years of war and pain,
Ulysses' comrades tempt the main;
Long tost about by every wind,
At length an island shore they find,
Where Circe, great Apollo's child,
Held sway, and on the strangers smiled.
She gave them cups of drink delicious,
With poison sweet, with drugs pernicious.
Their reason first gave way; and then
They lost the forms and souls of men,
Ranging about in shapes of beast,
Some like the largest, some the least: –
The lion, elephant, and bear,
The wolf, and e'en the mole, were there.
Ulysses, he alone escaped,

Refusing Circe's cups to drain;
And, as his form was finely shaped,
And god-like wisdom graced his mind,
The goddess sought his soul to gain,
By poisoned draughts of varied kind:
In fact, like any turtle-dove,
The goddess cooed, and told her love.
Ulysses was too circumspect,
Such coign of vantage to neglect,
And begged that all his comrades should
Resume their manhood's matural mould.
"Yes," said the nymph, "it shall be so,
If they desire. You ask them, go."
Ulysses ran, and, calling round
His former comrades, said, "I've found
A method sure, by which again
You may resume the forms of men;
And, as a token that 'tis true,
This instant speech returns to you."
Then roared the Lion, "I'm no fool,
Your offer really is too cool.
What! throw away my claws and teeth,
With which I tear my foes to death?

No! Now I'm King. – In Grecian land
I should a private soldier stand.
You're very kind, but let me rest;
I choose to be aregal beast."
Much with this rough-roared speech distressed,
Ulysses next the Bear addressed,
And said, "My brother, what a sight
Are you, who once were trim and slight!"
The Bear replied, in accents gruff,
"I'm like a bear – that's quite enough;
Who shall decide, I'd like to know, sir,
That one form's fine, another grosser?
Who made of man the judge of bears?
With fair dames now I've love affairs.

You do not like my shape? 'Tis well;
Pass on. Content and free I dwell
Within these woods, and flatly say,
I scorn mankind, and here shall stay."
The Prince the Wolf accosted then,
And, lest refusal came again,
Said, "Comrade, I'm in deep distress,
For there's a lovely shepherdess

Who echo wearies out with cries
Against your wolfish gluttonies.
In former days your task had been
Her sheep from every wolf to screen:
You led an honest life. Oh, come,
And once more manhood's form resume."
"No, no," replied the Wolf; "I'll stay:
A ravenous wolf you call me. Pray,
If I the sheep had eaten not,
Would they have 'scaped your spit and pot?
If I were man, should I be less
A foe unto the shepherdess?
For just a word, or slight mistake,
You men each other's heads will break;
And are you not, then, wolfish, too?
I've weighed the case, and hold it true
That wolves are better far than man:
I'll be a Wolf, then, whilst I can."
To all, in turn, Ulysses went,
And used this selfsame argument.

But all, both great and small, refused
To be of beast-life disabused.
To range the woods, to feed and love,
To them seemed all things else above.
"Let others reap the praise," they cried,
"Of noble deeds: we're satisfied."
And so, fast bound in Pleasure's chains,
They thought that free they roamed the plains.

O Prince! I much had wished to choose
A tale which might teach and amuse.
The scheme itself was not so bad;
But where could such a tale be had?
I pondered long: at length the fate
Of Circe's victims struck my pate.
Such victims in this world below
Were always, and are even now:

To punish them I will not strike,
But hold them up to your dislike.

The Companions of Ulysses

The Cat and the two Sparrows
To the Duke of Burgundy

Of equal age, lived closed together
A Sparrow and a Cat;
And he of fur and he of feather
Grew so familiar, that
The bird could fearlessly provoke
His formidable friend in joke.
To peck out eyes the one with beak pretended,
The other with protruded claws defended.
The Cat, however, truth to say,
Was always gentle in his play;
And though he showed his claws, took care
His little chirping friend to spare.
The fretful Sparrow, much less meek,
His tiny fury tried to wreak
On Master Cat, who only purred,
And thence this truth may be inferred,
That friends should never, in dissension,
Let quarrel grow to strife's dimension.
Still old acquaintance ne'er forgot
Kept their strifes from growing hot,
And battle never sprang from play.
  But yet it chanced, one luckless day,
A neighbouring Sparrow heedless flew
To where Miss Chirp and Master Mew
Had lived so long in amity.
At first 'twas well; but, by-and-by,

The birds grew jealous, and in rage
Gave vent to wrath none could assuage.
The Cat, aroused from hearth-rug sleep,
Endeavoured first the peace to keep,
But finding that in vain, declared,
"What! let this stranger Sparrow come
To eat my friend in his own home?
It shall not be." His claws he bared,
And soon, without a spoon or fork,
Of Master Chirp made but short work.
The Sparrow eaten, said the Cat,
"A most delicious morsel, that!"
And as no other bird was near,
Next swallowed his companion dear.

From this what moral shall I learn?
Without a moral fables are
But empty phantoms – deserts bare.
Some glimpse of moral I discern,
But I'll not trace it; I've no fear
But that your Grace will see it clear.
For you 'tis only simple play;
But for my muse in any way

'Twere toil. In fact, I'll not the truth let fall
For you, who need it not at all.

The Miser and the Ape

A man was a Miser; every one knows
That his was a vice which grows and grows:
This was a man that filled jars and buckets,
Old stockings and coffers, with pistoles and ducats.
'Tis a maxim of mine that such things left unused,
I mean pistoles and ducats, are simply abused.
To secure all his wealth from the lover of stealth,
My Miser had built him a home,
Surrounded by waves with their foam,
And there with a pleasure the which
To some seems but poor, to some rich,
He heaped up his wealth with delight,
And every day, and each night,
He counted the sum, and re-counted,
And gloated to see how it mounted;
But, somehow, count well as he might,
The gold pieces never came right.
And the source of this grievous disaster
Was this, that an Ape, than his master
More wise, to my mind, took a pleasure
In flinging to seaward his treasure.
  The Miser secure,
  With his double-locked door,

  Was wont to leave silver and gold
  All loose on his table, untold.
"Ah! ah!" said the Monkey, one day;
"I'll fling this in the sea; 'twill be gay."
Now for me it were hard to decide
If the Master or Ape were the wiser,
'Twould be half for the Ape, half for Miser.
Well, as I've said, the Ape, one day,
Laying hands on Master's gold,
Many a ducat flung away,
With sovereigns new and angels old.
With huge delight he tried his skill,
And ducks and drakes made with a will,
Of golden coins which mortals seem
To think, of mortal goods the cream.
In fact, had not the Monkey heard
The key within the key-hole stirred,
And feared its Master, every coin
Had gone its comrades to rejoin,
And 'neath the waves with golden flecks
Had lit the gloomy floor of wrecks.
Now, blessing on each Miser's head,
Both whilst he lives and when he's dead.

The two Goats

Since goats have ever clambering browsed,
By Nature's gentle force aroused,
They've wandered far and wandered free,
Enjoying sweets of liberty.
Their greatest pleasure is to find
Paths all unknown to human kind:
A rock, or hanging precipice,
Suits these wild animals' caprice:
No wall can make their gambols cease.
Two white-foot Goats, then, thus inspired,
And with adventurous spirit fired,
Deserted pastures too well known,
And chose their routes, each one his own.
But though each separate pathways took,
It chanced they reached the self-same brook,
O'er which, for bridge, a plank was thrown,
That scarce would have sufficed for one.
The stream was deep, the flood was wide,
And should these dames have terrified;
But, spite of danger, each young lady

Advanced upon the plank unsteady.
And now, by aid of history,
Louis le Grand I seem to see
Philip the Fourth advance to meet
Upon the isle of conference.
Well, step by step, with agile feet,
Our ramblers, with a proper sense
Of what was due to ancestry,
Refused to yield; for one Goat, she
Could claim that Polyphemus laid
Her sire at Galatea's feet;
The other, just as boldly, said
Her dam was Amalthæa sweet –
The goat who gave her milk to Jove,
Who rules below, and reigns above.
Neither would yield, so both fell down,
And there we leave our Goats to drown.

Of moral I've not much to say:
But such things happen every day.

The two Goats

To the Duke of Burgundy
In Answer to a Request for a Fable on
"The Cat and the Mouse."

To please the youthful Prince whom courtly fame
    Destines entempled in my works to be,
How shall I write a fable with this name –
    Le Chat et la Souris? ("The Cat and the Mouse.")

How can I represent in verse a maid
Who, sweet in aspect, yet still ruthless played
With hearts her charms snared, as you see
    Le petit Chat does *la Souris?*

Shall I sketch Fortune, and show her deceit? –
Tell how she gulls the world with the old cheat?
Treating poor self-complacent friends you see
    Comme le Chat does *la Souris?*

Shall I depict of all earth's royalty
The only one her restless wheel that stays?
The one who wars with Europe's chivalry;
And with the strongest of his foemen plays,
    Comme le Chat with *la Souris?*

But as I write, there comes, insensibly,
The plan that suits me, if I don't mistake;
I should spoil all if lazy I should be:
Mockery the Prince of my poor muse would make,
    Comme le Chat of *la Souris.*

The old Cat and the young Mouse

A young Mouse, small and innocent,
Implored an Old Cat's clemency: –
"Raminagrobis, let me live!
Your royal mercy, monarch, give!
A Mouse so little, sir, as I
A tiny meal can well supply.
How could I starve a family?
Host, hostess, only look at me;
I fatten on a grain of wheat:
A mite my dinner makes complete.
I'm thin, too, now; – just wait a bit,
And for your children I'll be fit."
Thus to the Cat the Mouse, aggrieved;
The other answered, "You're deceived.

Is it to me you talk like that?
Go, tell the deaf and dumb – not me:
Old Cats don't pardon, so you'll see.
The law condemns, and you must die:
Descend, and tell the Fates that I
Have stopped your preaching, and be sure
My children's meals will not be fewer."
He kept his word; and to my fable
I add a moral, as I'm able:
Youth hopes to win all by address;
But age is ever pitiless.

The sick Stag

In a land where stags abounded,
   One fell very sick indeed;
And he saw his bed surrounded
   By a dozen "friends in need."
"Gentlemen!" he muttered, "leave me,
   Leave me, I implore, to fate:
Since your tears can only grieve me,
   And your solace comes too late."
Not a bit; – their lamentations
   Lasted for a week, or more;
While they took their daily rations
   From his very scanty store.
Bit by bit his food diminished,
   Under such attacks as these;
Til the sufferer's course was finished
   By starvation – not disease.

For comforters of every kind
Some fee is necessary, mind;
And nobody will give advice,
Or shed a tear, without his price.

The sick Stag

The Bat, the Bush, and the Duck

A Bat, a Bush, and Duck, one day,
Finding home business would not pay,
Resolved their purses to unite,
And risks of foreign trade invite.

Soon with factors, counters, agent,
And all the merchants' usual pageants,
Ledgers, day-books, and all that,
Surrounded, they grew rich and fat.
All went on well, till, lucklessly,
A cargo, trusted to the sea,
And traversing a rock-bound strait,
Ill-piloted, endured the fate
Of all the other treasures which
King Neptune's sea-roofed vaults enrich.
Great cries of grief the trio uttered, –
That is to say, they only muttered:
For every little merchant knows
That credit loves not traders' woes.
But, spite of every cautious plan,
The tale through all the city ran;
And now Duck, Bush, and Bat were seen
Ready to wear the bonnet green,
Without or credit or resources,
For none would ope for them their purses.

All sorts of creditors daily arrived,
With bailiffs and writs; and the door scarce survived
  The continual thrum
  Of their creditors' glum;
And, of course, the Bush, Bat, and the Duck were
                                        intent
To find means this importunate crowd to content.
The Bush, with his thorns, caught the men that
And said, with a sort of a pitiful cry,   [went by,
"Pray, sirs, can you tell in what part of the sea
The wealth of myself and my partners may be?"
Whilst that diver, the Duck, plunging down out of
                                        sight,
Went to find them, he said, if he possibly might.
But the Bat, followed daily by bailiffs and duns,
At noon all the haunts of the human race shuns;
And, stricken with shame, to keep quite out of sight,
Hides in ruins all day, and fles only by night.

Many a debtor have I known –
Neither Bush, nor Bat, nor Duck –
Who even had not such ill luck
As was upon this trio thrown,
But simple lords, who, shunning snares,
Sneaked always down by the back stairs.

The Quarrel of the Dogs and the Cats; and, also, that of the Cats and the Mice

Discord has always ruled this universe:
Our world of this could many facts rehearse.
This goddess over countless subjects reigns;
The elements not Jupiter himself restrains;
Nor these four potentates alone wage war:
In many races there's a ceaseless jar.
A house once, full of Dogs and Cats, grew free
Of strife, at last, by many a grave decree.
The master fixed their hours, and every meal,
And let the quarrelsome his horsewhip feel.
They live, at last, like cousins, almost brothers,
And furnish quite examples to all others.
At length peace ended; – some stray tempting bone,
Some broth, or little preference to one shown,
Made both belligerents half crazy run.
To plead the grievous injury that's done,
I've heard that learned writers of old law
Attribute this to some small legal flaw.
Be what it might, they both made angry claims,
And set the kitchen and the hall in flames.
Some loud for Dog and some for Cat cried out:
The Cats went mewing, the Dogs whined about.
They deafened every one. Cats' advocate
Referred to the decree; and the debate
Ceased at that word; but still they searched in vain
Where it was hid, and sought and sought again.

The Mice had eaten it; then, lo, once more
The Mice were sufferers – many, many a score
The old Cats swallowed – some, with cruel claws,
Expounded to the Mice their code of laws;
Laid ambuscades; caught them in many ways.
And from their master obtained food and praise.
Mais à nos moutons. Not beneath the skies
Lives there a creature without enemies.
'Tis Nature's law; and how is purblind man
The secret of God's mysteries to scan?
It is God's will; further I do not go:
We waste our time in trying but to know.
Man is, at sixty years, a wondering fool,
Fit to be whipped, and sent again to school.

The Wolf and the Fox

How comes this general discontent?
Here is a man, for lack of wit,
Longing to live beneath the tent
The soldier's longing so to quit.

A certain Fox aspired to be
A Wolf; and who's prepared to say
The Wolf may not think luxury
Consists in the lamb's peaceful play?

It much surprises me to find
A poet prince, but eight years old,
Who writes prose of a better kind
Than I can verse – aye, twenty fold –
Though long experience makes me bold.

The thoughts throughout his fable spread
Are not a poet's work, I know.
They're numerous and better said;
Unto a prince the praise we owe.

I play upon a simple pipe:
That is my talent – just to please;
But soon my hero, growing ripe,
The clarion will make me seize.

I am no prophet, yet I read
The starry signs that promise give.
His glorious acts will Homer need;
Homer, alas! he does not live.

The Fox said to the Wolf, one day, "My dear,
I have but old tough hens for my poor cheer!
One wearies of the food; but you feed well,
And with less hazard. I, where people dwell,
Slink round, while you keep prudently away.
Teach me your trade, my noble comrade, pray!
Make me the first of all my race who slew
A good fat sheep, and took him for a stew!"
"I shall not be ungrateful," the Wolf said;
"'Tis well, I have a brother newly dead;
Put on his skin." Fox took it, and obeyed.
The Wolf then bid him not to be afraid
Of all the mastiffs of the shepherd's flock:
The Fox learnt of his maxims the whole stock,
First blundered much, then studied all he could,
And, lastly, well the precepts understood.
Just as he finished, there came passing by
A drove of sheep. He runs at them – they fly.
The new-made Wolf spreads terror everywhere;

And frightened bleatings fill the troubled air.
So in Achilles' arms Patroclus came: –
Mothers and old men shudder at his name.
The sheep see fifty wolves; and, in full cry,
Dogs, sheep, and shepherds to the village fly.
One only, as a hostage, left behind,
Is by the villain seized. Upon the wind,
Just then, came crow of lusty chanticleer:
The pupil snapped the fowl, and without fear,
Threw by his school-dress, all his task forgot,
And ran off, heedless of his future lot.
How useless was this counterfeiting then!
The changed suit hindered not the watchful men.
They follow in his track the self-same day,
And when they find him, they are quick to slay.

From your unequalled mind my poor muse drew
The story and its moral, plain but true.

The Crab and its Daughter

Sages are often, like the crabs, inclined
To backward step, and leave their goal behind.
This is the sailor's art, and, now and then,
The artifice of deep, designing men,
Who feign the opposite of their intent,
To put their adversaries off the scent.
My subject is a trifle; but how wide
The field on which its morals may be tried!
Some general may conquer, should he heed it,
An army with a hundred chiefs to lead it.
His plans of march and counter-march may be
At first a secret, then a victory.
No use in prying, when he would conceal;
From Fate's decrees one cannot make appeal.
The tide grows insurmountable, at length;
Against a Jove the gods may waste their strength.
Louis and Fate seem partners now, in glory,
And draw the world along. But to my story.

Said Mother Crab to Daughter Crab, one day,
"How *can* you step in such an ugly way?
Do try to go a little straighter, dear!"
The little Crab made answer, with a sneer,
"Look at yourself! It's very well to talk,
But it was you who taught me how to walk:
From you, and from your friends, I took my gait;
If they go crooked, how can I go straight?"

She told the truth – for lessons that we learn
    From family examples last the longest.
They teach us good and evil, in its turn;
    And oft the latter lessons are the strongest.

As to the way of walking, let me add,
    That turning backs has often merit in it
In war, for instance, it is far from bad,
    If people do it at the proper minute.

The Eagle and the Magpie

The Eagle, queen of the broad sky,
Met, one day, in a field, the Pie –
In mind and language different,
In plumage, and in every bent.
Chance brought them into a by way:
The Magpie was afraid to stay.
The Eagle, having dined but lately,
Assured her calmly and sedately.
"Come, let's be social," said the Eagle, then;
"And if the lord of gods and men
Sometimes is weary of the king
Who rules the universe, the thing
Is clear, that ennui may e'en vex
One who serves Jove. Amuse me! – come,
And chatter as you do at home;
It is not me you will perplex."
The Pie began at once to gabble
On this and that, on lords and rabble;
Just like the man in Horace – just,
Good, bad, indifferent, all on trust;
Talking incessant, and still worse
Than the poor fool in the famed verse.
She offers, if it please his grace,
To skip about, and watch each place
He wishes. Jove knows that the Pie
Was well constructed for a spy.

The eagle answers, angrily,
"Don't leave your home, my tattling friend.
Adieu! I have no wish to send
A gossip to corrupt my court,
And spread each lying, false report:
I hate a gossip." Quite content,
Maggy cared little where she went.
To dwell among the gods or kings
Is not the pleasantest of things;
That honour has its pangs also,
Detractors, spies, and many a foe,
Gracious and bland enough in face,
But false in heart, infest each place,
And make you odious. In courts wear
Coats of two colours, or take care.

The Eagle and the Magpie

The Hawk, the King, and the Falcon
To Monseigneur The Prince de Conti

As the gods are forgiving, they wish that the lords
Whom they send to rule over us creatures below,
Should control the proud use of their conquering
                                      swords,
And to subjects the mercies of charity show.
O Prince! 'tis well known that you think in this way
That you conquer your foes, but still pause ere you
                                       slay;
And in this, for you're one who no passions subdue,
Achilles, as hero, was far beneath you.
This title of hero, in fact, should belong
But to those who do good. This was always the case
In the ages of gold; but now absence from wrong
Of a very grave character gives men the place.
So far are you, Prince, from deserving this stain,
That for half your good actions you merit a fane.
Apollo, the poet, who dwells in the skies,
Sings already the praise of your name, 'tis believed;
Fast in heaven the walls of your mansion arise,
For of glory enough on the earth you've received.
May the sweetest of charms that god Hymen can
For you and the Princess, eternally live: [give,
For you fully deserve it; in token of this
I will point to your gifts, both of riches and bliss.
To those qualities wondrous, which, owned but by
                                       few,

To grace your young years, Jove has lavished on you.
Your spirit, O Prince! with such grace is combined,
That which most to prize a sweet puzzle we find;
For, sometimes, esteem takes our homage by force,
And then love leaps in with impetuous course.
But to sing all your praises and merits were long;
So changing my key, in a far humbler song
I'll tell you a tale, how a fierce bird of prey
Assaulted a king, and got safely away.

'Tis seldom falconers contrive
To take a new-fledged Hawk alive;
But one so taken, to a King
Was made a humble offering.
The bird, if true the story be,
No sooner saw his Majesty,
Than straight the Royal nose he clawed,
And then the Royal forehead gnawed.
"What! clutch a mighty monarch's nose?
He wore no crown, then, I suppose?"
Had he wore crown and sceptre, too,
'Twere all the same, the creature flew,
And King's nose clawed, like common nose.
Of course, an uproar loud arose,
Such as my verse could scarce describe,
From all the startled courtier tribe.

The King alone was calm and cool:
For calmness is with kings a rule.
The bird kept his place, and could not be persuaded
To vacate the strange throne he'd so roughly invaded.
His master, in vain, with threats and with cries,
Showed him his fist, but he would not rise.
And it seemed, at length, as though the bird –
Insolent creature! – would cling to that feature
Until the next morning's chimes were heard.
The greater the efforts to make him let go,
The deeper he dug in each keen-pointed toe.
At length he relaxed, of his own fickle will;
Then the King said to those round about, "Do not kill
The poor bird, nor the falconer trouble, for each, in
His several way, has obeyed Nature's teaching: –
The one has just proved himself falconer good,
And the other a real savage thing of the wood.
And I, knowing well that kings clement should be,
Grant both full pardon: so let them go free."
Of course, the courtiers all declared
That such great mercy ne'er was shown:
And had the trouble been their own,
Nor man nor bird would have been spared.
Few kings indeed had acted so,
And let the woodman freely go.
They 'scaped right well; but boor and bird

In nothing in this matter erred,
But only this, that, woodland-bred,
They had not learnt enough to dread
The neighbourhood of courts; but this small lapse
May be excused in such poor folk, perhaps.
The following story Pilpay places
Where Ganges nourishes dusk races;
Where man ne'er dares to spill the blood
Of any living thing for food;
"For how can we tell," they say, "that
This creature was not present at
The siege of Troy – a hero, then –
And that he'll not be so again?
For we Pythagoreans are,
And think that different forms we bear
At different seasons – pigeon now,
And then a hawk, and next a cow.
At present we are men; and so
Through every change of form we go."

The tale of that bold bird who clutched the King
Is told two ways. The second now I'll sing.
A woodman that, by luck or wit,
A Hawk had seized, went off with it,
To lay it at his monarch's feet.
Such captures we but seldom meet –

Once in a hundred years; indeed,
'Tis written in the falconer's creed
That woodman who a Hawk can catch
In nest, is any woodman's match.
Through all the crowd of courtiers, then,
Our huntsman, happiest of men,
Thrust with his prize, at last secure
His fortune now was firm and sure.
But, just as he had reached the throne,
Seized with a rage before unknown,
The savage bird, untamed as yet,
In spite of chained foot, turned and set
His claws deep in his master's nose.
All laughed, as you may well suppose –
The courtiers and the monarch, too;
Such very comic sight to view,
I'd give a crown, though it were new.

If Popes may laugh, I'm not quite sure
But kings could not their lives endure,
If they might laugh not – 'tis divine;
And Jove, though mostly saturnine,
With all his comrades, laughs, at times,
Enough to shake these earthly climes.
And Jove laughed loudest when, I think,
Poor hobbling Vulcan gave him drink.
Whether or no, 'tis well arranged
That gods should laugh, my subject's changed,
With reason; for 'tis time to ask
What moral lies beneath the mask
Of falconer unfortunate?

This simple lesson I will state: –
To every land each cycle brings
More foolish woodmen than good kings.

The Fox, the Flies, and the Hedgehog

Wounded and weak, and dripping fast with blood,
A Fox crept wearily through mire and mud.
Quickly attracted by the hopeful sight,
A Fly – a restless, winged parasite –
Came to show sympathy – and bite.
The Fox acused the gods on high,
Thought Fate had vexed him cruelly.
"Why attack me? – am I a treat?
When were the Foxes thought good meat?
I, the most nimble, clever beast,
Am I to be for flies a feast?
Now Heaven confound the paltry thing
So small, yet with so sharp a sting!"
A Hedgehog, hearing all his curses
(His first appearance in my verses),

Wished to set the poor beast free
Of the Flies' importunity.
"My neighbour," said the worthy soul,
"I'll use my darts, and slay the whole."
"For Heaven's sake!" poor Reynard says,
"Don't do it! Let them go their ways.
These animals are full, you see:
New ones will bite more greedily.

Such torments in this land are seen,
Courtiers and magistrates, I mean.
Great Aristotle likens flies
To certain men; and he was wise.
But when such folk get full of gold,
They're less importunate, I'm told.

Love and Folly

All is mysterious with Love, –
  His bow and arrow, torch, and wings.
Tis not a day's work in a grove,
  To master these momentous things.

Explain them my poor muse can not;
  My object is but, in my way,
To tell of Cupid's wretched lot,
  And how he lost the light of day.

Whether that fate be ill or well
  For those whom Cupid since has met,
Lovers alone can rightly tell:
  I cannot, though I've felt his net.

Folly and Love together played,
  One day, before he lost his sight;
But yet, as people will, they strayed
  From friendship, and got stung by spite.

Disputes are really melancholy!
  Love wanted all the gods and men

As umpires; but impatient Folly
  Preferred it settled there and then;

And gave poor Cupid such a blow,
  That both his pretty eyes were seared.
For blessed sight gave blindness – lo!
  Their heaven's blue brightness disappeared.

His mother, Venus, heard his grief,
  And cried for vengeance, like one mad,
On Jove and Nemesis, – in brief,
  On gods of all kinds, good and bad.

The case, she said, was very strong:
  Her blind son would require a stick
And dog, to help him walk along.
  Alas! for cruel Folly's trick.

The gods poor Cupid's case discussed, –
  And boys and girls in love decide,
Decreeing that it's only just,
  Folly should Love in future guide.

Love and Folly

The Crow, the Gazelle, the Tortoise, and the Rat
To Madame de la Sablière

I, by means of verse, would raise
A temple to your lasting praise.
Already its foundations lie
Based on that art which comes from high,
And on the name of her whose fame
Adoring clouds shall there proclaim.
I'd write above its portal-stones,
"This fane the goddess Iris owns;"
But not the Iris who for Juno
Goes out with messages, as you know;
A different Iris, whom the lord
Of gods, and Juno, too, were glad
To serve, if they her summons had,
When she such honour would accord.
Th'Apotheosis placed on high
Should show the people of the sky
My Iris to a throne conducting, –
A throne of sunlight's sole constructing.
In frescoes, on the panels placed,
Should all her life's sweet tale be traced;
A charming story, and one far
Remote from all the tales of war.
Deep in the Temple's chief recess
A painting should in part express
Her form, her features, her bright smiles,
And all the thousand artless wiles
By which she gods and men beguiles.
Low at her feet should there be shown
All the great men the world may own,
Great demi-gods besides, and even
The natural habitants of heaven;
For certain 'tis that they to whom
Men pray, to Iris burn perfume.
The artist's care should chiefly be
To make her eyes her soul express.
But, ah! to paint her tenderness
'Twere all in vain to try; may be
No art upon the earth resides
Which for a task like this provides,
To paint a soul in which combine
Man's strength with graces feminine.
O Iris! you who charm us all,
Before whose heavenly grace we fall,
You whom before ourselves we prize
(But, mind, I am not making love,
For love's a word you don't approve),
Yet even from this rough sketch may
A better likeness rise, some day.
The project of your sacred building
I've just for artist-purpose filled in

The foreground of a story which
Is so with rare-found friendship rich,
That, haply, it may favour find
With one that is so good and kind.
Of friendship monarchs seldom dream;
But he who gains your heart's esteem
Is not a king devoid of love;
No, he your gentle thoughts approve
Is a brave mortal, who would give
His life, that some dear friend might live.

A Rat, a Gazelle, and a Tortoise and Crow
Lived together as friends, in a desolate place;
And, as they took care to indulge in no show,
Man failed for some time the companions to trace.
But, alas! for poor beasts there's no safety from man,
Whatever concealment their instincts may plan;
To the heart of the desert, the depths of the sea,
Or to heaven's own vault, 'tis in vain that they flee.
The Gazelle, one sad day, was at innocent play
When a dog– cruel dogs! whom the men treat as
                                                    brothers,
Though beasts, to assist them to capture the others–
Unluckily snuffed at her scent, and, pursuing,
Led on his fierce master, to cause her undoing.

When dinner came that day, the Rat
Said, "What can Miss Gazelle be at?
She surely dreads some new attacks,
Or else our friendship's bonds relax!"
"Ah!" then the Tortoise, sighing, cried,
"If Heaven wings would but provide,
Such as our Crow has, I would fly,
And all around the country spy,
To find what accidents withhold
Our friend. Her heart's as good as gold."
The Crow, without a word, took flight,
And soon had poor Gazelle in sight,
Tied up with cords against a tree,
A hapless piece of misery.
At once the Crow, without a pause,
Flies back, nor seeks to probe the cause,
The whys, the wherefores, or the when
Which make Gazelles the prey of men.
Nor loses time, for action meant,
In a pedantic argument.
The Crow's report was duly heard,
And then the Crow a vote preferred
That two should speed, without delay,
To where their friend in bondage lay,
But that the Tortoise, lying still,

Should serve the counter, – guard the till;
For, whilst the Tortoise' step is slow,
Gazelles die quickly, as we know.
The words were scarcely said, when forth
The angry Crow and Rat went north,
To where their dark-eyed, dear Gazelle
Lay, victim of man's purpose fell.
The Tortoise, also, not behind-hand
To lend to any one a kind hand,
Toiled thither, also, grimly swearing
That he his house must still be bearing.
Arrived at the place where the Deer was confined,
Sir *Gnaw-net* (the Rat is so properly named)
At once set his teeth the hard cordage to grind,
And in less than two minutes the friend was reclaimed
The hunter coming up just then,
Cursed like a thousand sporting men;
And Master Rat, with prudence fraught,
A cozy hole directly sought,
Whilst Crow swarm safely up to tree,
And dear Gazelle in woods ran free.
Just then the hunter, in a state
Of hunger most disconsolate,
Perceived the Tortoise on his path,

And, thereupon, subdued his wrath.
"Why should I," said he, "vex myself?
This beast will grace my supper-shelf."
And thus the hapless Tortoise soon
Had been condemned to knife and spoon,
Had not the Crow the dear Gazelle
Taught how to act the lame man well.
The timid deer, with halting feet,
Went forth, the hunter's eyes to meet.
The man threw off, without delay,
All that his eager steps might stay –
The Tortoise, with some other things.
Of course the Rat undid the strings
That held the bag where Tortoise lay,
And all four friends got safe away!

'Tis Pilpay that has told this tale;
And if upon the god of song
I chose to call, I might prolong
This quadrupedal history,
And write another Odyssey.
And if, to please you, I should take
This work upon me, I should make
The Rat the hero; yet, 'tis true

That each had work, and did it, too.
The Tortoise, though with mansion weighted,
The case in point so clearly stated,
That Master Crow at once took wing,
To spy the land, and message bring;
Whilst dear Gazelle, with female cunning,
Before the hunter lamely running,
Gave to Sir Gnaw-cord time to bite
The strings which held the Tortoise tight.
So each one, in his several way,
Fought a good fight, and won the day.
On whom shall we the prize bestow?
On the good heart, as you'll allow.
What will not friendship dare for those
On whom its gentle tendrils close?
That other feeling, love, is not,
Compared with friendship, worth a jot;
Although, to tell the truth, its pains
Distract my heart, and fill my strains.
It is Love's gentle sister you
Protect, and I'll adore her, too;

And, blending Friendship with your name,
Throughout the world her joys proclaim.

The Forest and the Woodman

A Woodman, with too strong a stroke,
The handle of his brave axe broke,
   Broke it beyond repair;
For, though he ranged the Forest-side,
Of proper trees both far and wide
   The scanty wood seemed bare.
Then to the sylvan gods he prayed,
   That they his steps would sweetly guide
Unto the spot where they had made
   That branch for which he sighed.

To gain his bread himself he'd take
Far, far away; and, for their sake,
   Would spare both fir and oak.
"Respected are their charms and age,
And graceful in the poet's page" –
   'Twas thus the Woodman spoke.

The innocent Forest gave the bough.
   The Woodman hacked both oak and fir!
The groaning Forest soon found how
   Her gift brought death to her.

Behold the way the world doth spin.
Some men – say, politicians – win
   A place: then bite their friend!

Of them I tire. But should dear trees
Bear such rude outrages as these,
   And I not mourn their end?
In vain I sing: it is no use;
   Although my dart stings where 'tis hurled.

Ingratitude and gross abuse
   Are no less in the world.

The Forest and the Woodman

The Fox, the Wolf, and the Horse

A Fox, still young, though rather sly,
  Saw, first time in his life, a Horse.
Just then a stupid Wolf passed by,
  And Reynard saw a game, of course.

"Come, see this thing that's feeding near;
  He's grand. I view him with delight!
Is he more strong than us, my dear?
  Think you with both of us he'd fight?"

Replied the Wolf, with laughter – "Now
  Draw me his portrait: then I'll tell."
The Fox said, "Could I write, or show
  On canvas all his beauties well,

"Your pleasure would be great indeed.
  But, come – what say you? He may be
Some easy prey, on whom we'll feed,
  By Fortune sent to you and me."

The Horse, still feeding on the plain,
  Scarce curious to see the pair,
Planned flying with his might and main,
  For wolves have tricks that are unfair.

The sly Fox said, "Your servants, sir;
  We wish to know your name." The Horse
Had brains; so said, "My shoemaker
  Has put it round my shoe, of course.

"Read, if you can. There is my name."
   The Fox had store of craft in need:
He cried, "My parents were to blame;
   They taught me not to write or read.

"'Tis only mighty wolves who learn
   To read: they read things in a breath!"
Our flattered Wolf here made a turn;
   But vanity cost him his teeth!

The clever Horse, as he drew near,
   Held high his hoof: his plan he saw.
It cost the reading Wolf most dear, –
   Down came the hoof upon his jaw.

With broken bones, and bloody coat,
   Upon the ground the poor Wolf lay.
"Brother," the Fox said, "only note
   The truth that we've heard people say.

"With wisdom, what had been your case?
   No pain would need to be discussed.
This Horse has stamped upon your face
   That 'unknown things wise men mistrust.'"

The Fox and the Turkeys

Against a Fox, a tree served well
The Turkeys for a citadel.
The cunning rascal made the round,
And sentries at each opening found.
"What! these fools mock me, then?" he cried,
"And at the common lot deride?
Forbid it, gods! forbid it, pride!"
And this vow of his chivalry
He soon performed, as you will see.
The moon came just then shining out,
As if the Turkeys' foes to rout;
But he, no novice in assault
Like this, was not, of course, at fault;
And from his bag of schemes so sly
Drew one, to trap the weak and shy.
He feigns to climb, with rampant paws,
And next apes death, with close-fixed jaws.

He then revives, resuscitated:
No harlequin so much elated:
Raises his tail, and makes it shine,
And in the moonlight glitter fine.
No single Turkey dares to sleep,
But ceaseless, tiring watch they keep.
Worn out, they try their eyes to fix
Upon their foeman's wicked tricks;
At last, half giddy, one by one
Fall headlong, and his game is done.
He puts them carefully aside,
Till nearly half of them have died;
Then the bold rascal quickly bore
Away the heap, to fill his store.

If dangers we too closely heed,
'Tis ten to one they come indeed.

The Fox and the Turkeys

The Ape

There was a certain Ape in Paris:
Like many another Ape, he marries.
He chose a wife; and then, like some
Bad husbands, beat her deaf and dumb –
Aping their ways. The poor soul sighed,
And, after that, at last she died.
Their infant cries, but cries in vain,
And sorrows, o'er and o'er again.
The father laughs: his wife is dead,
And he has other loves instead,
Whom he will also beat, I trow;
He's often drunk, that well I know.
From one who's aping others look
For nothing good; whether a book
He makes, or work performs. Yes, all,
Upon whichever one you fall,
Are bad – the author ape the worst,
And of all monkey creatures first.

A Scythian Philosopher

A Philosopher once, who, in Scythia born,
Had somewhat, with study, his brain-pan outworn,
Made his mind up, for pleasure and profit, to seek
Repose for a time in the land of the Greek;
And there he made friends with a man of the kind
Whom Virgil so well in the Georgics defined:
A man who's a king, for himself he controls,
And a god, for he blends his own will with men's
                                    souls.
He found him with pruning-knife grasped in his hand,
Pruning here, snipping there, in all parts of his land,
As tranquil as Jove; here he cut off a twig,
There lopped off a branch to make others more big;
For Nature, experience had taught him, is prone
To waste in rash gifts all the wealth of her throne.
The Scythian, brought up in town, was downcast,
And looked at the ruinous waste quite aghast,
And exclaimed, "My dear friend, lay your pruning
                                    hook down,
And let Nature, judicious, take care of her own;
For, at best, you are taking much pains to deflower
The fruits which Time's tooth will but too soon
                                    devour."
The old man replied, with a rustical grace,
"I cut useless ones off to give useful ones space."
Struck by wisdom like this, with no moment's delay,
The Scythian homewards at once took his way;
And no sooner had got there but took up a bill,
And at cutting and hewing showed wonderful skill:

Hewed branches, snipped twigs, and persuaded his neighbours
To share in his rude horticultural labours.
The result is soon told: hacking trees without reason,
In summer or spring – taking no thought of season –
Must lead to results which no words can belie;
For the trees thus instructed instinctively die.
Now, the Scythian stands for a symbol of those
Who wish all the pathways of pleasure to close;
Who'd hoot at ambition, forbid a new dress,
And from lexicons banish the sweet word, *caress*.
For myself, though by custom not given to swearing,
I'll say that, by Jove, such old dolts there's no bearing;
They wish us to choke whilst we've plenty of breath,
And whilst full of life's vigour to simulate death.

The Elephant and Jupiter's Monkey

An Elephant had words, one day,
With a Rhinoceros, they say.
They settled they would fight it out.
But, while the matter was about,
Jove's Monkey, like a Mercury, came:
Giles was, historians say, his name.
The Elephant, a brute ambitious,
Was pleased to find the heaven propitious.
Eager for fame, he smiled to see
So dignified an embassy.
But Giles, though wise in all essentials,
Is slow presenting his credentials.
At length he comes to pay respect,
Yet still shows somewhat of neglect;
Speaks not a word: no single mention
Of the great deities' attention.
What care those living in the skies
If perish Elephants or flies?
The potentate's compelled to speak:
"My cousin, Jupiter, this week
Will see, from his Olympic throne,
A pretty combat, as he'll own;

And his Court, too, will see it partly."
"What combat?" said the Monkey, tartly.
"Pooh!" said the Elephant; "you know
'Bout the Rhinoceros, and the blow;
'Tis property that we dispute.
In a long, tedious Chancery suit
Elephantor and Rhinocere
Are warring, as you've heard up there."
"I'm pleased to learn their names, good sir,"
Said Master Giles; "but, King, you err
If you think we of such things heed."
The Elephant, surprised indeed,
Said, "Who, then, come you now to aid?"
"I come to part a blade of grass
Between some ants. To every class
Our cares of sovereignty extend.
As for your wars, my noble friend,
The gods have not heard of them yet;
Or, if they have, they do forget.

The small and great are, in Jove's eye,
Guarded with like equality."

The Madman and the Philosopher

A certain Madman, as the story goes,
    Threw stones at a Philosopher, one day.
The latter said, "My friend, I don't suppose
    You care to work so hard, without your pay.
Here, take this crown; how deeply I regret
    I cannot better recompense your trouble!
Go, pelt yon gentleman, and you may get
    A larger sum – perhaps as much as double."
Pleased at the chance, our fool begins to throw
    Big stones at a patrician; but, instead
Of giving gold, the lackeys mauled him so,
    That they departed leaving him half dead.

Such fools there are in kingly courts,
    Who raise the laugh at your expense;
But can you check their silly sports,
    Or stop their loud impertinence?
If any words or any blows
    Of yours are powerless to hush them,
Just get them to be rude to those
    Who have sufficient force to crush them.

Book XII, Fable XXII

The English Fox
To Madame Harvey

A good heart is in you with sense allied,
And scores of other qualities, well tried;
A nobleness of soul and mind, to guide
Both men and things; a temper frank and free.
In friendship firm, though tempests there may be.
All this deserves, we know, a pompous praise:
But pomp displeases you; so I'll not raise
My voice, but simple be, and brief. I would
Insert a word of flattery, if I could,
About the country that you love so dear.
The English are profound: in this their mind
Follows their temperament, as oft we find.
Deep, deep they dig for truth, and without end
The empire of the sciences extend.
I write not this to win good will from you;
Your nation are deep searchers, it is true.
Even your dogs, they say, have keener scent than ours;
Even your dogs, they say, have keener scent than ours;
Your foxes are of craftier mental powers:
I'll prove it, by an artful stratagem,
The most ingenious ever planned by them.
A wicked Reynard, chased quite out of breath
By the untiring dogs, and dreading death,
Saw a tall gallows, where dead badgers hung,
And owls and foxes were together strung –
Cruel examples for the passer-by!
Reynard in ambuscade prepared to lie,

Like Hannibal, who, when the Romans chased,
Baffled their armies, and their spies disgraced.
Old Fox this was! his enemies soon ran
To where he lay for dead. The barking clan
Filled all the air with clamour long and loud.
The master whipped away the noisy crowd:
The trick deceived him. "Come, you dogs!" he cried,
"Some puppy's saved the rascal, who ne'er tried
To climb the gibbet where such honest folk
Repose. Some day, he'll find the gallows a rough joke,
Much to his loss." And, while the dogs give tongue,
Back to his larder goes the Fox just hung.
Another day he'll try the self-same plan,
And leave his brush and four paws with the man.
Tricks won't do twice. The hunter ne'er had thought
Of such a scheme, had he been nearly caught,
Not from the want of wit, at all, you see,
For who can say the English want *esprit?*
But their contempt for life has often led
To evil in such dangers, it is said.

And now I once more turn to you, –
Not for more flattery. 'Tis true
All long eulogium does but tire:
I, a poor player on the lyre,
With flattering songs, and little verse,
Amuse the mighty universe,
Or win a distant nation's praise.
Your Prince once said, in former days,
He valued very far above
All studied praise one word of love.
Accept the humble gift I bring,
Last efforts that I mean to sing:
But poor indeed, and all unformed,
Yet were they by new fervour warmed,
Could you but make this homage known
To her who fills your country's zone
With sprites from Cytherea's isle;
I speak (you know it by your smile)
Of Mazarin, Jove dear to thee,
And Cupid's sovereign deity.

The English Fox

The Frogs and the Sun

The daughters of the mud obtained
Help from the star-king, while he reigned.
Nor war, nor any like disaster,
Could harm them under such a master.
His empire was the most serene!
The pond-queens (Frogs, I really mean:
For why not give their honourable name?)
Against their benefactors plotted; shame,
Imprudence, pride, and base ingratitude,
Good Fortune's children, roused the restless brood.
They could not sleep a wink (to trust their cry):
They would have stirred the world to mutiny
Against the eye of nature – the great sun.
It had begun to burn them: he must run
To arms, and gather all his powerful band,
Or he'd be driven from his own fair land.
The croaking embassies would go
Through all the regions, to and fro,
To make the whole world hear their case,
And gather pity from each place.
All the world seemed bent on this,
That four marshes took amiss.
Still this rash complaint went on:
Still this grumbling at the sun.
Yet in vain the noise and riot, –
Frogs must, after all, be quiet;
For, if the sun is once inflamed,
They will very soon be tamed,
And the Frog Republic will
Find they've calculated ill.

The League of the Rats

A Mouse, in very deadly fear
Of an old Cat, that kept too near
A certain passage, being wise
And shrewd, went straight, without disguise,
To ask a neighbour Rat, whose house
Was close to that of Mister Mouse.
The Rat's domains, so fair and snug,
Were under a large mansion dug.
This Rat a hundred times had sworn
He feared no Cat that yet was born;
Both tooth and paw he held in scorn.
"Dame Mouse," the lying boaster cried,
"*Ma foi!* how can I, ma'am, decide
Alone? I cannot chase the Cat,
But call and gather every Rat
That's living near. I have a trick; –
In fact, at nothing I will stick."
The Mouse, she curtsied humbly; then
The Rat ran off to call his men,
Unto the office, pantry named,
Where many rats (not to be blamed)
Were feasting at their host's expense,
With very great magnificence.
He enters, troubled – out of breath.
"What have you done? – you're pale as death,"
Says one. "Pray, speak." Say he, "Alas!
Friend Mouse is in a pretty pass,
And needs immediate help from you.
Raminagrobis, in my view,
Spreads dreadful carnage everywhere.

This Cat, this hideous monstrous Cat,
If Mice are wanting, calls for Rat."
They all cry out, "'Tis true! to arms!"
And some, they say, 'mid war's alarms,
Shed tears; but no one stops behind:
They all are of the self-same mind.
They pack up cheese in scrip and bag;
No single nibbler dares to lag.
With mind content, and spirit gay,
 It is to them a holiday.
The Cat, meanwhile, quite free from dread,
Has gripped the Mouse by its wee head.
At charging pace the Rats, at last,
Come; but the Cat still holds it fast,
And, growling, faces the whole band.
At this grim sound the Rats, off hand,
With prudence, make a swift retreat,
Fearing their destiny to meet.
Each hurries to his humble hole,
Nor seeks again the warrior's goal.

The League of the Rats

Daphnis and Alcimadura
(An Imitation of Theocritus)
To Madame de la Mesangere

Amiable daughter of a mother fair,
For whom a thousand hearts are torn with care;
Yours are the hearts whom friendship holds in fee,
And those that Love keeps firm in fealty.
This preface I divide 'tween her and you,
The brightest essence of Parnassus dew.
I have the secret to perfume for you
More exquisitely sweet. I'll tell thee, then;
But I must choose, or I shall fail again:
My lyre and voice will need more power and skill;
Let me, then, praise alone a heart that's still
Full of all noble sentiments, – the grace, the mind,
Which need no master but the one we find
Blooming above you. Guard those roses well,
And do not let the thorns o'ergrow, *ma belle*.
Love will the same thing say, and better, too;
Those who neglect him, Cupid makes to rue:
As you shall see. Alcimadure the fair
Despised the god who rules the earth and air.
Fierce and defiant, she roam'd through the wood,
Ran o'er the meadows, danced as none else could,
Obeyed caprice alone, – of beauty queen,
Most cruel of the cruel; she had been

Daphnis and Alcimadura

For long beloved by Daphnis: of good race
Was the poor lad, who doated on her face, –
Loved for her very scorn – nay, more, I vow,
Than had she loved him with an equal glow;
Yet not a look she gave, nor word to cheer,
Nor his complaints would ever even hear.
Weary of the pursuit, prepared to die,
Down at her door despair had made him lie.
Alack! he wooed the winds; – she, blithe and gay,
Still kept her door shut, – 'twas her natal day;
And to her beauty's throne she spread fair flowers,
The treasures of the garden, and spring hours.
"I hoped before your very eyes," he cried,
"Had I not been so hateful, to have died.
How can I wonder that you do deny
This last sad pleasure of fidelity?
My father I have charged my heritage
To offer at your feet: the pasturage,
And all my flocks, – my dog, of dogs the best;
And my companions will, then, with the rest,
Found a small temple, where continually
Your image, crowned with flowers, shall ever be.
My simple monument shall be near it,

And this inscription on the stone I've writ –
'Of love poor Daphnis died. Stop, passer by!
Weep, and say he was slain by cruelty
Of fair Alcimadura.'" The Fates at last
Cut the thin thread, and his vexed spirit passed.
The cruel maiden came forth, proud and gay:
In vain her friends beseech her but to stay
A moment, on the corse to shed one tear;
She still insulted Cupid, without fear:
Bringing that very evening o'er the plain,
To dance around the statue, all her train.
The image fell, and crushed her with its weight.
Then from the cloud thus spoke the voice of Fate:
"Love, and delay not: the hard heart is dead."
The shade of Daphnis raised its pallid head,
And on the banks of Styx stood shuddering;
While all vast Erebus, with wondering,
Heard to the shepherd the fair homicide
Excuse her cruelty and foolish pride.
But as to phantom Ajax Ulysses sued,
And Dido's death the guilty lover rued,
So from the maiden's shadow turned the swain,
And did not words of mercy to her deign.

The Arbitrator, Almoner, and Hermit

Three saints, by holy fervour fired,
To gain the heights of heaven aspired;
But, as the well-known proverb says,
Rome can be reached by various ways,
So these by different methods planned
To gain the shores of Canaan's land.
One, touched by the expense and care
Which luckless suitors have to bear,
Offered cases to determine
Without a fee, or wig, or ermine.
Since human laws were first began,
Lawsuits have been the curse of man;
Absorbing half, three-fourths, or all
Of days which, at the best, are small.
To cure a state of things so vicious,
Our Umpire thought his plan judicious.
The second of our saints declares
The sick sole object of his cares;
And I praise him: in truth, to me
This seems the truest charity.
But sick men, troublous then, as now,
Our good man vexed enough, I vow.
Capricious, restless, petulant,
Each moment brings a separate want;

And, if no other fault they find,
They cry, "To such and such he's kind:
Spends all his days and nights in caring
For them, and leaves us here despairing."
But these complaints were small to those
Which harassed, every day, the heart
Of him who, well-intentioned, chose
To act the Arbitrator's part.
The plaintiff and defendant, both,
T'adopt his sentences were loth;
And swore, with all their might and main,
His partiality was plain.
By such abuse as this disgusted,
The Umpire and the Almoner
Each unto each his woes entrusted;
And each agreed he could not bear
To be so shamefully mistrusted.
This being so, they sought a glade
Which neither suns nor winds invade,
And there, beneath a rugged mountain,

Beside a clear and babbling fountain,
They found their friend the Hermit saint;
So each one having made his plaint,
Asked his advice. "Your own pursue,"
Replied their friend; "for who but you
Can know your several wants? To know
One's self makes gods of man below.
And let me ask you, have you found
This knowledge where vast crowds abound?

No; trust me, it can only be
The fruit of sweet tranquillity.
Shake but the water in your vase,
And you no longer see your face;
But let it once more still remain,
And straight your likeness comes again.
'Midst worldly scenes you'll never learn
The love for which we all should yearn.
Believe me, friends, the desert's best
For him who'd study his own breast."

The Arbitrator, Almoner, and Hermit

To each the Hermit's words seemed good,
And, henceforth, each one sought the wood.

Of course, there's always work to do,
Whilst men still sicken, and still sue,
For lawyers and for doctors; and
They'll never perish from the land,
Thank mighty Jove, as long as fees
And honours greet their services.
But in such common toils the mind
Can seldom its true likeness find.
Oh, you, who give your lives away,
And serve the public every day, –
You, princes, judges, magistrates,
Exposed to all the angry fates,
Who, when no other ill oppresses,
Are slain by Judas-like caresses, –
To you yourselves are all unknown;
And if some moment is your own,
For self-reflection, ere it flies
'Tis spoilt by hateful flattery's lies.

This lesson shall conclude these pages;
May it be blessed to future ages!
To Kings I give it, to the wise commend:
How could my volume better end?

Index

List of
Full-Page Illustrations